TOTAL QUALITY MANAGEMENT

TOTAL QUALITY MANAGEMENT

For Students of Affiliated Colleges of **Anna University**
Chennai

THIRD EDITION

R S Naagarazan
Prof. & Director
Arunai Engineering College
Tiruvannamalai
Tamil Nadu

A A Arivalagar
Associate Professor
Department of Mechanical Engineering
Adhiparasakthi Engineering College
Melmaruvathur
Tamil Nadu

NEW AGE
ANNA

An Imprint of

NEW AGE INTERNATIONAL (P) LIMITED, PUBLISHERS
New Delhi • Bangalore • Chennai • Cochin • Guwahati
Hyderabad • Kolkata • Lucknow • Mumbai
Visit us at **www.newagepublishers.com**

Published by New Age International (P) Ltd., Publishers
First Edition: 2005
Third Edition: 2015

BRANCHES

- **Bangalore** 37/10, 8th Cross (Near Hanuman Temple), Azad Nagar, Chamarajpet, Bangalore-560 018
Tel.: (080) 26756823, Telefax: 26756820, **E-mail: bangalore@newagepublishers.com**
- **Chennai** 26, Damodaran Street, T. Nagar, Chennai-600 017
Tel.: (044) 24353401, Telefax: 24351463, **E-mail: chennai@newagepublishers.com**
- **Cochin** CC-39/1016, Carrier Station Road, Ernakulam South, Cochin-682 016
Tel.: (0484) 2377004, Telefax: 4051303, **E-mail: cochin@newagepublishers.com**
- **Guwahati** Hemsen Complex, Mohd. Shah Road, Paltan Bazar, Near Starline Hotel, Guwahati-781 008
Tel.: (0361) 2513881, Telefax: 2543669, **E-mail: guwahati@newagepublishers.com**
- **Hyderabad** 105, 1st Floor, Madhiray Kaveri Tower, 3-2-19, Azam Jahi Road, Near Kumar Theater Nimboliadda, Kachiguda, Hyderabad-500 027, Tel.: (040) 24652456, Telefax: 24652457
E-mail: hyderabad@newagepublishers.com
- **Kolkata** RDB Chambers (Formerly Lotus Cinema) 106A, 1st Floor, S.N. Banerjee Road, Kolkata-700 014
Tel.: (033) 22273773, Telefax: 22275247, **E-mail: kolkata@newagepublishers.com**
- **Lucknow** 16-A, Jopling Road, Lucknow-226 001
Tel.: (0522) 2209578, 4045297, Telefax: 2204098, **E-mail:lucknow@newagepublishers.com**
- **Mumbai** 142C, Victor House, Ground Floor, N.M. Joshi Marg, Lower Parel, Mumbai-400 013
Tel.: (022) 24927869, Telefax: 24915415, **E-mail: mumbai@newagepublishers.com**
- **New Delhi** 22, Golden House, Daryaganj, New Delhi-110 002
Tel.: (011) 23262368, 23262370, Telefax: 43551305, **E-mail: sales@newagepublishers.com**

ISBN: 978-81-224-3818-5

₹ 175.00

C-14-08-7840

Printed in India at Print-O-Pack, Delhi.
Typeset at Excellent Graphics, Delhi.

PUBLISHING GLOBALLY
NEW AGE INTERNATIONAL (P) LIMITED, PUBLISHERS
7/30 A, Daryaganj, New Delhi-110002
Visit us at **www.newagepublishers.com**

Preface to the Third Edition

While thanking the dedicated teaching faculty and motivated students for their great response to this textbook, the authors have decided on revising this book as it has served for more than 6 years.

The revisions in the ISO 9000, QS 9000 and ISO 14000 families necessitated this latest edition. Although the revisions in the ISO 9000:2008 version introduced only clarifications to the existing requirements of 2000 version, some changes were intended to improve its consistency with ISO 14001:2004. There were no new requirements. For example, the QMS being upgraded needs to be checked to see if it is following the clarifications introduced in the amended version. The revision in 14000 families includes aspects such as PDCA cycle for implementation and the Greenhouse gas accounting.

Based on the feedback from the distinguished members of the fraternity, minor changes and corrections have been included in the text. A paragraph on Six sigma technique has been added to cater for the revised syllabus. Once again we thank those persons who sent their comments and suggestions to include the revision upon the updated standards. Our sincere gratitude is due to the publishers, the New Age International Publishers, New Delhi, who agreed to release the revised edition at the earliest. This shows that we are all on the right track of continual improvement. The authors welcome any suggestions to improve this presentation such that it continues to inspire the Teachers and the Learners.

R.S. NAAGARAZAN

A.A. ARIVALAGAR

Preface to the First Edition

The initial thrust in the industrial scene was, 'To Produce and Flourish'. Later, it shifted to 'Produce Quality and Flourish'. Further, it was modified to 'Assure Quality and Flourish'. All over the globe, now the trend is 'Manage Quality and Flourish'. In this era of globalisation, the WTO have established influence over 180 countries to mutually develop and survive through ISO and Quality Management Systems.

The Quality Management and Improvement have gained larger significance in this context. The Anna University has rightly responded to this situation and introduced the subject 'Total Quality Management', as a core subject, for all specialisations of the engineering graduate curriculum.

As a teacher who had handled Statistical Quality Control, Quality Assurance and Reliability at the UG and PG levels, for more than thirty five years in a University, the first author has ventured to write this text book. The second author has more than ten years of teaching the quality-related subjects in the engineering colleges, at the UG level. This has provided us the motivation to write this book.

This book covers or discovers all the topics included in the syllabus of the Anna University, extensively. A reference table of the factors for the Quality Control Charts, Numerical Examples and the Questions for Short Answers, are also included, to sustain the interest of the student community. I trust, that the teaching fraternity and the student community will find this book useful, in deepening their knowledge and familiarising with the applications and in succeeding in their career.

The authors wish to record their deep sense of appreciation to Anna University for including the subjects Professional Ethics and Total Quality Management, which according to their experience and experiment with life, are inseparable and essential ingredients for happiness and success. We thank all the authors quoted, whose research and findings have kindled our interest in writing this book.

The authors wish to record their deep sense of gratitude, to Mr. E.V. Velu, M.A., M.L.A., our beloved Chairman, Arunai Engineering College, Tiruvannamalai, who have been generous and shown real motivation to us, in writing this book. Our thanks are due to the Principal, AEC, our colleagues, and the laboratory staff, M/s Sivakumar T., Ms. Sivagami K., and Ms. Sudha, who have helped us in the preparation of the manuscript and illustrations. We thank profusely our spouses, who have shown patience during the shaping of this book, and for their proof reading and facilitation in our endeavour.

Words are not sufficient to appreciate the speed and precision with which M/s New Age International (P) Ltd., Publishers, New Delhi, have acted upon, in turning this work to a fine form and for the timely release of this book.

The authors invite the comments and suggestions for the improvement, from the teachers as well as the students. We care for continual improvement, and to achieve the satisfaction of our customers.

R.S. NAAGARAZAN
A.A. ARIVALAGAR

Syllabus

GE6757 **TOTAL QUALITY MANAGEMENT** **L T P C**
3 0 0 3

Objectives:

- To facilitate the understanding of Quality Management principles and process.

UNIT I: INTRODUCTION **(9 periods)**

Introduction – Need for quality – Evolution of quality – Definition of quality – Dimensions of manufacturing and service quality – Basic concepts of TQM – Definition of TQM – TQM Framework – Contributions of Deming, Juran and Crosby – Barriers to TQM.

UNIT II: TQM PRINCIPLES **(9 periods)**

Leadership – Strategic quality planning, Quality statements - Customer focus – Customer orientation, Customer satisfaction, Customer complaints, Customer retention – Employee involvement – Motivation, Empowerment, Team and Teamwork, Recognition and Reward, Performance appraisal – Continuous process improvement – PDSA cycle, 5 S, Kaizen – Supplier partnership – Partnering, Supplier selection, Supplier Rating.

UNIT III: TQM TOOLS & TECHNIQUES I **(9 periods)**

The seven traditional tools of quality – New management tools – Six-sigma: Concepts, methodology, applications to manufacturing, service sector including IT – Bench marking – Reason to bench mark, Bench marking process – FMEA – Stages, Types.

UNIT IV: TQM TOOLS & TECHNIQUES II **(9 periods)**

Quality circles – Quality Function Deployment (QFD) – Taguchi quality loss function – TPM – Concepts, improvement needs – Cost of Quality – Performance measures.

UNIT V: QUALITY SYSTEMS **(9 periods)**

Need for ISO 9000 – ISO 9001-2008 Quality System – Elements, Documentation, Quality Auditing – QS 9000 – ISO 14000 – Concepts, Requirements and Benefits – TQM implementation in manufacturing and service sectors.

Total 45 Periods

Contents

CHAPTER 1

Introduction

1.0 DEFINITION OF QUALITY

Various definitions have been given to the term Quality, in line with changes and challenges in the industrial environment over time. Some of the definitions are listed as follows:

- Quality means conformance to specifications and standards.
- Quality is the conformance to requirements (Philip B Crosby).
- Quality is fitness for use.
- Quality means productivity, competitive costs, on-time delivery and the satisfaction of the customer.
- The quality of the product is decided by customer's needs, conformance to specifications, assured performance level, safety, effective packaging, on time delivery, efficient technical service and caring for the customer's feedback.
- Quality means getting every one to do what they have accepted to do, for the first time and every time.
- The degree to which a set of inherent characteristics fulfils requirements. The requirements are the needs and expectations that are stated, generally implied, or obligatory (ISO : 9000-2008).
- Quality is what the customer say it is.
- Excellence in everything.
- Quality *satisfies* the (expressed needs) customers, *delights* them by fulfilling their unstated or implied needs, and as per the current trend, quality is to *enchant* the customers.

1.1 DIMENSIONS OF QUALITY

Various dimensions of quality are listed as follows:

1. *Performance*: It is the main operating characteristics of a product. It is also called Functionality or Operationality.

   Example: Acceleration, maximum speed and comfort in an automobile.

2. *Features*: Enhancement, which is supplementing the product's basic function. Ex: remote control switch in a color television set, free movie on a omni-bus journey.
3. *Reliability*: Probability that a product is performing its intended function over its intended life and under the stated conditions.
4. *Conformance*: The extent to which the product's design and operating characteristics, satisfy the pre-determined standards.
5. *Durability*: Measure of product's useful life, before it physically deteriorates or it is replaced.
6. *Serviceability*: Time consumed in servicing, courtesy, competence and ease of repair or reconditioning of a product.
7. *Aesthetics*: Human response to a product—how it looks, feels, sounds, tastes or smells (appeals to senses).
8. *Reputation*: Impressions formed about the product quality from tangible and intangible features of the product, brand image, good will and the reputation of the organisation.
9. *Maintainability:* It is a measure of the ease with which the equipments can be maintained, to keep them in usable condition.
10. *Availability:* It is a measure of probability that the equipment is kept in running condition.
11. *Manufacturability:* It is the ease with the product can be manufactured or service can be provided. This includes the design, process planning, finishing, assembly, packing, and delivery.

Continuous improvement along any of these directions increases the customer value. But to determine which dimension is most important to customers, the quality managers have to necessarily understand the customer's needs.

For example, the manager should know, Who buys? and Who uses? The mother who buys baby biscuit packets, may expect a low cost and nutrition and the child who consumes the biscuit may fix priority to the taste.

1.2 QUALITY PLANNING

The steps that are adopted in quality planning include the following:

1. The objectives of quality system are initially listed.
2. The customers are identified.
3. The needs of the customers are listed.
4. The strategic planning which includes planning for the customer-supplier partnering, infrastructure of the organisation, total involvement of the organisation, information processing, education and training.
5. Design the product features that satisfy the customer's needs, and for optimization of the design.
6. Design and development of the processes.
7. Providing the infrastructure, establishment of teams, provision of resources, and training the personnel.

8. Quality improvement: Optimise the process capability and the quality control measures.

These steps ensure that the processes yield higher revenue at lower costs, enabled employees and satisfied customers.

1.3 QUALITY COSTS

QUALITY IS FREE, BUT ONLY TO THOSE WHO ARE WILLING TO PAY HEAVILY FOR IT–PHILIP CROSBY

1.3.1 Quality Cost Elements

Quality costs are defined as the elements of costs associated with non-achievement of product quality as envisaged by QMS.

The quality costs are classified into the following types:

1. **External failure cost**: This consists of costs incurred due to actual non-conforming products or service after delivery to the customer. This includes:
   (*a*) Cost of investigations on customer complaints including necessary field service.
   (*b*) Returned goods.
   (*c*) *Retrofit and recall costs*: Due to design deficiency the parts are redesigned, recalled and retrofitted.
   (*d*) *Warranty claims*: Cost of claims including repair costs, cleaning costs, price reduction negotiated in lieu of warranty and replacement.
   (*e*) *Liability costs*: claims including product and damages suffered.
   (*f*) *Penalty costs*: Punishment costs according to contracts or government rules, and for proven lack of performance.
   (*g*) *Customer goodwill*: Costs incurred, due to dissatisfaction of customer.
   (*h*) *Lost sales*: Contribution to profit lost due to reduction in sales because of quality problems.
2. **Internal failure cost**: Costs associated with non-conforming products, such as, cost of scrap, rework, repair and reconditioning. This consists of:
   (*a*) *Design failure cost*: Cost due to design inadequacy, which includes design corrective actions, rework due to design changes, and scrap due to design changes.
   (*b*) *Purchase failure costs*: Cost of purchased material rejection, cost of purchased material replaced, suppler corrective action costs, rework of supplier rejects etc.
   (*c*) *Operation (Product/service) failure costs*: This covers a major portion. Costs associated with non-conforming product/service discovered during operations, during material review, during corrective actions, rework or repair, scrap costs, and internal failure labor costs.
3. **Appraisal cost**
   (*a*) *Purchasing appraisal costs*: Receiving inspection or source inspection at supplier's facility or incoming inspection and control program..
   (*b*) *Manufacturing (Operations) appraisal costs*: Machine set up pieces or destructive testing, process control measurements, laboratory support, outside certification.

(c) *External appraisal costs*: Test during field during field trials of new products and evaluation of field stock and spare parts.

(d) Review of test and inspection data.

(e) *Miscellaneous quality evaluation costs*: In dispatch rooms, store rooms, packaging and shipping.

4. **Prevention cost**: The cost of prevention of poor quality consists of:

(a) *Marketing/customer/user*: Costs incurred in collection, continued survey of customer quality needs, including feed back, and contract and document review.

(b) *Product/service/design*: Cost of translating customer needs into designs and documents for manufacture, including field trials.

(c) *Purchase*: Cost of quality assurance of supplier parts, supplier reviews, supplier rating, purchase order technical data review, and supplier quality planning.

(d) *Manufacturing*: Cost of assuring capability and readiness of operations to meet quality standards, Quality control planning, QC training, design and development of QC measurement and control equipments, and operator quality education.

(e) *Quality administration*: Cost incurred in administration of salaries, quality program planning, quality performance reporting, quality education, quality improvement documenting, evaluating quality costs, and quality audit.

5. **Hidden quality costs**: Cost of redesign-wherever necessary, cost of changing the manufacturing methods because of the inability in meeting the quality requirements, cost of changes in software, and the scrap cost that has not been reported.

6. **Cost of lost opportunity**:

(a) Income lost by orders cancelled or lost.

(b) Losing to competitors due to the inability to meet the customer's requirements.

(c) Reduced number of repeated orders or quantity in each repeated order.

(d) Loss of customers, who change to competitors to fulfill their requirements.

(e) Loss of prospective customer, due to the loss of good will.

A sample result of the cause of the lost costs is shown in Table 1.1, as an illustrative example, for a production shop.

Table 1.1 Loss due to poor quality

Cause	% of total loss
Human error	10
Poor inspection	10
Poor specifications	15
Design fault (materials, design)	35
Poor planning	15
Miscellaneous	15

Cost of quality/Annual sales = 0.25 in manufacturing industries

= 0.50 in service industries

1.3.2 Quality Cost Models

A classical model called Juran's model for optimum quality level is illustrated in Fig. 1.1.

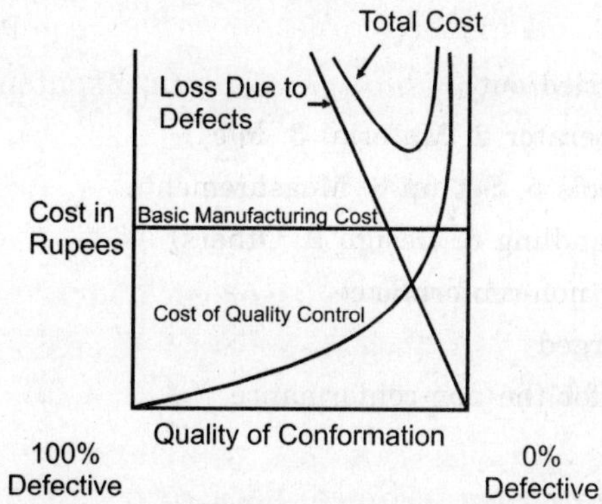

Fig. 1.1 Juran's classical model for quality costs

These models accept a trade-off between quality and cost.

1.4 COST ANALYSIS

1.4.1 Activity Based (Management Accounting) Costing

The activities such as transporting, inspection, receiving, shipping and order processing consume resources but also add value. A flow chart may be prepared to identify all the activities that add value and the ones that do not add value.

Once the activities are identified, the effects of time delays and inefficiencies are estimated. This helps the managers in making correct decisions on product design, process improvement, costing, product mix and continual improvement, and also reduces overhead expenses.

Techniques for cost estimation

1. Collecting data from accounting system.
2. Collecting data from existing reports.
3. Estimation of cost where data are not available.

Failure data

Data are collected from classified departments responsible for the non-conformance and the product or service concerned. Typical forms are illustrated in Tables 1.2 to 1.3 for internal failure and Table.1.4 for external failure.

Table 1.2 Form (Product defects)

1.	Part No., Name, Product No.
2.	Last operation carried out
3.	Description of the non-conformance
4.	Causes
5.	Dept. responsible for the non-conformance
	Account to be charged, with cost of non-conformance
6.	Qty of non-conforming items
7.	Cost of non-conformance

Table 1.3 Scrap report

1.	Part No.	Order No.
	Part Name	Product No.
2.	Last operation carried out	
3.	Defect code: (1. Operator 2. Material 3. M/c 4. Tools 5. Set up 6. Measurements 7. Handling 8. Design 9. Others)	
4.	Operation causing non-conformance	
5.	Account to be charged	
	Dept. responsible for the non-conformance	
	Account credited	
6.	Quantity scrapped	
7.	Total cost of non-conformance	

Table 1.4 External failure data

1.	Part name
2.	Product No.
3.	Date of Manufacture
4.	Period of time used
5.	Description of non-conformance
6.	Type of non-conformance
7.	Extent of non-conformance
8.	Cause of non-conformance
9.	Correction required
	(*a*) How was the failure noticed?
	(*b*) How did the product fail?
	(*c*) Reason for failure
	(*d*) Effect of failure

Various elements of quality costs are summarized as shown in the Table 1.5 for comparison clarity.

1.4.2 Trend Analysis

Quality cost data are collected from monthly reports, and classified by cost category, product category, by plant category within the organisation.

The graphical representation of this trend is shown in Fig. 1.2. The X-axis for this graph represent time periods, namely month or quarter or year.

Trend analysis is an effective tool, but some deviation or fluctuation may also be present due to chance variation, as in the case of control charts.

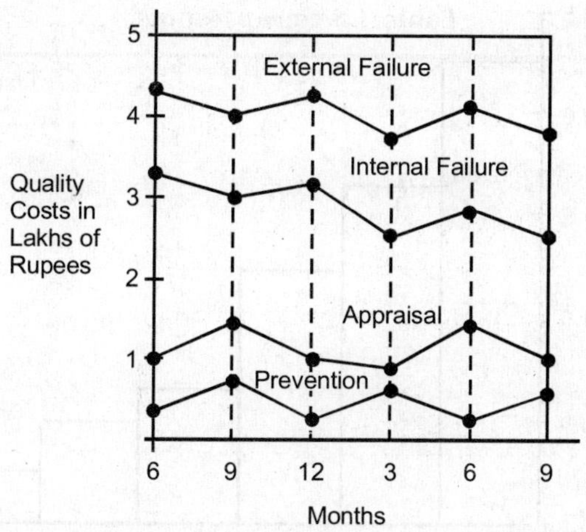

Fig. 1.2

Table 1.5 Cost of quality matrix

Costs	Design	Purchase	Manufg.	Adminstn.	Marketing
(A) Prevention costs : Quality, planning, training	Design qualilty program, development of quality standards, product /service, qualification, tests	Supplier review, supplier rating, supplier quality planning, purchase order, technical data review	**QC** planning, operations quality planning, operator quality education program	Administration expenses, quality performance reporting, quality, documents, quality education, quality audit	Marketing research, customer perception survey, contract review
(B) Appraisal costs: Test/ field trial inspection, instruments, audit	—	Incoming inspection, source inspection	Operations inspection set up inspection, purchaser external measurements, outside certification	—	—
(C) Internal Failure costs: scrap, rework	Product upgrading, design change	Purchase material, replacement, material loss, rework of supplier rejects	Material review, labour cost	—	—
(D) External failure costs: Returned goods, recall, warranty claims, penalties, lost sales	Yes	—	—	Yes	Yes

1.4.3 Pareto Analysis

Different elements of cost of external failure is shown in Fig. 1.3. Major items i.e., constituting large amount of costs are termed as, vital few and other items are termed as, trivial many. These diagrams may be constructed for quality costs by persons, by equipments, by departments or by product line or by category, by element or by non-conformities etc.

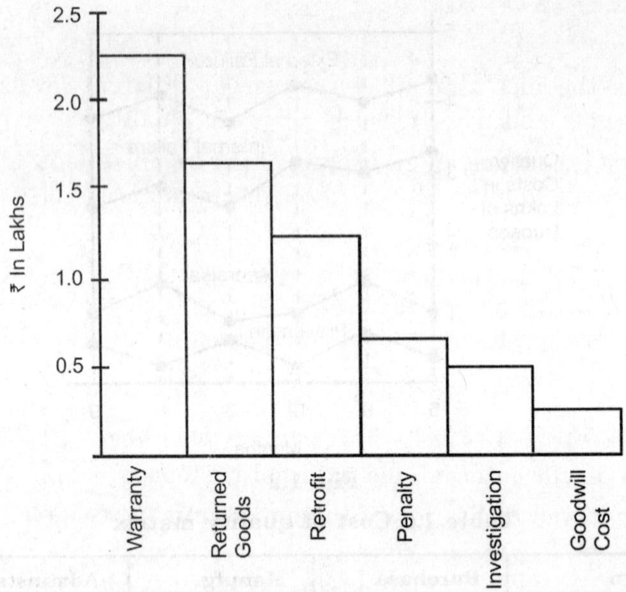

Fig. 1.3

Attention is given to vital few items, to reduce the costs and the trivial many be ignored, for the present. This method is discussed in greater detail, in Chapter 3.

1.5 STEPS IN REPORTING ON QUALITY COSTS

1. Commitment and support of management is initially obtained.
2. Teams are formed.
3. Select a department as a sample.
4. Obtain cooperation and support from the users and suppliers.
5. Define quality costs and classify.
6. Identify characteristics for quality control, in each class.
7. Determine sources of quality control study.
8. Select the appropriate quality control charts.
9. Establish procedure to QC study.
10. Prepare reports and circulate.

Some of the useful cost ratios are listed as follows:

(*a*) Operation failure costs/production costs.

(*b*) Operations appraisal cost/production costs.

(*c*) Purchasing quality cost/materials cost.

(*d*) Design quality costs/design cost.

(*e*) External failure cost/net sales.

1.6 BASICS CONCEPTS OF TQM

(*a*) What is TQM?

"Total" stresses the idea that all employees at different levels of the organisation understand the concepts and work towards achieving quality.

"Quality" means excellence, in all aspects of the organisation. "Management" refers to the commitment towards quality results, through optimum use of resources.

This starts with strategic planning and given effect through product design, manufacturing, testing and sales. It ensures continual improvement. It starts with people, and extends through all levels, from top to bottom. Thus it is seen that, TQM is the art science and technology of utilising all the available resources, optimally, to achieve excellence.

(*b*) Core Concepts

1. A committed management which ensures long term organisational support.
2. The focus on the internal and external customers.
3. Involvement and utilisation of the entire human resource.
4. Continuous improvement of the activities.
5. Treating suppliers and customers as partners.
6. Determine the performance metrics for the activities.

These concepts are described briefly as follows:

1. Management must participate fully in the quality program. A quality council must draw up a clear vision, specify long term objectives, implement and guide the program, with the feed back obtained from the employees. Management must participate in quality improvement teams and also train other teams. It is thus found, that the TQM is a continual activity, that must be built in the culture. TQM principles and procedures must be let known to all people.
2. For an effective TQM program, the customer focus is a proper place to start with i.e. by satisfying internal customers. Hence the dictum, 'Act right, the first time and every time', for getting the customer satisfaction.
3. TQM is an organisation-wide responsibility that is to be shared by everybody. All people must be trained in TQM, statistical process control, and other quality improvement methods. Inclusion of internal customers, as well as, internal suppliers on project teams is a useful approach, because they understand the process better than any one else. Persons must not merely to execute their jobs, but also think about how the job can be improved. People must be empowered to perform the activities in an optimal manner.
4. There must be a continual striving to improve all processes. Quality improvement strategies, such as timely delivery, accounting errors, customer satisfaction, cycle time and scrap reduction, and supplier management, are the most preferred places, to start with. Statistical process control, benchmarking, quality function deployment, ISO 9000 and design of experiments are very effective tools for problem solving.
5. The purchased product is about half of the sales; hence, the supplier quality must be excellent. A supplier partnering relationship is beneficial to both. The attention should be on quality and life-cycle costs, rather than the price.

6. Performance metrics such as downtime, percentage nonconforming, absenteeism, and customer satisfaction are to be determined, for each functional area. These should be communicated to all, so that every one in the organisation understands the status. Quantitative data are more useful to measure the continual quality improvement activity.

The TQM provides a quality product or service to customers, which results in, an increase in productivity at lower cost. With high quality and low price, competitive position and the market share will be increased. This sequence allows the organisation to achieve the objectives of profit as well as growth easily. Further, the employees gets job security, which will motivate them to work further and attain excellence.

Thus we see that, the TQM brings in a cultural change, in the organisation, over a period of time.

(*c*) Total Quality

Total quality implies that all persons in the organisation are committed to product or service by 'doing the right thing, right the first time, and every time' and in providing value to customers. These steps lead to the full customer satisfaction. Thus, we see that TQM combines the human needs, pride, esteem, and excellence into the job.

The customer's needs are transformed into product or service design features. Process produces the products to satisfy customer's requirements. The feedback from customers are sent to the product designer who re-fixes the materials, shape, colour, dimensions and methods. Feedback of inspection results are given to the manufacturing planning and product design engineer. Every body in the organisation is producing an output—product or service. Thus, every employee in the organisation who performs the following operation is an internal customer. The ultimate purchaser of the product or service is the external customer.

(*d*) Internal Customers

Example 1.

For the department:	*Internal customer is:*
Purchasing	Operations/Manufacturing
Manufacturing	Marketing
Production management	Sales
Finance	Manufacturing
Design	Manufacturing
Machine shops	Assembly
Assembly	Testing
Testing	Packing
Packing	Dispatch
Sales and Service	User

Example 2. For an Educational Institution, the *internal* customers are:

Students	Faculty members
Administrative staff	Technical staff
Menial staff	Hostel staff
Maintenance staff (Civil, Elect, Water, etc.)	Infrastructure staff (Transport, Communication, etc.)

(e) External Customers

Example 1. For an educational institution, the *external* customers are:

Parents	Industries (employers)
Affiliating universities	Government
Sponsors of research projects	A.I.C.T.E./ U.G.C.
Foreign Universities	Public

1.7 HISTORICAL REVIEW

1.7.1 Quality Era

Table 1.6 Quality era

Characteristics	**Inspection 1800s**	**SQC 1930s**	**Quality assurance 1950s**	**Strategic quality Mgt 1980+**
1. Primary concern	Detection	Control	Coordination	Management
2. View of quality	A problem	to be solved	Proactive attack	A competitive opportunity
3. Emphasis	Product uniformity	Uniform product with less inspection	Designers role	The market and consumer needs
4. Methods	Gauging, measurement	Statistical quality tools	Programs and systems	Strategic planning, goal setting
5. Who is responsible?	Inspection dept.	Manufacturing and engineering departments	All departments	Every (Team) one in the organisation
6. Orientation and approach	Inspects quality	Controls quality	Builds in quality	Manages in quality

The characteristic feature for the era from 2008+ is Sustained Quality Management. Besides the economic aspect, the environmental impact is given importance.

The ISO is reported to be actively preparing for ISO 9001:2015, wherein the QMS is designed to include the economic growth, the environmental integrity and the social equity aspects for sustainable development.

1.7.2 History of Quality

Table 1.7 History of quality

	Periods		**Milestones/events**
A	Before industrial revolution	1850s	Cottage industry approach
B	After industrial revolution	1870+	Skilled tradesman, standards, Inspection
C	After World War I	1919+	Statistical quality control
D	After World War II	1945+	Reliability, maintainability
		1951	Deming prize
E	Quality	1960+	Quality motivation, quality circle, quality assurance
		1962	Zero defect

F	Quality system	1979	Integrated quality program
		1983	Total quality control, TQM, strategic planning
G	Quality standards	1987	Quality standards ISO 9000
		1988	Indian standards IS 14000
		1991	Taguchi methods, Design of experiments as tool for quality improvement
H	Recognition and Reward	1991	Golden Peacock National Quality Award instituted by Institute of Directors, New Delhi
		1992	Rajiv Gandhi National Quality Award instituted by B. I. S.
		1994	Indian Quality Standards—revised
		2000	Indian Confederation of Indian Industry award for business excellence Indian Quality Standards—revised
		2000	International Asia Pacific Quality Award, instituted by Asia Pacific Qlty. Orgnsn., Philippines
		2001	National Institution for Quality and Reliability Awards, sponsored by Lucas TVS, Bajaj Auto, GKD, Susira, TVN Kidao, and T.S.Krishna
I	Juran Quality Medal	1997	Instituted by Ramakrishna Bajaj (Indian Merchant Chamber)
J	Revision of	2008	Revision of 9000 standards to include environmental integrity
K	Annual award	2013	Century International Quality ERA Convention, Geneva. This is based on criteria of QC100 quality model.
L	Social Equity	2015	Planned Revision of 9000 standards to include the social equity aspects also for sustainable development.

1.8 PRINCIPLES OF TQM

1. *Delight of the customer:* Customer satisfaction means, bringing in the best that fulfils the customer's desires and needs. Now the concept is extended to customer delight, which means fulfilling the unspelt desires, and also the customer enchantment, which means that the customer is motivated towards a better or creative use of the product or service.
2. *Management by facts:* Ethical decisions are made, based upon factual information, rather than on pressure or opportunity.
3. *Human based management:* Participation by all employees of organisation i.e., everyone is involved. The more the people are involved, the greater will be their

commitment to customer's satisfaction. Performance appraisal and recognition and reward system motivate as well as empower the employees.

4. *Continual improvement:* TQM as a management process implies that we should improve, or else our competitor will continue to improve and the customer will turn away from us.
5. TQM stands on quality system measures, documentation and records. Process measurements should be applied to all activities.
6. TQM starts with education and training and development of the human resource.
7. Quality planning is an essential step, to measure and control quality.
8. Strong leadership is needed to establish credibility and implement TQM.
9. TQM should not have any weak links or processes.
10. Team work and team accountability are necessary to solve the problems.
11. Human oriented technology is essential.
12. TQM is a corporate culture. Corporate goals and individual attitudes must coincide for effective implementation.

1.9 LEADERSHIP PRINCIPLES

The leadership should create order that is coherent, consistent, and controlled. The leader anticipates and identifies the impediments and remove them. They motivate others to achieve excellence.

Essential characteristics of a quality leader may be summarised as:

1. *Specific Vision:* Clarity in thought.
2. *Enthusiasm:* Motivation of the self.
3. *Integrity:* Self-knowledge, self control and unbiased.
4. *Commitment:* Commitment to quality achievement.
5. *Curiosity:* Willingness to learn.
6. *Courage:* Willingness to take calculated risk.
7. *Empower:* Delegate rather than direct the employees.
8. *Recognition and reward the team work:* Empower and develop the people to achieve the quality goals. Collaboration with mutual understanding rather than competition is favoured. Teams should share willingly the information. The leaders devote their efforts to train the human resource rather than supervise and control.
9. *Sense of honour:* Pride in his/her duty and clarity of purpose.
10. *Communicative:* Communication is the vital link that holds TQM efforts together.

1.9.1 Fiedler's Theory

According to Fiedler, the performance of a group depends upon:

1. Motivational system of the leader.
2. The extent to which the leader has effected control.
3. Leader-member relationship, task structure and leader's authority.

1.9.2 Role of Leadership in Continual Quality Improvement

1. Identify the customers focus and needs.
2. Plan the framework for quality.
3. Educate, train, empower and develop the employees.
4. Getting the employees' involvement and commitment.
5. Improvement in the process.
6. Measurements and use of statistical tools.
7. Recognition and reward system integration with the management practice.

1.9.3 Leadership Concepts

The successful leader should understand the human nature, their basic needs and abilities. To be effective, the leader understands that:

1. People need security as well as independence at the same time.
2. Employees are very sensitive to external rewards and punishments and yet strongly motivated.
3. People prefer hearing a kind word of praise from the superior. The leader should 'Catch them doing something right', so that he/she can pat them on the back.
4. People can process only a few facts at a time. Hence the leader should start with simple things.
5. People trust their gut reaction more than the statistical data.
6. People distrust their leaders, who are merely rhetoric, but do not follow any principle in actions.

1.10 ROLE OF SENIOR MANAGEMENT

The duties of senior management may be listed as:

1. Senior management must adopt, 'Management by moving around' methodology. They should visit customers, suppliers, departments within the organisation and the plants and outside the organisation. MBWA reduces the paperwork and ensures the first hand (on the spot) information, and facilitates immediate solution.
2. *Commitment by senior management:* The TQM expert should discuss the priorities of the company before initiating specific TQM plans. After a few discussions, a TQM strategic plan with objectives, metrics of excellence, and bench marking are developed and projected. Thus, the senior management inculcates commitment in the people to execute better.
3. Senior management must familiarise with the developments in knowledge on quality improvement by referring books, journals, and attending seminars.
4. *Management resource planning:* Provide the organisational structure including the steering committee, group level, department level, and the resources to implement and for improvement.
5. *Quality policy dissemination:*

   (*a*) The policy is to be communicated to all the employees for their understanding, acceptance and commitment to quality, by lectures at suitable functions.

Articles, in-house magazines, circulars, notices, use of utility items with a message or slogan on quality, messages on letter heads and other stationery items, are the means of propagating the importance of quality, to the employees.

(*b*) Unofficial grape-vine channels of employees are also effective.

(*c*) Communication externally, with suppliers, customers, the media and quality experts are also effective.

6. *Competency development:* Training and group meeting of the trainers on TQM program, development of soft skills for team work, development of communication skills and the knowledge and applications of analytical methods and statistical techniques are essential.
7. *Review on goals:* Review the appraisals, improvements, establish or revise the recognition and reward systems of the efficient and effective functioning of the teams.

Through these steps, the senior managers should be able to develop faith and confidence and remove the impediments such as fear, anticipate and demolish the resistance to change and effect a change in the corporate culture.

1.11 QUALITY COUNCIL

Quality council is mainly set up to provide overall directions and guidance.

Quality council consists of the chief executive officer, senior managers of design, marketing, finance, production and quality departments, a labour union representative and a coordinator. The coordinator will report to the chief executive.

The coordinator builds the two-way trust, reports the team needs to the council, gives back the council expectations to the team and briefs the council on the team's progress. The coordinator assists the team leaders, discusses on the problems and shares their experience through regular meetings.

The duties of quality council members are as follows:

1. They identify the core values, establish the vision statement, mission statement and quality policy statement.
2. Draft the strategic long term plan with goals and periodical quality improvement programs with objectives.
3. Install education and training plans.
4. Monitor the cost of non-conformance, continually.
5. Decide on the performance metrics for the organisation, approve and monitor them.
6. Continually identify the problems and plan to improve the processes, especially the ones, which lead to external and internal customer satisfaction.
7. Install cross-functional schemes and departmental teams and regularly monitor their progress.
8. Install or update the recognition and reward system, to keep motivating the people constantly.

In the quality council meeting, the following matters are normally discussed: Progress report on teams, customer satisfaction report, progress on goals achievement, new project teams, if any, and benchmarking report.

1.12 QUALITY STATEMENTS

Quality statements declare the core values and concepts, vision and mission and quality policies of the organisation. Once developed, they are reviewed and updated sometimes. These statements form part of strategic planning. Each of the award winning organisations, invariably have a vision of and mission on, what quality is and how to achieve it.

(*a*) Vision Statement

It is a brief declaration on the expectations of an organisation. It is the ideal state which an organisation strives continually to achieve. Visions are eternal, inspirational and shared fully within the organisation. For example:

Indian Overseas Bank	We grow with people
IBM	Service
Apple	Computing for the masses
Disney theme park	Happiest place on earth
Southern Railway	We care

Successful visions provide a guidance for decision making. The desired goals revealed by the vision, provide the criterion for effective decision making. Some organisations strengthen the significance of vision statement by incorporating the same, in the uniforms or badges of the employees and official letter heads.

- TI is a good company; one reason is that, I am a part of it—TI manual.
- Customers receive what they order, without nonconformities, on time, in the right quantity, booked and billed on time... People enjoy their work. The organisation makes a profit—Commercial organisation.

(*b*) Mission Statement

The mission statements explain the following: Who we are? Who are our customers? What we do? How we do it? It provides a clear statement of the aim for the employees, projected customers and suppliers, as well.

The mission statement declares exactly where the organisation is going. It answers the basic question, namely, How does the organisation intend to *win in the business?* In short, the mission statement defines the organisation's leadership and shows its direction.

Examples:

1. To meet customers' transport and distribution needs and by being the best at moving their goods, on time, safely and damage free—A Railway Company.

2. We are here to bring out and enlighten the hidden technical skills and abilities of youth, with high quality technical education and proper discipline—A Technical Educational Institution.

3. An ice cream company in USA, in its mission statement, 'wants to sell all natural ice creams and concoctions' and 'improve the quality of life locally, nationally, and internationally'. Such mission statement truly excite the employees and stretch them. An effective mission statement gives people a sense of direction to profitability and the inspiration to feel that they are part of the big and important role. It should be specific, descriptive and yet aspirational.

(c) Quality Policy Statement

This provides a direction to all employees in the organisation, as how they should provide products and service to the customers. It is drafted by the chief executive, upon the feedback from the employees and finally gets approved by the quality council.

Some of the *characteristics* of the policy statement may be highlighted as:

(*a*) Quality first, always.

(*b*) Fulfils the needs of the customers.

(*c*) Excel in the competition.

(*d*) Quality improvement, continually.

(*e*) Utilise the entire human resource.

A quality policy declaration for an institution, is a must as per ISO 9000.

Example: Mody is a quality company. Quality is the basic business principle for Mody. Quality means providing all our customers with creative products and services that satisfy their requirements completely. Quality is the concern of each employee—Mody Corporation.

Some examples of statements that include vision, mission, quality policy and core values are given as follows:

1. DELTA has a clear corporate vision....To be the benchmark company in the chemical industry through superior performance, exhibited in the following ways:

- Acting on established principles of excellence in environmental safety, health and welfare.
- Satisfy the aspirations of its customers.
- Utilising all resources in efficient and effective manner.
- Improving the processes, continually.
- Maintaining sustained values for customers, employees, suppliers and all stakeholders.
- Promoting ethical environment of trust, respect, and transparency—Delta Company.

2. We strive to bring out and nurture the talents and skills of youth, with quality technical education, motivate them to be self-disciplined and develop in them, the competence to face the challenges of globalisation by:

Providing excellent infrastructure and conducive environment to learn and grow.

Total commitment to comply with all the requirements of QMS.

Continually improving the effectiveness of the Quality Management System.

Responding to, the changes in both technology and applications, globally.

Associating with leading industries and research institutions, in the transfer of knowledge from the laboratory to the field. —Technical Institution

1.13 STRATEGIC QUALITY PLANNING

Strategy

It may be defined as the coordinated, coherent and sustained efforts, to achieve one's long term goals or according to market fluctuations. In fact the strategy determines the *structure* of the organisation.

The steps involved in strategic quality planning are as follows:

1. Study on the market share, customer needs and expectations and aspirations.
   (*a*) Study the competitors and factors such as, what is the field like? Life cycle of the product, drivers of profitability, SWOT analysis on competitors, expenditure on R and D, sales force, who are our main customers? Who are their main customers?
   (*b*) What the competitors have done in the immediate past?
   (*c*) What you have done in the immediate past to win the competition? It may be new product, stealing persons from other organisation, a special product or a new technology. If you have lost persons or a special product or technology, invest in continually upgrading the hardware or software and save the equipment from obsolescence.
   (*d*) What are the threats in a year ahead?
   (*e*) What is your utmost winning move to retain customers?
2. Decide on objectives such as the customer needs and satisfaction, and customer supplier partnership, and the strategies to adopt. e.g. globalisation, 'six sigma', service add-on, innovation, adapt a new technology, merger, acquisition and invest in new capacity are some of the strategies adopted.
3. Alignment:
   (*a*) *Design*: Design the required organisation structure as estimated for the present and for the projected future scenario.
   (*b*) *Resource planning*: Provision of necessary and sufficient resources including the employment of right people in the right jobs as drivers, for effective implementation and improvement.
   (*c*) Design methods of policy implementation and communication so that all employees understand, accept and commit themselves to realise the objectives.
4. Deployment:
   (*a*) Training to develop team spirit, in communication skills, and analytical and statistical techniques for performance and continual improvement.
   (*b*) Install appraisal, metrics of performance, recognition and reward system.

Some of the tools recommended for *qualitative analysis* are:

(*i*) Affinity diagram, to map out logical or sequential links among related classes.

(*ii*) Bench marking, search for the best practices and adoption, to ensure excellent performance.

(*iii*) Brain storming for generating ideas.

(*iv*) Cause and effect or Fishbone diagram or Ishikawa diagram to analyse the results and find the root causes.

(*v*) Flow chart, for procedure study.

(*vi*) Tree diagram to analyse the inter-relationships among goals and measures.

Some of the tools for *quantitative analysis* are:

(*i*) Control charts to monitor, sense and control deviations.

(*ii*) Histogram or frequency distribution diagram: To fix priority while decision making.

(*iii*) Pareto diagram: For identifying and acting on the critical few factors or areas and considering trivial many, later.

(*iv*) Scatter diagram or correlation diagram: To identify the reliable relationship between the cause and effect.

1.14 DEMING PHILOSOPHY

W. Edwards Deming had proposed *fourteen* principles concepts towards quality achievement. These principles are summarised as given below:

1. Create constancy of purpose for improving products and services with a plan. Publicise the aims and purposes of the organisation's long range goals, resource allocation for innovation, research and development, training and continuous education for the employees.
2. Adopt the new philosophy: Focus on the customer satisfaction, prevention of non-conformance, rather than detection and correction, and customer satisfaction are a few of the examples of new philosophy.
3. Cease dependence on mass inspection to achieve quality: To improve the process and reduce its cost, use of statistical techniques should be adopted. Acceptance sampling, is to be eliminated completely.
4. End the practice of selecting the suppliers, based solely on price. Price is meaningless, without quality. Minimise total cost by working with a single supplier, thereby developing a long term ethical and economical relationship, loyalty and trust with the suppliers.
5. Identify the problems and work to improve the system—continuously (Kaizen). Management must locate and correct problems, such that quality and productivity are continuously improved and the cost reduced. The focus should be on prevention of problems. Responsibilities are assigned to the teams, so that the root causes of the problems are removed, and the process improved continuously.
6. Institute training on the job: Each employee is to be trained in quality improvement skills, communication skills and problem solving methods.
7. Adopt and institute leadership: Management must provide supervisors with training on analytical methods and all these listed points, so that the philosophy can be implemented 'in toto'.
8. Drive out fear and create mutual trust, nurture a climate for innovation. Fear is caused by lack of job security, anticipated physical harms, performance appraisal by superiors, ignorance of organisational goals, poor supervision and poor knowledge of the job. Driving out fear, is the primary step to success.

   All the employees are to be treated with dignity and trust. Only then, they can provide ideas and act upon for improvement.

9. Breakdown barriers between staff areas:

   Impediments exist internally among levels of management, among departments, and within departments. Externally, they exist between the organisation and its customers and suppliers. They thrive, because of poor channels or methods of communication, competition, fear, personal prejudice or even enmity. This will optimise the efforts of the team or groups.

10. Eliminate slogans, exhortations on and targets for the people:

    Exhortations that demand for increased productivity without providing tools can demoralise the organisation. These may express the management's desire, but do not result in a better product or service.

    Goals should be set such that they are achievable and the methods are known and made available, to all the employees.

11. Eliminate work standards that prescribe numerical quotas for the work force and numerical goals for management. Instead of fixing quantity, the management must concentrate on the methods for improvement and quality. Quota and work standards give importance to quantity, rather than quality.

    Rather than quotas, the management must learn the capabilities of the process and methods, and concentrate on efforts to improve them. Internal goals set by the management without a method, is similar to the construction of a building without foundation. It is a false approach.

12. Remove the barriers that rob employees of pride of workmanship and eliminate the annual rating or merit rating system:

    Loss of pride in workmanship occurs in organisations, because of the following reasons:

    (*a*) Workers are unaware how to relate their efforts to the organisation's missions.

    (*b*) They are blamed for system failure.

    (*c*) Poor designs leading to waste of product or service.

    (*d*) Inadequate training.

    (*e*) Punitive supervision.

    (*f*) Inadequate or faulty equipment and tools provided for performing the job. The elimination of barriers may be a long-term commitment by the management. When workers feel proud of their work, they will grow fully and successfully, in their job and out of their job.

    Management must communicate all employees, the job descriptions, provide appropriate tools and materials, and insist on the employees' understanding of their roles and contribution to execute and improve the process.

13. Institute a vigorous program of education, retraining, and self improvement for every employee:

    A long term plan to train and educate the employees continuously must be made by management. Deming's principles and the organisation's mission should form the basis, for such education program. Every employee should be retrained, if the requirements of the organisation are revised to meet the challenges and changing environments.

14. Put everybody in the company to work and accomplish the transformation, for good: Management's important responsibility is for the continuous improvement of the process. Create a sructure in top management that will emphasise the preceding thirteen points every day.

The principles may be aptly called, **'codes of ethics for Quality'.**

1.15 PHILIP CROSBY'S 14 POINTS ON TQM

The steps developed by P. Crosby are similar to that of Deming. These steps were developed as steps for 'Zero defects program' and are also referred to as 14 points on TQM.

1. MANAGEMENT COMMITMENT. The quality movement begins with the top management. The top management should be convinced of the need for quality improvement. They should formulate clear policies, communicate them to all employees, and assign duty and responsibility to every employee.
2. QUALITY IMPROVEMENT TEAM. A team of departmental heads is formed to oversee the improvements in their departments as well as in the organisation as a whole.
3. QUALITY MEASUREMENT. Improvement measures are to be established suitable to each activity so that improvements are gauged, and areas in need of improvement are identified.
4. COST OF QUALITY. The cost of quality is estimated to identify the areas where the improvements would be profitable.
5. QUALITY AWARENESS. The quality awareness among the employees is to be raised, so that they understand the importance of product conformance and the costs of non-conformance.
6. CORRECTIVE ACTIONS. Corrective actions are incorporated as per steps 3 and 4.
7. ZERO DEFECTS PLANNING. The quality council initiates a program towards this objective.
8. SUPERVISOR TRAINING. All levels of management are to be trained towards the implementation of quality improvement program.
9. ZERO DEFECTS DAY. A day may be arranged to propagate the idea of zero defects.
10. GOAL SETTING. Goals are to be set for the individuals and their groups.
11. ERROR CAUSES REMOVAL. Employees are encouraged to report any problems which prevent them from implementing error-free activity.
12. RECOGNITION. For the outstanding performance or for meeting the quality goals, the employees should be given public and non-financial appreciation.
13. QUALITY COUNCIL. This council consisting of professionals, and department heads should meet regularly to discuss on the problems and means of solution.
14. DO IT ALL OVER AGAIN. Steps 1 to 13 are repeated to continually improve the quality.

1.16 JURAN'S 10 STEPS FOR QUALITY IMPROVEMENT

The ten steps enunciated by Juran for quality improvement are given as follows:

1. Build awareness of need and opportunities to improve
2. Set goals for improvement
3. Organise to reach goals
4. Provide training
5. Carryout projects to solve problems
6. Report progress
7. Give recognition
8. Communicate results
9. Keep score
10. Maintain momentum by making annual improvement part of the regular systems and processes of the organisation.

1.17 CLAUS MOLLER'S PRINCIPLES

Claus Moller has developed the concept of *personal quality* as the starting point for quality movement and improvement. He believed that 'charity begins at home' and the quality efforts begin with the individual. The twelve principles of Claus Moller are listed as follows:

1. Set personal quality goals
2. Establish own personal quality account
3. Check how satisfied others are with your efforts
4. Regard the next link as a valued customer
5. Avoid errors
6. Perform tasks more effectively
7. Utilise the resources well (fully)
8. Be committed
9. Learn to finish what you start
10. Control your stress
11. Be ethical
12. Demand quality.

Thus it is found that in all the theories propounded by various quality gurus, the quality management is certain to begin with management commitment, and through effective employee involvement, results in the customer satisfaction. The means may vary with individuals or teams, but their coherent efforts converge towards the customers' satisfaction, delight and enchantment as well.

1.18 BARRIERS TO TQM

1. Absence or lack of top management's commitment. For example, TQM will not succeed if senior management is only motivated by outside pressures, such as needing to please the board of directors or meet an accrediting agency's standards.

If employees see discrepancies in what management says and what it actually does, they will lose interest and faith in TQM. There should be specific commitment on time as well as other organisational resources.

For successful implementation, the management must clearly communicate to all people, the objectives for adopting TQM and be consistent in its application of those principles. In the absence of this commitment, the morale will be the casualty.

2. Inadequate knowledge or understanding of TQM principles and methodology.
3. Failure to accept TQM as a cultural revolution, i.e., a change in the organisational culture or the mind set of the employees:

From result orientation	to	Process and result orientation
From company orientation	to	Customer and company orientation
From task orientation	to	People and task orientation

The following observations made from the psychological studies are relevant here:

(*a*) People change, when they want to, and to meet their own needs

(*b*) People have to be convinced themselves of the need to change

(*c*) People must be moved from a state of fear to mutual trust and participation

(*d*) People tend to lose motivation, without involvement or participation in decision making, and without recognition and reward of their work.

4. Improper planning: Absence of long term vision, mission, and goals by the top management. Three components of successful TQM planning are:

   (*a*) Obtaining company-wide commitment,

   (*b*) Communicating company vision, mission, and goals, and

   (*c*) Providing open communication about the company's new focus. A time frame such as Gantt chart, should be developed and posted in public areas, so that everyone remains focussed on TQM. The plan can be flexible, so that adjustments and improvements can be made as the culture evolves.

5. Absence of continuous training and education: Senior management should conduct training programs on principles of TQM, in group discussion, communication skills, education program, essentially on quality improvement techniques, problem identification, and problem solving methods. Training and education should be both formal and informal. Senior management personnel may be involved in training the employees, to demonstrate management's commitment to TQM and to ensure that the principles are consistently taught to all employees. Informal training could include circulating articles on, or displaying information about TQM on company noticeboards.

6. Inadequate use of empowerment and team work: Complacency in team work will inhibit TQM progress. Ineffective teams that fail to stay focused or complete their tasks are a big expense to organisations. To be effective, teams need trained facilitators, a mission, a time frame for completing projects, members who represent the functional areas to be improved, and accountability. The mission of the

team must not be overwhelming; some tasks need to be broken down into manageable phases.

Whenever possible, teams' recommendations and solutions should be implemented, as this sends a powerful and positive message to employees about the importance of the empowerment and team work.

7. The Management related barriers are:
   (*a*) Fear of senior management losing control
   (*b*) Apprehension and doubts of the senior management, about the efficacy of the TQM methodology
   (*c*) Lack of leadership qualities
   (*d*) Failure in or faulty delegation of authority
   (*e*) Lack of motivation at the senior level and
   (*f*) Managers do not support each other.
8. Incorrect or insufficient or incompatible organisational structure and isolated individuals and departments. Autocratic organisational structure and management policies can lead to implementation problems. As team work is an essential part of TQM environment, the isolation of the individuals and departments will dissolve over time. Tools such as brain-storming, cause and effect diagram, and work flow diagrams are successful in identifying the discrepancies and misinterpretations that are often the root cause of such feuds.
9. Inefficient or ineffective measurement techniques and lack of access to data and results. Having no measurement process or ineffective measurement techniques, failing to maintain accurate and reliable data, and failing to provide sufficient access to data run counter to TQM principles. Data are critical to decision making in this culture. Key quality characteristics should be measured consistently, so that credible and reliable data are produced and decision makers can make proper and timely decisions. Quick and easy access to data and also quick and efficient data retrieval are necessary. Decision makers must also be trained in data analysis and interpretation, so that measurement serves its intended purpose.
10. The Customer related barriers may be listed as:
    (*a*) Inadequate attention to internal and external customers and the public.

    Managers, too often, assume they know what customers need and expect, which results in misdirected efforts and investments. Training to anticipate, sense and interpret the changing needs and aspirations of the customers and appropriate sampled surveys and feedback, are initiated by many high profile companies, when a new product is launched.

    (*b*) Lack of social responsiveness.
    (*c*) Risks and benefits to the public are ignored or not evaluated.
11. Inability to build a learning organisation that provides for continuous improvement. A person, even though on the right track, will get run over, if he/she just sits there! One should move forward on the track, rather than standing still, to survive the risks including competition.

❑❑❑

CHAPTER 2

TQM Principles

Only a customer can define the purpose of a business .

—Peter Drucker

2.1 CUSTOMER SATISFACTION

The department of customer satisfaction is responsible to deal with the customer complaints. This department monitors and classifies the complaints, review, identify the schemes that are expected to improve customer service and provide satisfactory response to customers.

What do the customers expect? Most of the customers expect the following attributes from the goods/services: Values, brand image and also good performance. Customers favour the delivery with right quality, in right quantity, at the right time, at right cost and at the right place in addition to safety, and ethical transactions of the organisation.

Customer satisfaction is obtained along three different types of needs, according to Kano of Japan, namely,

(*i*) Dissatisfiers which are the needs that are expected in a product or service.

(*ii*) Satisfiers which are the needs that customers feel they desire.

(*iii*) Exciters/delighters which are the creative features that customers had not expected, at that point of time.

Satisfiers are identified through market study. Over a time span, the exciters/delighters become satisfiers as the customers familiarize with them and ultimately turn into dissatisfiers.

The profit is based on quality, customer satisfaction, good will and reputation promoted by the satisfied customers. Tracing the customer needs, analysis and reporting of customer attitudes, trends on product quality, safety, and reliability, data on field trials, after sales service call rate, ethical advertising, customer education, accounting errors, mutual trust, polite and quick response, and the spare parts availability, promote the customer satisfaction.

It is observed that the customer satisfaction is a combination of the following factors:

(*a*) Technology (hardware and software), product, price, quality and responses, delivery and appropriate communication.

(*b*) Perceived knowledge of the company, cost of the product, and personal expectations, needs and attitudes.

(*c*) Apart from cost, the quality and the consistency of the customer service are very relevant in the present day context. In fact, the service paradigm in the industry is broken, so that the customers are not just satisfied but they are delighted that they tell the friends as well as strangers, how good is *your* organisation. Typical examples of high customer satisfaction scores in the service industries are Federal Express (FedEx, courier), United Parcel Service (UPS), and Dell (Computers) in U.S.A. according to a recent survey, released by the National Quality Research Center at the University of Michigan.

Various steps to evaluate the customer satisfaction are listed as follows:

(*a*) Study the buying procedures of each customer organisation and map them with respect to individuals.

(*b*) Determine the factors of buyer-seller interactions.

(*c*) Analyse the trends of the above and formulate the indices, to represent of all relevant features such as repeat orders, switching suppliers, and number of customers lost, as well as gained.

2.1.1 Factors in Determining Customer Satisfaction

1. Quality of supply.
2. Product installation/Commissioning.
3. Product performance, ease of operation and control.
4. After sales service.
5. Reliability.
6. Maintainability.
7. Serviceability.

For the questionnaire on customer satisfaction listed in Malcolm Baldrige National Quality Award, students are advised to refer, Arora[3] (p. 401)

2.2 CUSTOMERS PERCEPTION OF QUALITY

2.2.1 Customer Perceived Quality

It is the subjective assignment resulting from image, advertising, or brand names. Consumers do not always have complete information about a product or service. A product's durability, for example, cannot be readily observed; it must be inferred from various tangible and intangible aspects of the product. In this case, images, advertising, and brand names–*inferences* about quality rather than the reality itself–can be critical. The customer impression of quality is the essence of *perceived* quality.

The quality of the product or service as perceived by the customer may be different from the quality as perceived by the organisation. A feature that is satisfactory to one customer may be disliked by another. For example, some people prefer to take coffee with less sugar (with bitter taste) and some prefer to take 'chicory' coffee with lather.

A survey by the American Society for Quality showed that the following are the factors that influence the user perceptions of quality:

1. Performance
2. Features
3. Service
4. Warranty
5. Price
6. Errors in documentation
7. Errors in delivery and
8. Reputation and good will

It is obvious from this, that the product quality and service are more important than price.

1. *Performance:* It means 'fitness for use' which shows that the product or service is ready for the customer's use at the time it is sold. The related considerations are:
   (*a*) Reliability
   (*b*) Availability and
   (*c*) Maintainability.
2. *Features:* Attributes or features of a product or service are psychological, time oriented, ethical and technological. These are in fact, secondary characteristics of the product or service.
3. *Service*: Service is defined as the results generated by the activities between the organisation and the customer and by the organisation's internal activities, to meet the customer needs[8].

   Customer service may be measured mainly by (*a*) the *consistency* in service provision, which is very relevant, effective feature to impress, satisfy, and also delight the customer. Some of the other factors such as (*b*) number of requirements fulfilled, (*c*) number of misunderstood requirements, (*d*) time taken for repair or replacement, and (*e*) the time lag between the order and exact replacement, indicate the quality of customer service. Providing excellent customer service is different from and is more difficult to achieve than a good quality product. Customers may or may not complain, but some organisations obtain feed back from them. A data base on the promptness or time lags in effecting the service, response time to service calls, and number of reminder calls etc is built by the organisation and fed back to the employees periodically. The activities may be divided into sub-processes, analysed, and improved continually to minimise the time lag.
4. *Warranty:* It represents the manufacturer's promise on quality, supported by a guarantee on customer satisfaction. It also represents a commitment to assure a level of service or replacement of parts to satisfy the customer.

   In parallel, the warranty provides feed back on the product and service quality. It also compels the organisation to develop corrective and preventive system. The warranty encourages customers to buy a service by reducing the risks while in use and increases the sales from the present customers by continued trusted loyalty.
5. *Price:* Now-a-days, the customer is willing to pay a high price to get value. Customers are constantly valuing the products and services against the competitors, to know who provides a better value. But at the same time, the customers concept of value also changes. Frequently, organisations have to maintain contact with customers to identify, verify, and raise their perception of value on each product and service.

6. *Errors in Documentation*: Documentation errors in the invoice, delivery note and way bills not only delay delivery and payments but a lot of good will may be lost. Typographical errors in the amount or quantity or the address in the documents delay delivery and payment, cause litigation, anxiety and dislocation of consequent schedules for the buyer, and ultimately lead to the loss of good will.
7. *Errors in Delivery*: (*a*) Errors in handling the goods (*b*) Wrong items delivered, (*c*) Wrong or incomplete address and (*d*) Delay in delivery come under this category. Computerisation seems to be best way to eliminate such type of errors. Automated handling or sorting of items is also the other method adopted in the developed countries.
8. *Reputation and Good will*: The customer satisfaction depends up on the lasting experience with the company, beyond the product or service.

   Customers are ready to pay more, for popular brand name and they also become life long customers. It is estimated that the cost of winning a new customer is five times that for keeping the existing customer. Customer retention is major economic strategy for an organisation. Investing for customer retention has been reported to be more effective bottom line approach than spending resources to lower the operational costs. The feed back is a very effective means to study this.

   FEED BACK: Feed back from the customers must be obtained continually. Customers change their ideas, expectations and their suppliers. Prompt feed back enables the organisation and the front line people to: (*a*) Discover customer satisfaction or dissatisfaction, (*b*) Discover their relative priorities on quality, (*c*) Compare performance with competition, (*d*) Obtain the customer's needs and develop and (*e*) Establish opportunities for improvement

   In service industries such as banking, insurance and transport, the feed back has been playing important roles towards product or service development. There are statistical techniques to identify and analyse the errors, and various schemes for preventive and corrective actions.

2.2.2 Voice of the Customers

Several tools available to listen to the customer's voice are such as:

1. Comment cards.
2. Questionnaires.
3. Focus groups.
4. Toll free telephone lines.
5. Visit to the customers.
6. Report cards.
7. The internet.
8. Feedback from employes.
9. Mass customisation.
10. Customer satisfaction index.

1. Comment Card

It is a cheap method. A card is enclosed with the warranty card and packed along with the product, during sales. The card collects information on name, address, age, sex, occupation and the factor that influenced customer's decision to buy the product etc.

Comment cards are very much common in hospitality industry.

2. Customer Questionnaire

It is a familiar method to get opinions and perceptions on the organisation and its product and service. But it is time consuming and costly. Many survey seek the customer's response on 'one to five' scale grading. A sample surveys to elicit the relative importance of the qualities of the house wife as expected of the husband, is shown in Table 2.1

Table 2.1 Survey on dinner served

1. How often do you take dinner with your wife at home?

______ Not at all	______ Daily	______ When guest visit
______ When reminded		______ When it rains

2. How often do you expect to take dinner at home with your wife?

______ Not at all	______ Daily	______ Only on week days
______ When reminded		______When feeling sick

3. How satisfied are you with your wife's cooking?

______Very satisfied	______ Dissatisfied	______ Neutral
______Satisfied		______ Very happy

On a scale 1 to 8, rank the importance of the following to the happiness in life, where 1 is most important

______ Personal hygiene	______ Cleanliness of the house
______ Lawn maintenance	______ Romance
______ Faithfulness	______ Respect to mother in law
______ Thoughtfulness	______ Sharing purchase activities

To make surveys effective, it is necessary to bear in mind the following:

1. Clients (surveyed) and actual customers may be different.
2. Surveys raise customers expectations. Raising expectations and taking no actions disappoints them. Hence implementation of changes, should be planned immediately upon survey.
3. Depending upon the questions framed, the answer is obtained!

   A question, for example, Do you like 'Gujarathi' food?, provides information on custom, feelings or attitudes. But the question, How often you dine out? provides information on the behaviour of customers. Is there a 'Kwality' ice cream parlour within 6 km from your house? This question elicits customer's knowledge about the product.
4. The well structured question elicits a better answer.
5. If more time is spent in survey development, the time spent in data analysis and interpretation will be less.

6. Whom do you ask, is as important as, what you ask. Customers who are surveyed may be either the current or past customers, potential customers or may even be the competitors' customers. The survey analysis may begin with identifying the problems and opportunities. But finally it should lead to specific solutions.
7. Before collecting data, one should determine how the data are to be analysed.

3. Focus Groups

This method is very expensive. But it is very effective in collecting information on customer expectations and requirements.

A group of customers is gathered in a meeting, and a series of questions are answered. The structured questions probe into the participants' ideas, perceptions and also frank comments. In this method current, as well as, proposed products and services are included.

In this method, inherent feelings associated with a product or service, word association, discussion and relaxation techniques are used to identify customers future needs. Ex: A fast food company found that consumers preferred low energy foods during weekdays and energy rich dishes on weekends!

4. Toll Free Telephone (1800 xxx xxxx) Numbers

This method is most effective for obtaining complaints and feedback. Response can be faster and cheap.

5. Visits to Customer's Place of Business

By this approach, the organisation can proactively monitor the performance of the product, which is being used on the spot. This enables them to identify any of the specific or recurring problems.

6. Report Card

A specimen report card is shown in Table 2.2. The data are examined to locate the areas of improvement.

7. The Internet

Discussions and chat on the internet are monitored by some managers. Messages that compare the company's product with those of competitors can be studied. Monitoring the internet is less costly and can identify creative ideas. The customers' views are expressed through the organisation web pages, and the internet sites that take the customers' views and rank them.

8. Employee Feedback

Many times, the employees can offer suggestions on the hidden aspects of quality. Brainstorming sessions for the employees help in identification of many quality problems and solutions. Instead of seeking suggestions through the box, proactive feedback should be obtained.

9. Mass Customisation (Customised Production)

The ultimate aim is fulfilling the wants of the customers. In the past, it was very expensive. But mass customisation is a way of providing variety at affordable cost. Mass customisation is made possible by flexible manufacturing technology, just-in-time systems and by cycle time reduction.

Table 2.2 Quarterly report card—a specimen

Dear customers,

We are committed to improve continually. To assist us in our endeavour, we seek your feed back.
Please grade our performance in each class:

Scale: A = Excellent B = Very good C = Average
D = Poor F = Failing

1. Product quality Grade:______
   Comments:______
2. On time delivery Grade:______
   Comments:______
3. After sales service Grade:______
   Comments:______
4. Overall performance Grade:______
   Comments:______

Designation: Sign:

Organisation: Date: Seal:

It has been done in automobile industries. Depending upon customer's choice of seat coverings, colour, stereo system and AC system, products are manufactured.

Computers are assembled according to customer's requirements by adding or subtracting components built on one of several base systems. Customized production at assembly stage, provides the type of computer system they want at a reasonable cost. Modular furniture is another example of customized product, at the delivery stage.

10. Customer Satisfaction Index

The American Customer Satisfaction Index (ACSI) was established in USA for products manufactured and sold there. The index was based on the study through telephonic interviews and from samples of households, who have bought or used a company's product. The index measures eight sectors of economy namely

1. Manufacturing (Non durables)
2. Manufacturing (Durables)
3. Retail
4. Transportation, communication and utilities
5. Finance and insurance
6. Services
7. Public administration and government
8. e-commerce

Table 2.3 gives the comparison of scores in non-durable manufacturing sector and the base line scores for the e-commerce sector, in the USA.

Table 2.3 Typical ACSI scores

Sector / Industry	2000	2006	2013
National ACSI	73	75	76.3
Non-durable Mfg.	81	82.3	81.9
Processed food	81	83	83
Athletic shoes	79	76	80
e-commerce	73	78	81.1

The ACSI allows comparisons between companies and industry average and comparisons over time. Government services are found to have scored the lowest overall customer satisfaction rating. This is perhaps true in the Indian scene also. As per recent survey by the National Quality Research Center at University of Michigan, U.S.A., high satisfaction reported by the consumers with most of the Gas and Electric companies, the U.S. Postal Service and limited service (fast food) restaurants. Students are advised to browse the web sites www.asq.org and www.theacsi.org for further reports.

The actions suggested to obtain customer satisfaction include the following:

(*a*) Record the customer's experiences through feed back, and then act on it positively.

(*b*) Install procedures for complaint resolution which include empowering the front line employees.

(*c*) Analyze the complaints, but they may or may not fit into clear cut categories.

(*d*) Identify the deviation in the processes and eliminate the root causes.

(*e*) Upon obtaining the survey response, the senior management should contact the customers and solve the problems.

(*f*) Develop customer satisfaction measures and monitor them at regular intervals.

(*g*) Circulate the complaint details, and also the results of study and solutions, to all the employees in the organisation.

(*h*) Submit a monthly report on the complaints and corrective actions and preventive actions taken, to the quality council, for their evaluation.

(*i*) Whenever possible, anticipate the customer's expectations before, rather than after the complaint analysis.

Majority of the customer contact is initiated through the organisation's frontline employees. A small complaint given to a front line employee, frequently becomes a major complaint, when it goes to the management level.

Hence the frontline employees are to be trained on, customer focus and listening skills, so that they can discuss on their complaints and deal with the situations.

2.3 CUSTOMER COMPLAINTS

A complaint is any response or opinion of a customer upon a product or service, which does not meet his expectations.

The complaints imply different subsequent problems such as:

1. Satisfying the complainant: Restoration of service, adjustment, and restoration of goodwill.
2. Preventing a complaint recurring.
3. Identifying the vital few complaints.
4. In-depth analysis, upon discovering root causes.

The media for complaints are letters, survey results, telephone calls, facsimile, or email messages, feed back through sales or service personnel.

The steps to deal with complaints should have the following inputs:

1. Time frame for closure of complaints.
2. Time frame for performing various steps such as repair, replacement.
3. Feed back to inform the management, on the status of solutions.
4. Maintaining a record of number of customers lost and number gained.
5. Statistical records on class, frequency, and clearing time.

2.4 SERVICE QUALITY

The teachings of quality gurus, Deming, Juran and others have really revolutionised the manufacturing sector. But the results have been slow, in service sector or service activities.

Customer service is the set of activities an organisation uses to win the customers and retain their goodwill. This service is provided before, during or after the sales of the product.

2.4.1 Various Aspect of Service Quality

The customer service activities may be classified into two broad areas, namely 1. Internal customer service and 2. External customer service. They begin with the management commitment in mobilising the employee involvement, empowerment and commitment. This step improves the internal service quality of the employees and results in employee satisfaction. Then, by appropriate training of the employees towards execution, measurement, and feed back, the external customer service quality is improved. This results in customer satisfaction. The sustained and continual improvement on the sub-processes by the employees, results in customer retention.

Various steps towards improving the service quality are divided into the following categories:

A. Organisation

1. Identify each market segment.
2. List the requirements of the customers.
3. Communicate the requirements.
4. Organize the processes.
5. Organize the physical locations.

B. Customer Care

6. Fulfill the customer's expectations.
7. Obtain the customer's point of view.
8. Deliver what is promised.

9. Ensure that every one is treated as a valuable customer.
10. Listen and respond to all complaint.
11. Respond fully to the customer.
12. Set a clean and comfortable reception area, for the customer.

C. Communication

13. Optimise the trade-off between time and personal attention.
14. Use optimum number of contact points.
15. Provide pleasant, knowledgeable, and enthusiastic employees.
16. Write documents in customer friendly language.

D. Front-line Personnel

17. Employ people, who like customers.
18. Challenge them, to improve their methods.
19. Empower them, to solve problems.
20. Serve them, as internal customers.
21. Ensure that they are appropriately trained.
22. Recognize and reward their performance.

E. Leadership

23. Lead by example.
24. Listen to the front line persons.
25. Work for continuous process improvement.

The detailed discussion of these aspects is presented in the following paragraphs:

A. Organisation

To ensure the same level of quality for all customers, the organisation must record and then communicate its employees, the instructions for all tasks. A service quality manual is to be created with the description of quality standard for each service. Communicating the service quality standard for each task can be effected through training, video projection, private coaching, or meetings. Also, intranet sites can be established, so that the employees can find answers to frequently asked questions and contact people for further information.

The physical space must be sufficient to serve the customer. For example, a redesigned emergency room for the patients in a hospital, provided separate rooms for (*a*) first aid, (*b*) for less serious injuries and (*c*) for serious injuries, respectively. The less injured patients could save service time and get discharged quickly.

In another case, the students were provided with counters for administrative tasks, payment of fees, and disbursal of scholarship and thus offered better service, in an engineering college.

B. Customer Care

Every customer should be valued and treated like a friend. If they are treated with respect, customers will simply forgive, forget the mistakes and positively promote good will.

Henry Ford is reported to have said, "It is not the employer who *pay* wages–he only *handles* the money. It is the customer who pays the wages". This shows that employees must please customers, not bosses.

A sample code of ethics towards customer's care, reads as follows:

- Keep promises to customers.
- Listen and return calls to customer quickly.
- Share the customer's concerns, by referring to an appropriate employee, for action towards problem solving, when necessary.
- Treat our customers with respect, courtesy and professionalism, at all times.
- Give every customer an involved, committed and personal attention.
- Always maintain a clean and neat personal appearance, including the workplace.

C. Communication

Communicate daily with the customers. If they are talking to us, they can not be talking to competitors. The communication to their customers, has to be in commensurate with its level of service quality. A customer may be dissatisfied, if the claims in the advertisement and the results differ. The organisation may correspond with its customers, through telephone or an interactive voice response system or email. Organisation must create maintain a level of trust, by listening to them.

The web site should be customer friendly, as it creates and retains the good impression of the organisation to all the viewers.

D. Front-line Personnel

Customers are the most valuable asset of any company and should be attended to, by employees, who have been adequately trained to handle their complaints.

A good personality is the most important requirement, in front line employees. If employees are not happy, this will be reflected upon the customers. Customers may go frustrated by petty things. Front-line employees need to care, smile, converse with a pleasant voice, and thank the customer frequently for their transaction. These people must possess a positive attitude, *always*.

These employees also need training, to develop their written and oral communication skills and problem-solving skills. They should also be empowered to resolve complaints. More so, they should exhibit a genuine care for their customers. Customers understand and feel happy when someone empathises with them and genuinely trying to help. For example, when a professor found that the stitching missing in a new suit, purchased from a supermarket, he returned it. Upon returning the suit, the salesperson offered him a discount coupon for the next purchase, because he had spent some time at his disposal, to come to the shop for returning the suit.

To sum up, the front-line people deal with customers every day. They are also a valuable source of information, as they know better *what* the customer wants. They also need information and support from the management to effectively to deal with the public. Rewards are also given to them to encourage their efforts.

E. Leadership

Quality improvement can succeed only with management's involvement as well as commitment. Managers exhibit their commitment to service quality, by example. Every executive should be allowed to spend a few hours every month, behind a customer service desk.

2.4.2 Characteristics and Expectations

The important part of customer satisfaction occurs after the sale. Table 2.4 shows different characteristics and expectations, on various occasions.

Table 2.4 Characteristics and expectations

Characteristics	Expectations
Delivery	Delivered on time, in right time, at the right place, in undamaged condition
Commissioning	Necessary instructions on setup, or technicians or manual, supplied for complicated products
Use	Well drafted training manuals or instructions for proper use and avoiding misuse (Do's and Don'ts)
Field service	Appropriately trained technicians, to promptly attend repairs and replacement
Customer service	Customer service personnel to respond to questions and for clarifications
Warranty	Clearly written and ensuring prompt service on claims

Many organisations give importance to reactive service after the sale. Some of the examples include: (*a*) Preventive maintenance (service provided according to a prescribed schedule), (*b*) Annual maintenance schemes, upon paying an agreed amount as a percentage of the cost of product, (*c*) Service contract (service provided as required and agreed), and (*d*) a combination of the above.

An organisation working to upgrade its service quality, must stay at the proactive level. These proactive organisations maintain contact with their customers and monitor their service quality needs and expectations. This data is used to establish the organisation's strategy, for future service.

2.4.3 Translating Needs into Requirements

The Kano model, which is shown in Fig. 2.1, conceptualizes customer requirements. The model suggests three major regions of customer satisfaction. The first region of customer satisfaction, explains by the diagonal line, represents explicit requirements. These cover written as well as verbal requirements and are identified, expected to be fulfilled. Satisfying the customer would be relatively simple if these were fulfilled.

The second region of customer satisfaction represents innovations, as shown by the curved line in the upper left corner of the graph. The customer's written instructions may vague to conceptualize and define the product. These innovative ideas often excite and delight the customer. These ideas get converted as expected.

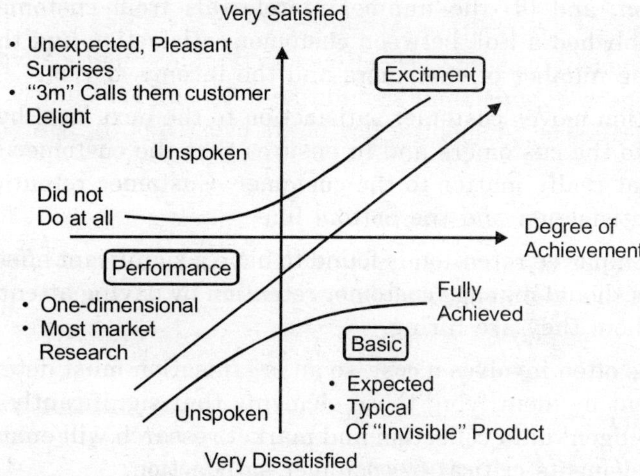

Fig. 2.1 Kano's model for customer satisfaction

The third and most important region of customer satisfaction represents undeclared or unspoken requirements, as shown by the curve in the lower right corner of the graph. The customer may not be aware of these requirements. Basic specifications often do not cater for real-world manufacturing requirements; many of them are based on industry standards or past practice. These implied requirements are the hardest to explain but prove very costly if ignored.

Customer satisfaction is a combination of the following factors:

(*a*) Technology (hardware and software), product, price, quality and response, delivery and communication, and

(*b*) Perceived knowledge of the product cost, company and personal expectation, needs and attitudes.

In fact, the customer does not buy a specification; the customer buys the product or service to fulfill his need. Peter Drucker once said, "Customers don't buy *products*, they buy *results*." People do not buy products; they are said to buy transportation or status. Customers are loyal to whatever helps them most, to achieve their desires fulfilled. Meeting a customer's need alone is not sufficient; the product must exceed the customer's needs.

A systematic approach of converting customer needs and demands, when designing a new product or service or when improving the existing product or service, called Quality for Design (QFD) is described in detail in Chapter 3.

2.5 CUSTOMER RETENTION

Customer retention is more powerful than customer satisfaction. Customer retention represents the activities that produce the customer satisfaction, create customer loyalty, which actually improves the bottom line. Sampled surveys on customer satisfaction, focus groups, and interviews, help in determining what customers think of a service or a product. But it is found that, what people *say* and think is often different from what they *do*. Customers may be delighted with the tropical scents and aromas as hair care products which are high priced, but still end up buying the local products. Hence customer satisfaction should also be measured, by using (1) cash register receipts, (2) market share, (3) the level of customer retention, and (4) the number of referrals from customers. The developed companies have established a link between customer satisfaction and the bottom line. The analysis identifies the number of customers and the income at risk.

Customer retention moves customer satisfaction to the next level by determining what is really significant to the customers and in ensures that the customer satisfaction system focuses on inputs that really matter to the customer. Customer retention is the vital link between customer satisfaction and the bottom line.

Similarly, high employee retention is found to have a significant effect on high customer retention. Companies should manage customer retention by paying attention to their current employees and to whom they are hiring.

Improved service often involves a cost, so an organisation must determine its return on the service investment by identifying those elements that significantly promotes revenues and market share. Diligent data collection and market research will enable the organisation to determine those elements critical to customer satisfaction.

The organisation must continually improve the methods of data collection the customer's needs and expectations. It is the quality council's responsibility to review the methods. Frequently maximizing the customer satisfaction and retention takes to better financial results.

2.6 EMPLOYEE INVOLVEMENT

Here lies a man who knew, how to enlist, in his service, better man than himself.

—On the tombstone of business titan Andrew Carnegie

2.6.1 Why Involvement?

Employee involvement is necessary because of the following reasons: The market is changing. The competition is emerging at the global level. Hence it is essential to familiarise the employees with modern technologies and process methodologies. Increased consumer awareness and expectations, changing business equations, to think creatively for solving problems, and to continuously learn and update the skill and knowledge, the employee involvement has to be ensured.

Employee involvement is possible by the following approaches: education, training, empowerment, participation in group activities (such as quality circle) and Kaizen.

By involving employees, empowering and bringing them into the decision making process the opportunity is provided for continual process improvement. Their ideas, expert knowledge potential, experience and creative thoughts of employees, promote quality and productivity.

- They help to implement and support decisions, in which they had a role.
- Employees have better ability to locate and pinpoint areas for improvement.
- Employees are better suitable to take immediate corrective actions.
- Employee involvement reduces misunderstanding between labor and management, by encouraging effective communication and cooperation.
- This develops morale by inculcating a feeling of 'belonging' to the organisation.
- Employees can cope with change, because they are familiar and able to control the work environment.

- The employees have an increased commitment to goals of their department, because they are involved.

Employee involvement is a way of life, vital to TQM. Employees hold the future in their hands. Change is an ongoing process that must occur, if an organisation should continue to exist in a competitive situation. It is observed that, people do not resist change: they resist being changed, and the problems arise, when a person's comfort zone is disturbed.

2.6.2 Human Resource Management

The principles to be followed managing the personnel are:

(*i*) People are to be treated with human dignity and ethical consideration.

(*ii*) The organisation hires human beings with body, mind and intellectual.

(*iii*) Management must bear in mind various human models—Social, organisation human, self actualizing human, whole human, rational being, to know them well.

(*iv*) Management must exhibit genuine interest in employee's opinions and conversations.

(*v*) Management has to tap the full potential of all employees.

(*vi*) Management has to behave rationally and ethically, with humans.

(*vii*) Most of the problems are with systems and not with people.

(*viii*) Management has to think why, what and how, not who.

People involvement are promoted by the following processes:

1. Team building, rather than individual.
2. Involving and leading, rather than managing.
3. Participative, consensus and democratic approach, rather than delegation.
4. Empowerment, self-control, rather than control.
5. Considering an employee as problem solver, rather than as problem creator.
6. Flattened structure, rather than pyramidal structure of organisation.
7. Continuous improvement, rather than short time improvement.
8. Value, action, measurement and reward rather, than punishment.
9. Participation in improvement teams (quality council), rather than individual role.

The employee involvement ultimately ensures the following:

1. Employee satisfaction.
2. Customer satisfaction.
3. Process improvement and better control.
4. Better benchmarking can be done better.

2.6.3 Psychological Basis for Employee Involvement

1. Maslow's Theory

The motivational theory was developed by Abraham Maslow. He explained motivation in terms of hierarchy of need at five levels, as shown in Fig. 2.2. These levels are survival, security, social, esteem and self actualization. Once a given level is satisfied, it can no longer motivate a person.

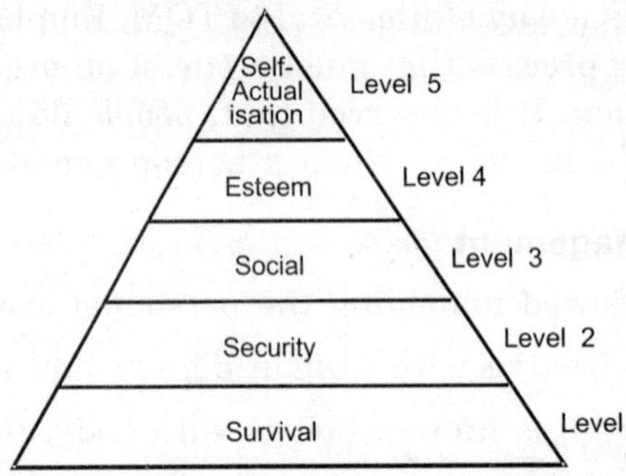

Fig. 2.2 Maslow's hierarchy of needs

At Level 1, in the work place, the needs are proper illumination, heating or air conditioning, ventilation, phone connection, data/voice access and computer information system. Level 2 mean space of safety place to work and job security which are essential for the employees. This includes not only job security but also having privacy on job such as a room with door and lock, storage of personal items and an ergonomic furniture and safe work environment.

As the humans are all social animals, Level 3 relates to our 'need to belong'. Giving an individual the opportunity to be part of the group, by feeling important and needed, will motivate the person. Employees should be provided with areas for social interactions, such as canteen, conference rooms and informal areas such as, water cooler and bulletin board.

Level 4 deals with esteem, pride and self worth. Everyone irrespective of the cadre or job wants to be recognized as a person of value to the organisation. Where possible, employee should be given offices or personal spaces. Visiting cards, work space size and office protocols also provide employees with, a level of self esteem within the organisation. Level 5 (self actualization) insists that individuals must be given opportunity to go as far as their abilities will take them as per the principle; 'Opportunity for all, according to their abilities! Many institutions have a policy of promotion from within, to motivate the employees under this principle.

It is relevant to note that as employees move up in the ladder of hierarchy, they will immediately revert back to the previous level, if they feel threatened. For example, if an employee staying satisfied in Level 3, a rumor of downsizing may cause an immediate return to Level 2.

2. Herzberg Two Factor Theory

Fredrick Herzberg's theory is an extension of Maslow's theory on employee motivation. He found that people are motivated by factors such as recognition, responsibility, achievement, advancement and the work itself. They are called motivators.

In addition, he found that, bad feeling are associated with low salary, minimal fringe benefits, poor working conditions, ill defined or unethical organisational policies and incompetent technical supervision. These factors are called dissatisfiers or hygiene factors, which mean they are preventable. These dissatisfiers are often 'extrinsic' and the motivators are 'intrinsic' in nature. The *presence* of extrinsic factors *does not* necessarily motivate the employees, but their *absence* results in *dissatisfaction* of employees. Absence of motivating factors does not make the employees dissatisfied, but when they are present, they provide strong levels of motivation, that leads to good performance of the individual as well as the organisation.

Herzberg's dissatisfiers are approximately equivalent to Maslow's lower levels and the motivators are similar to the upper levels.

Table 2.5 shows what is the ranking of wants of employees and the managers perception of employee wants, in the U.S. scene. Employee preference seem to agree with the theories of Maslow and Herzberg. But the managers' perceptions are found to be very much different. To make their efforts fruitful the managers must orient their action towards the motivators.

Table 2.5 What the employee wants?

Factors	Employee rating	Manager rating
Interesting work	1	5
Appreciation	2	8
Involvement	3	10
Job security	4	2
Good pay	5	1
Promotion/growth	6	3
Good working conditions	7	4
Loyalty to employees	8	7
Help with personal problems	9	9
Tactful discipline	10	6

By promoting team spirit and by adopting appropriate reward and recognition system, managers can reap the advantages of improved quality as well as productivity, along with employee satisfaction .

The concepts of effectively motivating the work force may be listed as follows:

1. *Know thyself:* Managers must know their own motivations, strength and weakness. This is best obtaining peers' and employees' appraisal on the manager's, anonymously. The managers are aware that the most valuable resource is human ware and success of management is based on the employees achieving their goals.
2. *Know your employees:* Managers should ask questions and listen to answers from employees. With the knowledge of their employees' interests, likes and dislikes the manager can influence them and help promoting their interest and achieving the goals of the organisation.
3. *Establish a positive attitude:* Managers are responsible for generating positive and action oriented attitude. Respect and sensitivity toward others, are vital for the development of positive attitudes. Get the employees' opinion on job related problems and treat their ideas as treasure and implement them.
4. *Share the goals:* Well-defined and achievable goals are needed and all the employees are to be communicated on them.

5. *Monitor the progress:* Managers should periodically review the performance and progress against set targets.
6. *Develop interesting work:* Managers should consider altering the employees' assignments by job rotation, job enlargement and job enrichment, to match their job interesting.

   Job rotation permits employees to change jobs within a department for a limited period of time. This breaks the boredom and provides better knowledge on the entire process and thus raising quality consciousness, leading to process improvement.

   Job enlargement combines the tasks horizontally and this makes every employee more responsible, leading to process improvement.

   Job enrichment combines tasks vertically, by adding managerial activities such as planning, scheduling and inspection. This promotes the employees' sense of autonomy and control over their work, which may also lead to process improvement.
7. *Communicate effectively:* Clear cut and effective communication provides employees with the knowledge about their work unit and the organisation.
8. *Recognise and celebrate success:* Recognize the employee's achievement as the most effective tool in the manager's tool box.

   These concepts are used at all managerial levels of the organisation.

2.6.4 Employee Survey

In these surveys, managers study the state of employee relations, identify trends, measure the effectiveness of program implementation, identify desired improvements and increase effective communication.

The quality council forms the group to choose the objective, develop a plan, to make root cause analysis and implement corrective actions.

Some of the features that are included in such surveys are:

(*a*) Psychological characteristics such as stress, fatigue, anxiety, self-esteem in the organisation.

(*b*) Management styles such as consideration for subordinates, initiating structure, commitment to quality.

(*c*) Job attitudes such as job satisfaction, social support at work and co-worker's commitment, and

(*d*) the work, including task variety, autonomy and importance.

Surveys may be conducted annually, preferably by external agency to maintain neutrality and anonymity. Data are analyzed and conclusions are then reported to the quality council, for further action.

This employees' feed back guides the management in continuing TQM efforts.

2.6.5 Empowerment

1. What is Empowerment?

Empowerment is permitting the employees, the authority and responsibility for the decisions on the activities of the organisation, which affect their jobs. It is a term which is also applied to the process of the employee participation in improving the working practices and in realising the organisational values and objectives, through team working, total quality management, problem solving and so on.

Empowerment should not be mistaken for delegation or job enrichment. Delegation refers to distributing and entrusting work to others. Employee empowerment means that the individual is held responsible for accomplishing an assigned task. The employee is the process owner that is, the individual is not only responsible but also answerable and accountable. Job enrichment focuses on enlarging the contents of an individual's job, whereas empowerment focuses on enlarging the context of the job, such as interactions and interdependencies to other activities of the organisation.

2. Empowerment Means a Paradigm Shift

	FROM	TO
RESULTS	Ends are important	Means are equally important
	By change and streaks	By systematic problem solving methods
	Focus on individual responsibility	Collective responsibility towards excellence
	Focus on quantity	Focus on quality
LEADERSHIP	Through adherence of rules	Through involvement by empowerment
	Independent decision making	Collective decision making (mutual dependence)
MOVE	Profit only motive	Customer satisfaction
TOWARDS	Short term policies	Long term orientation
	Internal, closed communication	Transparent communication
	Overall control	Autonomy to individuals
	Reactive	Proactive
	Rigidity	Experimentation
	Rare or stray innovation	Continuous opportunity for creativity and change management
	Monotony of work	Pleasurable work upgrading the employee

3. Why Empowerment?

Empowerment process has evolved in response to the trend towards a greater degree of responsibility and involvement among the employees, in running their organisations. The organisations have recognised that, the capacity of their employees improve and enhance the business performance, when they are informed and involved, when their skills and experience are recognised, and when they are encouraged to be creative, to innovate, and to take risks.

People generally want to assume more responsibility and be more in charge of their jobs and careers. They act in that way, in their daily personal life. Many people value the trust and responsibility obvious in a situation that supports empowered persons and their actions. When people who possess the data, education, and skills to act in a changed situation, realise their limits of empowerment, and convinced about the necessity for change, their resistance to that change disappears to a large extent.

2.6.6 Conventional Management Tools

Some of the conventional management tools used in this context are discussed as follows:

1. Forced Field Analysis

This method helps to determine the forces and factors that have influence on the goals. It enables understanding the promoting or driving factors, and the restraining or inhibiting factors with a view that positives can be strengthened and the negatives weakened or nullified. The procedure sets the objective, establish the criterion for evaluating the effectiveness of the improvement action, prioritize the forces on their importance and act to reinforce the promoting forces and reduce the inhibiting forces.

The procedure consists of: 1. Selecting a team of 5 to 7 members, 2. Identification of the barriers in achieving a goal, 3. Identification of the causes, 4. Identification of the solutions to a problem, 5. Deciding on current and correct situation, 6. Ranking and the positive or negative forces, 7. Writing the present situation on the diagram, and 8. Actions for the removal of the restraining forces and encourage the driving forces. Table 2.6 gives an example of the forced field analysis.

Table 2.6 Forced field analysis

Objective: To make profit	
Promoting/Driving forces	**Inhibiting/Restraining forces**
Good business ⟶	⟵ Lack of knowledge
Action ⟶	⟵ Short staffed
Skills ⟶	⟵ Low morale
Equipments ⟶	⟵ Poor equipments
Procedures ⟶	⟵ Poor quality
Culture ⟶	⟵ Short cuts on quality
People ⟶	⟵ Delayed output

2. Decision Making

Several approaches available for effective decision making, such as

1. *Autocratic:* Centralized authority, one person, the leader decides.
2. *Democratic:* Decentralized authority. Decision agreed upon views on problems and solutions, from concerned and responsible members.
3. *Majority rule (voting):* Decision based on the views of majority of the group members.
4. *Consensus:* Every one participates in discussion, understands the decision, supports and willing to implement the decision arrived at consensus method promotes commitment.

3. Nominal Group Technique

(*a*) In this approach, initially the ideas are elicited from the group, enlisted and categorized.

(*b*) The team leader scans all the suggestions to explain and discuss further.

(*c*) Every one in the group is asked assign the rank/points of importance to various listed ideas.

(*d*) Upon further discussion, the idea that scored highest is declared to be most important and then implemented.

2.6.7 Levels of Involvement

Various levels of involvement and their effects are presented in Table 2.7

Table 2.7 Levels of involvement

Ordinary level of performance	Competing level of performance
(*a*) Individual suggestion system	(*a*) Team proposal system
(*b*) Employee involvement means any one, not management	(*b*) Employee involvement means every one, in the organisation
(*c*) Win and lose, zero sum game for sharing information, knowledge, power and rewards	(*c*) Win and Win, non-zero sum games for sharing information, knowledge, power and rewards
(*d*) Less improvement per employee per year	(*d*) More improvement per employee per year

2.7 TEAM WORK

The employee involvement is put to optimum in using teams. Though the teams are very effective, they are not the solution for solving for all quality and productivity problems.

2.7.1 Definition and Scope

A *team* is defined as a group of individuals who have complementary skills and are committed to shared, meaningful purpose and specific objectives or goals. *Teamwork* is the cumulative sum of actions of the team, during which each person in the team subdues one's individual desires and opinions, to satisfy the objectives or goals of the group. They have clear set of roles and responsibilities, and hold themselves mutually accountable for the team's performance. The objectives are to be set clearly, and adopted a systematic and collaborative approach. Members of the team have to be focused on how they are inter-related to each other, to take note of the suggestions of colleagues, to build on previous information, and to resolve conflicts creatively. They will have to fix standards, maintain discipline, develop team spirit, and motivate mutually. They should ensure the completion of tasks and the needs of friendship, fulfilment of personal growth and self-esteem are also attained.

2.7.2 Why and How of 'Team Work'?

Why and how teams work, is explained in the following paragraphs:

(*a*) Team work succeeds because many heads are more knowledgeable than one. Abilities and expertise of each member of the team can be used effectively to solve problems. Many procedures are so complicated that one member cannot have thorough knowledge on entire process.

(*b*) According to the **synergy principle**, *the whole is greater than the sum of its constituents.* The interaction within the group gives results that exceed the contributions of each member.

(*c*) The team members develop mutual respect and appreciation with each other which enables them to do jobs better. The team spirit (*esprit de corps*) motivates them to do better.

(*d*) Teams provide the effective medium for improved communication, enabling successful solutions.

2.7.3 Types of Teams

The teams may be classified into four types based on their characteristics:

1. *Process Improvement Team:* Each members of this team, represent on operation or the process. The activity of the team is limited to that shop or department. A team may consist of six to ten members from shop and departments an external or internal supplier or customer may be included in the team. The life cycle of this team is usually temporary and is disbanded, once the objective is realised.
2. *Cross Functional Team:* Six to ten persons representing different functional areas such as engineering, marketing, accounting, manufacture , quality, and human resources, form this team. The customer and supplier may also be the members. A typical example of a cross-functional team is a design review team. This type of team is normally temporary. A product support team, may function as permanent to serve a particular product line, service, or a particular group of customers. This type of team serves beyond functional area boundaries.
3. *Natural Work Team:* This team consists of all the members of the shop or department. It differs from quality circle, since a manager is part of the team and the schemes for improvement are chosen by the management. The managers should anticipate reluctance of some employees to join this team and assist them in becoming comfortable in the team environment. Although 'team work' is possible, but without mutual understanding and unity of ideas and action, it can not be made a reality.
4. *Self-directed / Self-managed Work Team:* They are similar to the natural work team, but without a manager or supervisor. Hence they are the crux, of the organisation, as they are not only to execute the work but also to manage it. Usually a coordinator, by rotation, liaises with senior management. The team meets periodically to plan their activities, and decisions made by consensus. In addition, they are also responsible for recruitment, performance evaluation, customer relations, supplier relations, recognition and reward and training.

In a 'hydraulics unit', for example, the self directed team for assembly, deals with all aspects of the customer's order such as receiving the purchase order, manufacturing the components, assembly and testing the circuits,, shipping the valves, controlling the inventory, and processing all information.

In these cases, a gain sharing plan and a reward system for the team performance, instead of the individual performance is relevant. Some overlap may occur between these types of teams and the organisations are at liberty to modify them, to suit their goals.

2.7.4 Characteristics of Successful Teams

In order to make an effective team, it should have the following ingredients incorporated:

1. *Sponsor:* To liaise effectively with the quality council, there should be sponsor, a member from the quality council, so as to ensure the organisational drive and support.
2. *Charter for the team:* The charter is a document, which declares their mission, boundaries, the preamble of the problem, the authority and duties, and envisaged resources. It helps the members to identify their roles assigned, such as leader, recorder, timekeeper, facilitator, etc.
3. *Composition of the team:* The size of the team is normally ten or less number of members. If the teams are larger, maintaining commitment and control becomes difficult. Teams members are drawn from employees with different skills, perspectives, and expertise. The internal and external customers and suppliers may also be included, where found relevant.
4. *Effective training:* Members are to be trained in mathematical and statistical analysis, problem-solving techniques, group dynamics, communication and transactional skills.
5. *Ground rules:* The team must formulate its rules for operation and conduct. Frank discussion beforehand on this aspect, is beneficial, while implementation. The rules may be reviewed and revised, periodically, if found necessary.
6. *Clear cut objectives:* Without objectives and goals framed clearly, the team cannot function effectively. The criteria for success should align with the management policies.
7. *Accountability:* The team is accountable on performance. Periodic status reports are submitted to the quality council. The team has to review its performance and identify the weakness and to continue improvements.
8. *Decision making:* Rational, effective, factual or logical, ethical , and timely decisions are to be made by the team.
9. *Team Resources:* Funding, employee availability time and access to documents are essential for the successful function of the team.
10. *Trust:* Management must trust the team to function effectively. Mutual trust must exist among the members to think and act united.
11. *Open communication:* Members should discuss frankly and listen without interruption, among the team, speak with clarity and clarify any difference in views or doubts, that may arise.
12. *Proper leadership:* All teams require leadership to steer, even if the team is matured.
13. *Balanced participation:* Involvement of all members in the team's activities is promoted by voicing their opinions, utilising their expertise, and encouraging other members to take part.
14. *Cohesiveness:* Members should be enabled to interact with each other and act united and not to work as individuals or groups, with vested interests.

2.7.5 Roles of Team Members

Teams are usually chosen by the quality council. Each team consists of a leader, facilitator, recorder, timekeeper, and other members. Each member of the team is assigned definite roles and responsibilities.

The roles of the TEAM LEADER are the following:

- Ensuring the smooth and effective function of the team, assigning record keeping, coordinating activities, and supervising the drafting of reports and presentation.
- Facilitating the team activities, ensuring participation of all members in the meetings, preventing domination of individual members, actively guiding without domination, and promoting positive interpersonal behaviour.
- Serving as a contact point, between the group and the quality council.
- Coordination in implementation of the changes recommended by the group, within organisational constraints and team boundaries.
- Monitoring the status and achievements of the team and ensuring the completion of assignments in time.
- Preparation of the agenda of the meeting which includes time, date and location, and ensuring that the resources required for the meeting are available.
- Ensuring that the team arrives at a consensus and appropriate decisions.
- THE FACILITATOR is a non member of the team and is not necessary for a matured team. He/she does not get involved in the contents of meeting.

The roles of the facilitator of the team, are the following:

- Supportive to the leader, in forming the team, in the initial stages.
- Focuses on the team procedure; concentrates more with, how decisions are arrived, rather than the decisions themselves.
- Acts as an advisor to the team, by intervening, if found necessary, to move the team on track.
- Provides feedback to the members, regarding the effectiveness of the team activities.

THE TEAM RECORDER is usually selected by the leader and rotated periodically. The team recorder exhibits, the following roles:

- Records the major ideas of the discussion, the issues raised, decisions arrived and actions identified.
- Presents the details for the team, to review and then distributes them as minutes, after the meeting, in specified time.
- Participates in the discussion as a team member.

THE TIME KEEPER, who is again, normally selected by the leader and may be rotated on a periodic basis, exhibits the roles such as:

- Monitors the time, to make sure that the meeting runs to schedule, as prescribed by the agenda.
- Participates as a team member, in the discussions.

THE TEAM MEMBER, who may be selected by the leader, or quality council or is a member of a natural work team, discharges the following responsibilities:

- Contributes the best, by actively participating in discussion and sharing knowledge, expert ideas, and information, in a frank manner.
- Integrity: Respects other's contribution—does not criticize, complain, or condemn, openly or secretly.
- Listens carefully and seek clarifications, by questions.
- Promotes consensus on decisions and is prepared to negotiate on important points.
- Understands and is committed to the declared group objectives.
- Maintains mutual respect and is tolerant of individual differences.
- Responds positively, to the feedback on own behaviour.
- Exhibits a sense of honest and sincere appreciation.

2.7.6 Stages of Team Development

The four stages of team development are Formation, Interaction, Preparation and Implementation.

The first stage is FORMATION. In this stage, the members are made aware of the boundaries of their acceptable activities. Members prefer to do the work on their own, as there is normally a want of trust. Members are cautious with their communication and tend to be formal. Quite a lot of time is spent in organising and training. The facilitator gets the details of the problem from the management, selects the team members, then determines the type of training for the team members, and allows the team members to evaluate the problem.

In the second and most important stage, INTERACTION, the members start to realize the amount of work that lies ahead. There may be conflicts and the leader has to be patient and flexible, in working with the team. If the team does not have any conflict, it may be become stagnant. The leader should see that the conflicts do not become wide and disruptive, making the team is non-functional. The team members may be drawn from different hierarchy or functions with different goals, different perceptions, different levels of work ethics, and attitudes toward authority and family back ground. In such a situation, each member of the team may be asked, to list what the other side should do. Exchange these lists, select compromises that all are willing to accept, and test the compromise, to see if it meshes with the team goals. If managed properly, the conflicts may lead to positive movement toward the goals, innovation and creativity and adaptable solutions to the problems.

The third stage, PREPARATION, members begin to work together. Conflicts are converted to cooperation, cohesion, and constructive criticism.

The final and IMPLEMENTATION stage, is one where the members understand the project better, and begin performing by diagnosing and solving problems and choosing and implementing the changes. Once the team work is accomplished, it will be disbanded.

2.7.7 Common Barriers to Team's Progress

A list of barriers to the progress of the team, primarily due to the system is given below:

- *Insufficient training:* Teams can not be expected to perform unless they are familiar and trained in problem-solving methods, group dynamics, and communication skills.
- *Incompatible rewards and compensation:* In general, organisations plan nothing to reward team performance, because of the strong focus on individual rewards.
- *Lack of planning:* A lack of common direction or alignment on the use of collaborative efforts, internal competition, redundancy, and fragmented work processes affect the team progress.
- *Lack of management commitment:* Management must provide the resources and "buy into" the quality council/sponsor system. Teams' decisions should be implemented.
- *Access to information system:* Teams need access to organisational information such as business performance, competitive performance, financial data, etc.
- *Lack of union support:* Organisations need union support also, for the team to be successful.
- *Project scope too large:* The scope may not be clear to the team or the management might not guide the team properly.
- *Project objectives are not significant:* Management has not defined the role of the team to play.
- *No clear measures or metrics for success:* The team is not clear about the goals.
- *No time to do the improvement work:* Values and beliefs of the organisation are not compatible with the team's work. Individual and departmental rivalry interfere with the team's progress. The feuding team members hinder the progress.
- *Team is too large:* The organisation lacks methods for involving people in ways other than team membership.
- *Trapped in group-think:* Team members all have a mind-set that no actions are taken, until everyone agrees with every decision.
- Knowledge of these barriers helps the management to evaluate their own performance and take necessary corrective action to facilitate the team progress.
- On the participants side, the problems are due to overbearing, dominating and reluctant personnel. The resistance by first line supervisors also can affect the progress of the team work.

2.8 TRAINING

The training is very important for effective functioning of the team. The quality council has to establish these programs. This should be treated as an investment as the return is definite and large. Even small manufacturing companies have experienced a significant and positive relationship between their profitability and the management training. Trainers should be selected for their knowledge, and enthusiasm. The training must include theory and practical sessions. Wherever necessary, role-playing and case studies should be used.

The team members should be friendly with the trainer. The objectives of the program should be presented to the trainees. They must be encouraged to give feed back on the program and the team leaders should care and respond to the suggestions and make changes whenever found necessary. Employees will participate in the programs, wherein their views are incorporated.

To begin with, every one should know the objectives and contents of the training, suggestions, and feedback should be gathered, to get acceptance. Trainees must accept that the training will be of value to them. Now the program is adapted. Every individual should feel, that they are part of the progress. The final step is, to adapt to, what has been taught and learnt, through changes in behaviour and attitudes.

Trainees should learn on (*a*) group dynamics, (*b*) communication skills, (*c*) quality awareness, (*d*) specific problem-solving techniques, such as statistical process control, (*e*) safety, and (*f*) the technical aspects of the job.

The training should be action and results oriented, so that it succeeds. According to Juran, different types of quality training at different levels are offered in quality, as illustrated in Table 2.8.

Table 2.8 Who needs what, in quality training?

Subjects	Top management	Quality managers	Middle managers	Specialists	Facili-tators	Work force
Quality Awareness	x		x	x	x	x
Basic concepts	x	x	x	x	x	x
Strategic quality management	x	x				
Personal roles	x	x	x	x	x	x
Quality processes	x	x	x	x	x	x
Quality in functional areas		x	x	x		
Motivation for quality	x	x	x		x	

The role of a team leader is different from that of a supervisor. Supervisors, who act as team leaders, will have a different experience. The team leaders should share their responsibilities with other team members. They give team members, an opportunity to develop, on their own. To be an effective team leader, also require training. Knowledge and experience in human relations, motivation, conflict resolution, and communications, are often advantageous.

2.9 RECOGNITION AND REWARD

Recognition is a form of motivation, in which the organisation openly acknowledges the positive contributions of an individual or team, leading to the success of the organisation. This acknowledgement is delivered verbally or written form and may be by certificates or plaques. Reward is something tangible, such as lunch for the family or a cash award to promote good relationship. Recognition and reward, together, form a system for acknowledging that these people are valuable to the organisation. The recognition makes them feel like winners and creates positive energy—*both in their soul and purse!*

All employees should be involved in the planning and execution of the quality program. This activity is giver effected by a cross-functional team that represents different departments. It should be fully understood by the employees and reviewed periodically, so that it can be improved over time, since, the priorities of the employees or organisation may be refined, for better.

The system must *declare clearly*, the recognition criteria. Policies and procedures must be consistently and uniformly applied, throughout the organisation. The system should not declare ranking the individuals, because that would be counterproductive as they are identified as winners or losers. Recognition should be sincere and meaningful for the giver and the rewarded; it should not be aimed at manipulating people, but should recognize the efforts and the quantified results.

Jack Welch of General Electric said that one of the organisation's strengths was its ability to *celebrate* the best ideas[17]. That is what he did when one of his managrs created the 'Lloyd Trotter Matrix'. Energising the people with better ideas with celebration motivates everybody else to think and act proactively.

The reward may be delayed but the recognition should be in time. Rewards should be proportional to the quantum of saving or improvement. They should be of value and in many organisation, the employees are given the option to select the form of the reward, from various alternatives.

Employees prefer to be recognized, either as a team or as an individual. A person's pride in achievement, knowledge that the organisation cares, and publicising peer recognition are more favoured, than any reward. Apart from the framed picture or a medal, the recognition may be made through photographs on the notice board, articles in the in-house magazine or press, letters to the families, personal phone calls or notes, placing positive note in folders, and *increased* responsibility! Supervisors express the recognition also by *pat on the back*, on the spot, whenever the job is done well.

The forms of individual rewards may include a better housing plot allotment, gift certificates, gift to charity in the name of the recipient, trips or return tickets V.G.P Wonderland or Black Thunder or a hill resort such as Ooty or Simla. Group rewards, similarly, may include an outing for picnic, movies, cricket match, or Sircar's magic show, group lunch or dinner in a sea resort such as Mahabalipuram or Puri, or providing a laptop computer or PDA. A few typical reward practices followed in the west are listed in the Table 2.9, as examples. Many organisations have periodic celebration days, when awards are presented to the individuals and teams.

Table 2.9 Reward practices in the developed countries

Intrinsic rewards	Extrinsic rewards
* Non-monetary forms of recognition to acknowledge achievement of quality goals	* Profit sharing * Gain sharing
* Functions to acknowledge achievement of quality improvement goals	* Job security * Compensation time
* Regular communication for appreciation by managers and leaders to employees	* Individual based performance systems
* Performance appraisals—feedback from co-workers, subordinates or customers	* Quality based performance appraisals
* Formal suggestion system	
* Development based performance appraisals	
* Promotions based on quality achievement	

To sum up, an effective recognition and reward system, should:

(*a*) Serve as continual reminder, that the organisation cares more for quality and productivity.

(*b*) Offer the organisation a transparent technique to motivate high performers for their exemplary performance.

(*c*) Motivate the employees to improve the process.

(*d*) Boost the morale in the work environment by introducing a healthy competition among employees seeking recognition.

2.10 PERFORMANCE APPRAISAL

And yet, the ultimate test of management is business performance achievement, rather than knowledge remains, of necessity, as both proof and aim. —*Peter Drucker*

The purpose of the performance appraisals is to let employees know how they evaluate and provide a basis for promotions, salary increment, and counseling. There should be mutual trust between the employee and the appraiser. Employees should know the method of appraisal, including the contents and the frequency. The appraisal should bring out strengths and weaknesses, as well as how performance can be improved. The specimen appraisal formats are shown in Table 2.10.

Table 2.10 Formats for appraisal

Type	Description
Ranking method	Comparison of the employees by ranking highest 10 to lowest 1
Narrative method	Description of employee's strengths and weakness
Graphic method	Highlight the major duties performed by the employee and rating each duty with a scale—from 5 (excellent) to 1 (poor)
Forced choice	Places each employee in a class with assigned slots, *e.g.*, Excellent (15%), Very good (25%), Good (30%), Fair (20%), and Poor (10%)

Performance appraisals may be done either for the team or individuals. An important factor for successful appraisal, is the employee involvement. The employee should be given the opportunity to defend on the evaluation, including disagreement. Performance is to be based on standards that are developed and agreed upon by all the employees. Standards may specify an ideal level and acceptable level and it should change when situation warrants.

Performance appraisals should be used as a positive way to get employees involved. If employees are properly trained and counselled, then the performance appraisal can be a pleasant task for all employees, and can show how effective the employee is contributing to the development of organisation. Performance evaluation should be made error free. Culture, professional ethics, education level, and pre-conceived notions may affect evaluation. A fair evaluation helps a valuable employee and vice versa.

The appraisals are said to nourish short-term performance and destroy long-term planning according to quality experts. Another criticism, is that the individual appraisal kills the team spirit. A third point is, that we assume, that an individual is responsible for all results. Deming has found that majority of the problems are the results of the 'system'. Finally, the appraisals are often interpreted to be based on subjectivity and immeasurables. They have to be based on objectivity; although it may be difficult to measure some attributes, such as customer satisfaction and leadership.

Based on the objections discussed above, the performance appraisal system may be modified on the following lines:

1. Use of rating scales that have 3 or 5 rating categories, is preferred.
2. Adopt group evaluations, that are equally relevant as individual evaluation. The TQM activities emphasize on the team performance. Hence, this will encourage the team members to assist, support, and cooperate with each other, better.
3. External customer satisfaction indices may be included in the appraisal process. To accomplish this process, however, the customers and their requirements are to be identified, and the performance metrics determined using a rating scale. The evaluation is to be based on the change in the metrics, with the base line established initially.
4. Evaluation for process improvement in addition to results should be evaluated. One of the basic concept is continual process improvement. In spite of a time a lag between process improvement and the results from that improvement, it must be appraised periodically.

2.11 CONTINUAL PROCESS IMPROVEMENT

The process improvements are made by one or more of the following ways:

- Viewing all work as a process, whether it is associated with production or business activities.
- Making each process adaptable, effective and efficient.
- Anticipating changing customer needs.
- Controlling in-process performance, using measures such as scrap reduction, cycle time, control charts, etc.
- Eliminating waste and rework, wherever it occurs.
- Investigating the activities that do not add values to the product or service, with the aim of eliminating those activities.
- Eliminating nonconformities in all phases of everyone's work, even if the incremental improvement is small.
- Using benchmarking, to improve competitive advantage.
- Innovating, to achieve breakthroughs.
- Incorporating lessons learned into future activities.
- Using technical tools such as statistical process control, experimental design, benchmarking, quality function deployment, etc.

Continual process improvement is designed to utilize the resources of the organisation and to achieve a quality-driven culture. Every individual must think, act, and speak on quality.

2.11.1 Process

A 'process' refers to an activity, where there are some inputs and some outputs. Figure 2.3 illustrates a process model.

The inputs may be *human resource, material, money, data, methods, equipments* etc. Outputs may be *profit, information, products, service*, etc. The output of one process, can also be the input to another process. Output usually requires performance measures. They are designed to achieve certain desirable outcomes, such as customer satisfaction. The feedback is provided to improve the process. The process is the interaction of some combination of human resources, materials, equipments, method, measurements and the environment to produce an outcome such as product or service or an input to another process. It must be effective, efficient, under control, and adaptable. In addition, it must act within certain conditions imposed by policies and constraints or regulations. Such conditions may include, state or union laws, regulations and policies.

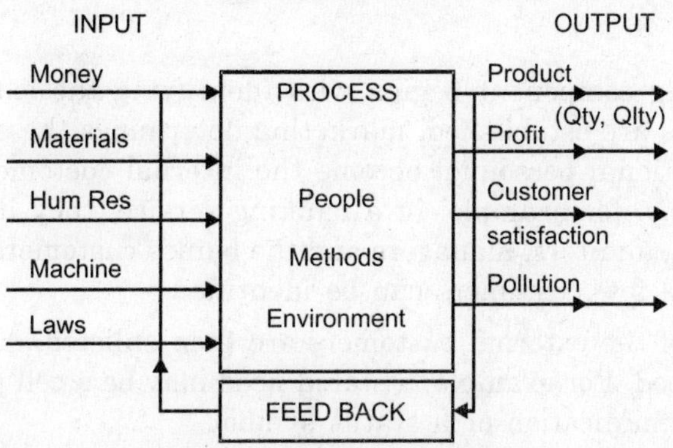

Fig. 2.3 A process model

The customer defines the purpose of the organisation and every process within it. Because the organisation exists to serve the customer, process improvements must be defined in terms of increased customer satisfaction, as a result of higher quality products and services. All processes have at least one owner. In some cases, the owner is obvious, because only one person performs the activity. The sub-processes may be owned by several individuals in an organisation. The ownership should be part of and responsible for the process improvement initiatives.

The improvement is defined in one of the *five* basic ways, namely, (1) reduce resources, (2) reduce errors, (3) meet or exceed expectations of downstream customers, (4) make the process safer and (5) make the process more satisfying to the person who does it.

(1) *Resources*: A process that uses more resources than necessary is a waste. e.g., Reports that are distributed to more people than necessary, lead to waste of stationery and time and also of file space.

(2) *Errors*: Errors indicate poor workmanship and necessitate rework. e.g. typographical errors that are detected after the computer print out, require opening the file, making the correction, and printing the revised document.

(3) *Expecations:* By meeting or exceeding expectations of customers, the process is improved. e.g. the better the casting, the less grinding is required, to make the surface finish better.

(4) *Safety:* A safer workplace is more productive, with fewer or no accidents and less compensation paid to workers.

(5) *Satisfaction:* A minor change, for example, an ergonomically designed chair, can make a significant change in the attitude of an employee towards one's work.

2.11.2 Approaches

Several approaches toward the *continual improvement* are:

1. Juran trilogy (a cost oriented perspective).
2. Shewhart's P D S A cycle (a scientific method).
3. Kaizen (a Japanese approach, more behavioural, than the other two).
4. The five S (a house keeping practice or work place management).

1. The Juran Trilogy

This approach has three components: Planning, Control and Improvement.

PLANNING:

1. The planning component begins with identifying the external customers. Once quality goals are established, marketing determines the external customers, and all organisational personnel become the internal customers. External customers may be many, for example, in a banking service, they include cashiers, tellers, loan officers, auditors, managers and the bank's customers. Using a pareto analysis, the vital few customers can be identified.
2. The needs of the external customers are then enlisted. A stated need may differ from real need. For example, a stated need may be a cell phone, whereas the real need is communication or a status symbol.
3. The internal customers are identified and their needs may be discovered, by being a user of the product or service or by communicating with the customer, through product satisfaction and dissatisfaction data or may be obtained by simulation study in the laboratory. These needs are then to be translated to requirements that are understood and adopted by the organisation and its suppliers.
4. In the next step, one has to determine and develop product or service features, which—(*a*) respond to customer needs, (*b*) meet the needs of the organisation and its suppliers, (*c*) are competitive, and (*d*) optimize the costs of all stakeholders, through QFD or Taguchi's quality engineering or quality by design approach. The design team consisting of all functional areas within the organisation, the customers and suppliers have to approve the final design. Then the processes to produce the product/service features, are developed another group. These activities include identifying necessary facilities, training, and operations, control, and maintenance of the facilities.
5. Converting plans to operations is the final step in the planning process. Process validation is necessary to conform or even ensure that the process decided will consistently produce a product or service meeting all the requirements.

CONTROL: The control needs the feedback loop and it consists of the following steps:

(*a*) List all the factors to be controlled and their units of measure.

(*b*) Determine the objectives for the controls and also the type of sensors to be adopted to measure the product, service or process.

(*c*) Measure the actual performance.

(*d*) Compare actual performance to the objectives.

(*e*) Act on the deviation.

SPC techniques such as Pareto diagrams, flow diagrams, cause-and-effect diagrams, check sheets, histograms, control charts, and scatter diagrams are the effective tools in achieving the control. In addition, the process capability such as C_p and C_{pk} are used to determine, if the process is capable and is centered.

IMPROVEMENT: This part aims at reaching the levels of performance that are significantly higher than current levels. Process improvement commences from establishing a quality council. The quality council identifies the improvement projects and forms the project teams and provides the teams with the resources to study the causes, to develop solutions and establishe controls to hold the gains. Process improvement achieved could be either incremental or quantum jump.

2. The PDSA Cycle

The basic Plan-Do-Study-Act cycle, was first developed by Shewhart and then modified by Deming. It is an effective improvement approach. Figure 2.4 shows a typical PDSA cycle. The four steps involved in this cycle are: Plan thoroughly what is to be done. Execute the plan, do it. Study the results, to know whether the plan worked as intended or deviated. Finally, Act on the results, by discovering what worked as planned and what worked against. Using this knowledge, develop an improved plan and the cycle is repeated.

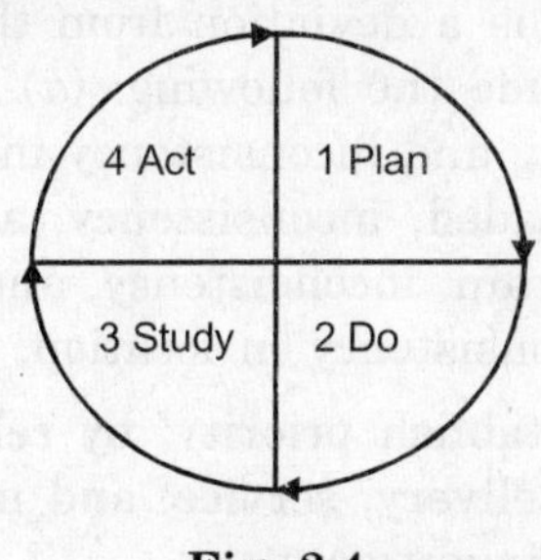

Fig. 2.4

3. Kaizen

'Kai' and 'zen' in Japanese, mean change for good. It indicates the philosophy that defines management's role in continuously encouraging and implementing small improvements involving every person. It is the principle of continual improvement whereby the process is made more effective, efficient, controllable and adaptable. Improvements are achieved with little expense, and with less sophisticated equipment or techniques. It concentrates on simplification by splitting the complex processes into their sub-processes and then improving upon them.

The need for 'kaizen' arises due to the changing environments such as (*a*) the customer expectations, (*b*) Product design, (*c*) Product quality, (*d*) People (the types of users and changing tastes of users), (*e*) Competition (change in the economy), and (*f*) Government rules and regulations (export, import policy, change in government, international standards, and influence of organisations such as W.T.O.). Changes are required to achieve excellence at the technical and managerial levels. If we do not move forward, time will push us backwards. Hence we must change our way of thinking and doing the jobs.

The Kaizen improvement gives attention on the use of the following factors:

1. Value-added and non-value added work activities.
2. Muda (muddling) which refers to the seven types of waste—Excess production, time delay, transportation, processing, inventory, wasted motion, and defective parts.
3. Principles of motion study and the use of cellular manufacturing.
4. Principles of material handling.
5. Documentation of standard operating procedures.
6. Five S philosophy.
7. Visual display for better communication.
8. Just-in-time principle to produce only in right quantities, at the right time, and with right resources.
9. Poka-yoke (fool proofing) to prevent or detect errors deviations.
10. Team dynamics, which include problem solving, communication skills and conflict resolution.

The *steps* for implementing kaizen are as follows:

1. *Identification of Problems:* Start with our area problems (to set our house in order, first) A problem is a deviation from the norm. A check list for problem identification may include the following: (*a*) on the human (strain in posture, environment or handling and inconsistency in the job and work load), (*b*) on the machine (strain, overloaded, inconsistency, and wastage including utilization), (*c*) on the material (strain, inconsistency, and wastage), and (*d*) on the method (strain on muscles, inconsistency in location, environment, and line)
2. *Prioritise Problems*: Establish priority; by relating the problems to the factors such as quality, cost, delivery, service, and material. Select the problem which does not warrant high investment.
3. *Analysis of the Problem*: (*a*) Follow the P-D-C-A cycle to analyse and implement the solution.

    In PLAN stage, the bad effects of the problem are identified. The causes of the problems are found. Determine the method (type of kaizen) to use. Find the solutions to reduce or eliminate the bad effects. Choose the optimum solution. In the DO stage, Get the approval from the department head and quality council, get the help from other departments if necessary, and implement the actions.

    In the CHECK stage, check whether the bad effects of the problem has reduced or eliminated, as planned. Check whether the method (type of kaizen) employed is as per the plan. Finally, in the ACT stage, standardize the new activity and rewrite the work instructions. Apply remedial actions for the remaining part of the problem, and prevent recurrence.

    (*b*) The Five Ws and two H Analysis.

The details of this methodology are discussed in Section 3.9.2.

4. *Selection of idea / solution*: The criteria for selecting the solution are the feasibility of implementation, time required and available for implementation, and the available resources including human labour involved.
5. *Reporting for Approval*: A report on the actions and the results is sent to be sent to the department head and to the quality council for approval and provision of the required resources.
6. *Implementation*: Upon getting the approval from the concerned, prepare a list of pre-requisites, clearly define the responsibility of the individuals, draw up daily schedule for implementation, and seek the guidance from specialists, if required.

An example of a kaizen-type improvement would be the change of the color of a welding cubicle from black to white to improve operator visibility. This change was found not only to result in a small improvement in weld quality but also a substantial improvement in operator satisfaction.

The differences between 'kaizen' and 'innovation' are explained as follows:

Kaizen	Innovation
1. It is a concept midway between the existing situation and the striking situation. It is a small improvement. It is the result of ongoing efforts.	1. It means a drastic improvement as a result of huge investment in technology/equipments.
2. It involves small steps.	2. It involves big steps.
3. It requires conventional know-how.	3. It requires technological breakthrough.
4. Continuous efforts are required to bring about kaizen.	4. High investments and high risks are involved.
5. It is process-oriented.	5. It is result-oriented.
6. Slow growth economy.	6. Fast growth economy.

4. The Five S

The Five S focuses on effective work place organisation and standardized work procedures. The five Japanese words have the following meaning:

SEIRI	meaning SORT (Straighten up the work place and remove unnecessary items, clearing)
SEITON	meaning SET (Systematic arrangement)
SEISO	meaning SHINE, (Sweeping, pleasant and clean environment)
SEIKETSU	meaning STANDARD (Maintain cleanliness and character spotlessly)
SHITSUKE	meaning SUSTAIN (Self discipline, monitoring, and training)

The need for Five S, is justified in many ways. An orderly mind alone can create well-ordered surroundings. The converse is also true. An orderly environment promotes an orderly mind. A dirty factory can not produce quality products. Clutter hides problems. A neat work place promotes easy and early discovery of abnormalities. Quality diagnosis becomes feasible then.

The Five S contributes to (1) Safety, (2) Quality, and (3) Productivity and also it facilitates the (4) Visual control. If clearing and arranging (Seiri and Seiton) are done well, then the work place has clean and more space, and also there is less clutter. Preparation for the work is easier, efficiency is higher, things do not get lost, and the general atmosphere is pleasant. All these conditions promote safety. When some machine parts are out of place, our clothing or limbs may get caught or when a hazardous chemical is spilled or without a label or in wrong location is contacted, it may harm the body and health. Thus it can be seen that orderliness promotes safety be it at home, office, shop floor or on the road.

The contribution of Five S to quality can be explained in many ways. A clean and orderly work place is a pre-requisite for making good products. A factory with poor house-keeping is bound to have quality problems such as:

(*a*) If the parts or materials look similar, they are likely to be mistaken while assembly or handling.

(*b*) If the rejected components or materials are not removed, they may get mixed with good ones in stores, and the rejects may be issued to the shop.

(*c*) Such a wrong mix in the shop floor may either go the next machine for processing or even to the customer.

(*d*) Some processing may be missed, as in the case of parts waiting for heat treatment getting mixed with parts that are already treated.

(*e*) Dusty parts or materials may lead to poor performance or poor impression of the customer.

(*f*) Materials might find their use beyond the shelf-life.

(*g*) Good amount of time is wasted in searching for the parts.

(*h*) Wear of the machine beds or guides is faster if they are dusty, and this reduces the accuracy leading to variability in results and nonconformities.

The Five S influences also the Productivity. Productivity is very much a function of morale. Good morale is promoted when people are trained to maintain their workplace in the ways mentioned below:

(*a*) The time spent is searching for the tools, spares, or paper or records is eliminated.

(*b*) Production loss due to a part or material or tool which is available but can not be traced is eliminated.

(*c*) Production loss arising out of use of wrong materials, mix-up of materials, and other such non-conforming are eliminated.

(*d*) Less machine or equipment break down, when maintained dust free.

(*e*) Lack of punctuality of any one member may affect the productivity of other members in a work place.

(*f*) Abnormalities which are likely to cause production stoppage can be spotted easily and also in time. e.g., a bin without requisite materials in the shop floor or a pile-up of rejection bins.

The Five S leads to easy and effective 'visual control' possible and hence improves the quality management. When house-keeping is poor, it is hard to separate the normal from the abnormal. When things lie all over, how does one spot anything unusual? With Five S in practice, the manager can easily find, 'This line seems to have high non-conformities today', 'there seems to be breakdown in the middle of the process, hence there is a pile-up there' and 'this line is not balanced properly'. There is no even flow of materials and so on. The visual control is achieved by the five S, and using clear signs, labels, colours, systems or orderly arrangement. The signs must be recognisable at a glance, and understandable to everyone. The visual control helps in storage operations also, e.g., the colour signs on meters and stripes on materials and foundry patterns ensure quality and safety. As part of standardisation, a Five S manual must be prepared. The manual containing charts and other visual displays with clarity should be made available while training the employees, new and old.

1. *Seiri means Clearing*. Take out unnecessary items and throw them away. This can be adopted in the factory floor (broken tools, old notices, scraps in heaps, used clothes, and rejected materials) or the office (old diaries, used/broken pens, outdated files, and broken furniture) or the house (old clothes, broken suitcases, used or useless tins and bottles, and broken toys). The items are classified as wanted, and unwanted. In the second case, they are sorted out as repairable or junk/waste and moved to the designated area periodically. If the items are in use, classify them based on the frequency of use and store them accordingly.

   The major benefits are that time is saved in searching, reduced fatigue, worry, anger, and tension, improved work efficiency and also safety. This corresponds to ISO 9001 #4.2.3 and 4.

2. *Seiton denotes Arranging*. Arrange everything in proper order so that it can be easily spotted and picked up for use. This is adopted in factory floor (unlabelled tool crib, cluttered shelves and lockers, and things lying on the floor), office (unlabelled file cabinets, shelves, tables, and papers lying all over), and the house (clutter, papers, litter even in drawing rooms, kitchen, and often in study rooms!). Without this, the search squads always go around looking for misplaced items. In some cases, this situation may lead to accidents or near-accidents.

   The steps involved in 'Seiton' are:

   (*a*) Analyse the present situation

   (*b*) Fix the address or storage place

   (*c*) Fix the method of storage, so as to facilitate easy retrieval.

   (*d*) Follow the rules. The factory floor including the aisles should be kept clear of any materials.

   It corresponds to ISO 9001 # 6.4.

   The major benefits are that time is saved in locating the material and place of storage, and by systematic movement of materials.

3. *Seiso indicates Sweeping*. The work place should be swept thoroughly so that there is no dust or dirt anywhere. This is applicable to the factory floor (dirty machines, dust on products and materials, dusty walls, roofs, and floor), office (dusty furniture, dirty office equipment, and windows), and the house (dirty furniture, windows, and exhaust fans). Cleaning reveals many potential equipment

problems existing but hidden. During cleaning one can identify the presence of defects, and causes of stain, dirt, and defects. This corresponds to ISO 9001 # 7.5.3.

4. *Seiketsu means Cleanliness (Standardising).* It includes washing things to disinfect or remove hazardous chemicals. It is applicable to the factory floor (after handling hazardous chemicals, control of fumes, and disinfecting for personal hygiene), the office (pests and rodents control, and personal hygiene), and the house (pests and rodents control and personal hygiene). Health and Safety features demand this practice of cleanliness. This corresponds to ISO 9001 # 7.5.5.

   The benefits are:

   (*a*) neat, orderly and uniform look improves the overall appearance, and

   (*b*) easy to identify by the customers, auditors, and the visitors with name tags.

5. *Shitsuke points to Training and Discipline.* Discipline includes safety and punctuality. Everything must be in its place. People are also to be in their place, at the right time, in the right attire. The management should train the people to practice 5 S with discipline, and they should make 5 S a habit. Without the fifth S, the first Four S will not stand. It corresponds to ISO 9001 # 8.5.1.

Training on Five S is given with the help of visual charts and display. Through this the message is understood well, stays clear in their minds, and is developed into habits. The charts and displays serve as reminders to employees. The new or transferred employees also can be trained easily on this.

To put it in a nut-shell, a clean workplace promotes high productivity, produces high quality, keeps the cost low, ensures delivery on time, is safe for people to work, and maintains a high morale in people.

R.I.L.[18] have introduced the Five S program successfully at their laboratories and shops for inventory and document management. In Chennai, TVS-Lucas, a leader among the pioneering industries, has implemented the 5 S programs successfully for two decades since.

2.12 SUPPLIER PARTNERSHIP

The purchased goods have been estimated to contain a major percentage of the cost of goods sold, in recent years. The supplier quality is hence found to have major effect, on the overall cost of a product or service. The customer (buying organisation) working with suppliers in partnering environment is able to achieve the same quality level, as achieved within the organisation.

Customers and suppliers strive towards the same goal, i.e., to satisfy the end user. If the supplier's quality is better, the supplier's long-term transaction is better, because the customer will get better quality product. With both the customer and the supplier having limited resources, by working together as partners, both are able to maximize their return on investment.

The procurements were based purely on price, in the past. The contracts were awarded to the lowest bidder. The quality and delivery aspects were ignored. Quality Guru like Deming, declared that customers must stop awarding contract based on the low bidder, because price has no basis without quality. He also advocated single suppliers for each item to help so that a long-term relationship of loyalty and trust can be built. Actions on this basis were found to have improved the products and services.

Another factor influencing the supplier relations was the just-in-time (JIT) concept. As per this concept, the raw materials and semi-finished products reach the manufacturing centre, in small quantities as and when they are needed, and not before. The JIT keeps the inventory costs to a minimum. Procurement lot size is small and delivery is frequent. The supplier then becomes, a JIT organisation. The supplier must be in a position to reduce considerably the set-up time or otherwise its costs will increase. More details are presented in Chapter 6.

Many original equipment manufacturers have reported to have developed strategic partnerships with their suppliers. Consequently the suppliers have been taking on increased product-development responsibilities such as product design, formation of specifications and component testing. This combined endeavours have resulted in, improved quality, reduced costs, and increased market share for both.

2.12.1 Principles of Customer Supplier Relations

According to *Ishikawa*, the following *ten* principles are recommended to ensure quality products and services and to promote satisfactory atmosphere between the customer and the supplier:

1. The customer as well as the supplier are fully responsible for the control of quality.
2. Both of them should be independent of each other and respect each other's independence.
3. The customer is responsible for providing the supplier with necessary and sufficient requirements, so that the supplier can know precisely, what to produce.
4. Both of them should enter into a contract, beneficial to both, with respect to quality, price, delivery method, and terms of payment.
5. The supplier is responsible for providing the quality to satisfy the customer and submitting necessary data upon the customer's request.
6. Both the customer and the supplier should agree upon the method to evaluate the quality of the product or service to the satisfaction of both parties.
7. Both of them should establish, in the contract, the method by which they can reach amicable settlement of any disputes that may arise.
8. Both of them should continuously exchange information, including the use of multifunctional teams, in order to improve the product or service quality.
9. Both the customer and the supplier should perform business activities, namely procurement, manufacture, inventory planning, and systems, so that a satisfactory relationship is maintained.
10. In business transactions, both the customer and the supplier should always hold the best interest of the end user.

Thus, it can be seen that the true partnership can flourish on long-term commitment, trust, and shared vision and yet, preserving their identity and independence.

2.12.2 Partnering

Partnering is a long-term commitment between organisations, for the purpose of achieving specific business goals and objectives, by maximizing the effectiveness of each of their resources. The relationship is built upon trust, dedication to common goals and objectives, and an understanding of their expectations and values. The benefits of partnering, are improved quality, increased efficiency, lower cost, increased opportunity for innovation, and the continual improvement of products and services.

The three basic elements to a partnering relationship are:

1. *Long term commitment:* Many of the problems require time to solve or processes need constant improvement. Hence, long-term commitment provides the desired environment for both parties towards continual improvement. The involvement must be total for the organisations from top to bottom.

   Apart from the strength of each party, investment in new machinery, systems and humanware are required, for fostering the commitment. The parties take risk in proportion to their anticipated rewards and the extent of the relationship. A supplier might not acquire new equipment or systems, without a long-term commitment.

2. *Mutual trust:* Mutual trust enables the resources and the knowledge of each partner to be combined to eliminate deficiencies. In course of time, partners share freely the information and adopt reduced controls. The trust provides the basis for a strong and live relationship. The purchase and inspection functions of the organisation must act within the overall goals and objectives. Free and frequent communication prevent wastage and disputes, while building the relationship.

   The parties should have access to each other's business plans and technical information such as product and process parameters. Further, they also share or integrate their resources, such as training programs, office systems, and equipment.

3. *Shared vision:* Each of the parties must be aware of the need to satisfy the end user or customer. To achieve this goal, there must be transparent and frank exchange of information on their needs and expectations. Shared goals and objectives develop a common direction and must be aligned with mission of each party. Employees of the both sides should function towards their common good. Their decisions are to be equitable and to be implemented as a team. This sharing of goals and plans helps in mutual strategic planning and is beneficial to both sides.

2.12.3 Sourcing

The three types of sourcing that are common, are: *sole, multiple, and single*. A sole source of supply means that the organisation is compelled to procure from only one supplier. This situation may exist because of factors such as patents, technical specifications, location of raw material, or the components being manufactured by different plant of the same organisation, or monopoly manufacture of the component.

Multiple sourcing means, purchasing an item from two or more suppliers. The transactions depend upon their performance through the price, quality, and delivery. The competition between them leads to higher quality, lower costs, and better service. Besides, the multiple sourcing eliminates disruption of supply due to strikes, *bundh* or *rasta roko, and floods.*

Single sourcing is the selection of one supplier for an item although several sources are available. This principle leads to, long-term contracts and partnering relationship. With a definite future demand, the supplier can direct it resources to improve the process. The advantages for the organisation are, reduced business and manufacturing costs, complete accountability, supplier loyalty, and a better end product with less deviations. On the other side, the supplier also gets the cost of transactions reduced. In this way, many companies could cut supplier base and, at the same time, improve the quality.

2.12.4 Supplier Selection

Normally the decision to produce or outsource (buy) should be made in the design stage. The answer to the following three questions explains the lead to the situation:

1. How critical is the item, to the design of the product or service?
2. Does the organisation have the technical know how to manufacture the components or semi-finished product from within? If not, should that know how be developed?
3. Are there any suppliers, who are specialists in manufacturing those components? If not, is the organisation willing to develop such a specialised supplier, externally? The answer, in terms of quality, safety, and the acquisition of technical knowledge helps in the selection of the supplier.

After the decision to outsource (buy), the selection of the supplier and the evaluation follows. One should make sure that,

1. The supplier agrees to the management philosophy of the organisation.
2. The supplier has a stable management system. To assess this, one should check, if the supplier has the declared objectives, policies and its commitment to quality or whether the supplier is an ISO certified organisation.
3. The supplier maintains high technical profile and has the potential for technological innovations.
4. The supplier can provide those raw materials and semi-finished parts required by the purchaser, and those supplied conform the quality specifications.
5. The supplier has sufficient capability to produce the quantity needed.
6. The price is right and delivery dates can be met and the supplier is easily accessible in terms of transportation and communication.
7. The supplier is sincere in implementing the contract provisions.
8. Does the supplier have a contract review system and how the differences and disputes, that may arise, should be resolved? Further, does the system provide for the inclusion of amendments or review of contracts?
9. Does the supplier have a track record of customer satisfaction and credibility?

A comparison of several suppliers with a numerical score of 1 to 5, for each condition listed, may be used. Small organisations use a written questionnaire and survey the potential suppliers by mail.

2.12.5 Supplier Rating (Rating of the Supplier)

The suppliers are usually rated by the customers with the following objectives:

(*a*) To obtain the overall rating of the supplier's performance.

(*b*) To ensure thorough understanding with suppliers with their past performance on quality, service, and delivery.

(*c*) To provide the supplier with a detailed factual record for corrective actions.

(*d*) To strengthen the customer—supplier relationship.

A reliable supplier rating system requires the following factors:

1. An internal structure to implement and sustain the rating program.
2. A regular and formal review of the process.
3. A standard measurement system for all suppliers. The supplier rating is frequently based on quality, delivery, and service, and in a few cases, machineability and cost are also included. The quality is given high weightage. Table 2.11 shows a typical scorecard (rating) for a manufacturer and seller of storage solutions for a computer industry. The weightage for characteristics such as quality, process control, technology, support, delivery, product technology, lead time and purchasing are indicated and a comparison is made of its suppliers. These reports are prepared periodically and the grades should be reported to each supplier.

Table 2.11 A sample supplier score (rating)

Product VVV			
Period Q2 05		**Supplier A**	**Supplier B**
Quality performance	**Maximum points**	**Actual points**	**Actual points**
Items returned: Normalised	30	28	29
Deduction (Maximum –10)		–10	–10
Yield multiplier	1	0.9	0.72
Penalty: field issues, stoppage of shipment, line purge at –15, –15, –5, respectively	30	15.9	13.4
Process control	8	7	6
Process technology	6	5	5
Sustaining technical support	6	2	3
On-time delivery	20	20	18
Product technology	10	10	8
Lead time	15	13	13
Purchasing and material support	5	5	2
Performance matrix total	**100**	**77.9**	**68.4**
Price index = target price/actual price	1	0.88	0.97
Score = performance matrix × price index	100	68.6	66.4
Total cost of supply = ((100–score)/100)+1	**1**	**1.32**	**1.34**

2.12.6 Relationship Development

In addition to partnering, supplier selection, principles of customer/supplier relations, and periodic rating, the processes such as inspection, training, teams and recognition and reward system etc. promote the growth of relationship between the customer and supplier.

INSPECTION: The objective of inspection is to eliminate, substantially reduce, or automate the inspection activity. The four common modes of inspection are 100% inspection, sampling, audit and identity check.

1. Initially, 100% inspection of the important quality characteristics, by both parties is followed.
2. As the supplier gains confidence in its quality performance, a change to sampling with statistical control is favoured. At this point, the customer changes to auditing the supplier's performance through random sampling of the submitted lots.
3. The supplier continues statistical process control and initiates its own auditing. The customer now, has complete confidence in the supplier and initiates identity checks, which verify the item number and quality for accounting and inventory control.
4. In the final stage, both customer and supplier perform only identity checks. The statistical process control and continual improvement continues. It is estimated that these four stages are realised in about five years in the developed countries.

TRAINING: In small organisations, the customer or consultant starts the training process. Larger organisations may include the supplier in their training. Such a training and the type of course contents may be part of the partnership agreement.

TEAM APPROACH: Customer/Supplier teams are established in a number of areas, such as product design, and quality system. Team meetings are conducted at both parties premises, so that, they achieve a better understanding of the processes.

RECOGNITION: Incentives are declared for suppliers to encourage their commitment to quality improvement. Incentives may be in the form of a preferred category of supplier, recognition published in the customer's newsletter or a display board exhibited in the supplier's reception area.

2.13 PERFORMANCE MEASURES

Change can't occur without laser-like accountability and metrics to measure how you are doing.

—Larry Bossidy of Honeywell

One of the core values for international quality awards, is the performance measures. Measures are important to know the success or failure.

Basic Concepts

Performance measures are needed to achieve the following objectives:

1. Establish the baseline measures to reveal trends.
2. Determine which processes need to be improved.
3. Indicate process gains or loses.
4. Compare the goals with actual performance. A thing that cannot be measured, cannot be controlled.

5. Provide information for individual and team evaluation.
6. Provide information to make informed decisions.
7. Determine overall performance of the organisation.

Typical Measurements

The details of the information required are listed as follows:

Human Resources: Absenteeism, lost time due to accidents, turnover, employee satisfaction index, number of suggestion for improvement, number of suggestions implemented, hours of training per employee, training cost per employee, number of active teams, number of grievances, etc.

Customers: Number of complaints, number of on-time deliveries, warranty data as part replacement, customer satisfaction index, time to resolve complaints, response time on enquiries, mean time to repair, dealer satisfaction, report letter, etc.

Manufacturing: Inventory turns, SPC charts, C_p/C_{pk}, amount of scrap or rework, nonconformities per million units, software errors per 1000 lines of code, machine downtime, actual performance to goal, number of products returned, cost per unit, etc.

Research and Development: New product time to market, design change orders, research and development spending to sales, average time to process a proposal, recall data, cost estimation errors.

Suppliers: SPC charts, C_p / C_{pk}, on time delivery, service rating, quality performance, accounting accuracy, average lead time, per cent of suppliers that are default free, JIT delivery target, etc.

Marketing/Sales: Sales expense to revenue, order accuracy, new product sales to total sales, new customers, gained or lost accounts, sales income to number of sales people, number of successful calls per week, etc.

Administration: Revenue per employee, expense to revenue, cost of poor quality, number of days accounts receivable past due, office equipment up-time, purchase order errors, vehicle fleet data, order entry/accounting accuracy.

2.13.1 Criteria

In case of any addition to the list of metrics, the following criteria are recommended for evaluating them:

1. Measures should be simple to understand by all those who use them.
2. *Few in number:* Two or three measures should be sufficient for any work group to concentrate upon.
3. *Should be developed by the user:* To ensure the ownership of the measures, they must be developed by the user rather than thrusted upon from top. However, in some cases, measures are mandated by the customer.
4. *Relevance to customer:* Measures must be relevant to the needs of internal or external customers. Control over important changes should be with the people who are held responsible for the performance measure.
5. *Improvement:* Measures are used to promote improvement, prevention, and strategic planning and not to identify poor performance and penalise those performers.

6. *Cost:* The cost of measurement should be considered. Cost and profit must be reflected in the improvement.
7. *Visible:* Unit measures should exhibited to the people concerned, in a central location, to constantly remind them of their goals.
8. *Timely:* Financial and accounting data are often presented too late, to take action upon. This may require that measurements are taken hourly or daily or weekly instead of monthly or quarterly, as in traditional accounting system.
9. *Aligned:* A set of several measures and indicators should be aligned with the organisational goals.
10. *Results:* Key result measures are to be guided and balanced by all stakeholders—Customers, employees, stockholders, suppliers, the public and the community.

Strategy

The quality council will obtain appropriate information from all of the stakeholders and refer the core values, goals, mission, and vision statement, and also the criteria discussed earlier. With this input the strategic measurement system is introduced.

The quality council should meet every month, to monitor current activities and plan the future ones. A report package on the following, namely:

1. Performance measures.
2. Narrative reports of competition, opportunities, and relevant events.
3. System audits, are prepared to assist the council.

2.13.2 Presentation of Performance Measure

The simplest of the *six* basic techniques for presenting performance measures, is the time series graph. The quantified performance measure is shown along the Y-axis and the time, in days or weeks or months, is shown along the X-axis. This graph shows the trends in the measure, favourable or unfavourable.

A second form of presentation, is the control chart (refer Chapter 3, for details).

A third method, is the capability index, which is defined as the ratio of the tolerance to the capability and C_{pk}. The two measures, one indicating the ability of the process to meet the specifications, and the other indicating the centering of the process on the target (refer Chapter 3), give the performance measures.

Another way of measuring quality, is Taguchi's loss function. This technique combines target, cost, and specifications into one measurement.

The fifth method of presenting performance measures is the cost of poor quality. Money attracts the attention of senior management effectively. The quality costs have been described, in detail, in Chapter 1.

The sixth method is, the National Quality Award. Some of the characteristics of the award systems are discussed below.

2.13.3 Criteria for Performance Excellence

Table 2.12 shows the seven categories of award and the twenty items with their weightage points. It is obvious that most of the score is for the results and not on procedures or tools.

The LEADERSHIP clause examines the organisation's leadership system and leaders' personal leadership. It examines, how senior leaders and the leadership system address, values, company directions, performance expectations, a focus on customers and other stakeholders, learning, and innovation. How the company addresses its social responsibilities and provides support to key communities are also examined.

The STRATEGIC PLANNING category examines how the organisation sets strategic directions and how it develops the critical strategies and action plans, to support directions. How plans are deployed and how performance is tracked, are also considered.

The CUSTOMER AND MARKET FOCUS category examines how the company determines requirements, expectations, and preferences of customers and markets. How the company builds relationships with customers and determines their satisfaction, are also examined.

The INFORMATION ANALYSIS category examines the selection, management, and effectiveness of use of information and data to support key company processes and action plans, and the company's performance management system.

The HUMAN RESOURCE FOCUS category examines how the organisation enables their employees to develop and utilise their full potential, aligned with the company's objectives. The company's efforts to build and maintain a work environment and work climate, conducive to performance excellence, full participation, and personal and organisational growth are also examined.

Table 2.12 Award categories and factors listing[1]

Category / Factor	Points
1. LEADERSHIP	
1.1 Leadership system	80
1.2 Company responsibility and citizenship	30
2. STRATEGIC PLANNING	
2.1 Strategy development process	40
2.2 Company strategy	40
3. CUSTOMER AND MARKET FOCUS	
3.1 Customer and market knowledge	40
3.2 Customer satisfaction and relationship enhancement	40
4. INFORMATION ANALYSIS	
4.1 Selection and use of information and data	25
4.2 Selection and use of comparative information and data	15
4.3 Analysis and review of company performance	40
5. HUMAN RESOURCE FOCUS	
5.1 Work systems	40
5.2 Employee education, training and development	30
5.3 Employee well-being and satisfaction	30
6. PROCESS MANAGEMENT	
6.1 Management of product and service and processes	60
6.2 Management of support processes	20
6.3 Management of supplier and partnering processes	

7. BUSINESS RESULTS		
7.1	Customer satisfaction results	125
7.2	Financial and market results	125
7.3	Human resource results	50
7.4	Supplier and partner results	25
7.5	Company-specific results	125
	Total points	**1000**

The PROCESS MANAGEMENT category, examines the key aspects of process management, including customer-focused design, product and service delivery, support, and supplier and partnering process involving all work units. How the key processes are designed, implemented, managed, and improved to achieve better performance, are also examined.

The BUSINESS RESULTS category, examines the organisation's performance and improvement in key business areas such as, customer satisfaction, financial and market place performance, human resource results, supplier and partner performance, and operational performance. Performance levels relative to competitors are also examined.

According to the study by Dr. Juran, on the winners of this award, the gains are accomplished by big as well as small organisations and the notable gains are in quality, productivity and cycle time.

❑ ❑ ❑

CHAPTER 3

Statistical Process Control

3.0 STATISTICAL PROCESS CONTROL

The Statistical Process Control is one of the effective tools for improving the product and service quality. There are seven basic techniques. In fact the first four techniques are not statistical. Further these tools not only *control* the process but have the capability to *improve* it as well.

3.1 PARETO DIAGRAM

Pareto A. an economist, conducted studies on the distribution of wealth in Europe. He found that there were a few people with a lot of money and many people with little money. This concept was applied to many fields and the phrase, 'Vital few and Trivial many', in Engineering also.

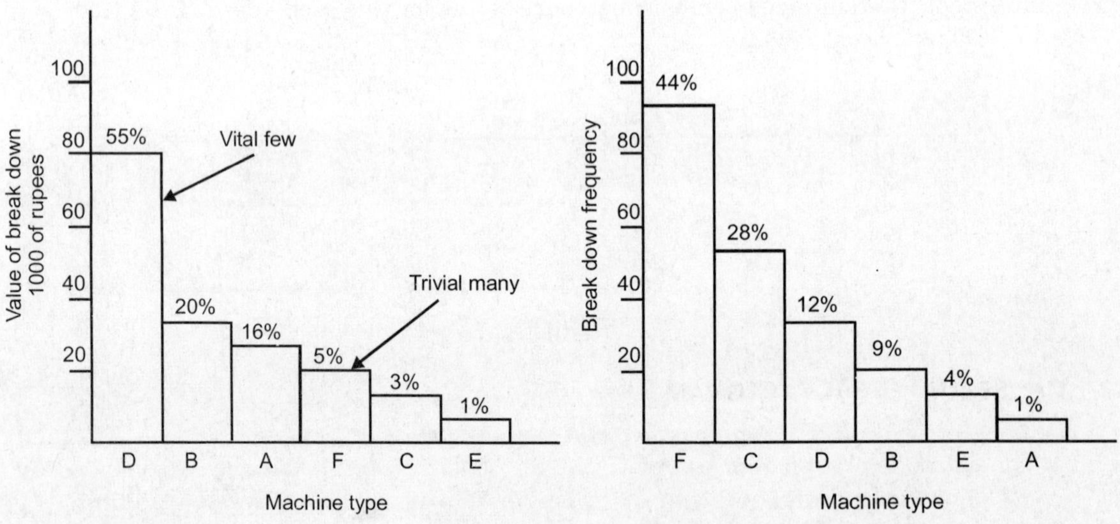

Fig. 3.1

A Pareto diagram is a graph where the data are classified in descending order from left to right, as illustrated in Fig. 3.1 The data classification could be complaints, breakdowns, causes, type of nonconformities, inventory values, etc. The vital few are grouped on the left and trivial many on the right. The Y axes represent cost of breakdown in rupees and frequency of breakdown, where as the X axes represent type of machines in both graphs. As can be seen from the graph, the machine D has the greatest cost, but F has the greatest frequency. The graph has the advantage of providing a visual impact, showing those vital few machines, that need attention. Resources are then directed to take necessary corrective actions. In the case discussed, 75% of the breakdown costs resulted from 25% of the machines (Types D and B).

Some examples of the, 'vital few' are: A few nonconformities account for the majority of customer complaints, a few errors account for the bulk of the process downtime, a few products account for the majority of the profit, a few items account for the bulk of the inventory cost.

The use of Pareto diagram is continual. Initially vital few items are identified for process improvement and improved. When the Pareto analysis is made next time, another item may be identified as critical and improved. This process continues until the nonconformities become an insignificant quality problem.

The Pareto diagram is a powerful quality improvement tool. It is applicable to problem identification and the measurement of progress.

3.2 PROCESS FLOW DIAGRAM

Fig. 3.2 shows a flow diagram, for the order booking activity for made-to-order flow valves. This diagram shows the flow of the product or service as it moves through the various processing operations. The diagram makes visualization of the entire system easy, identify the potential trouble spots, and locate control activities. It also hints at, who is the next customer. Improvements can be accomplished by changing, reducing, combining, or eliminating steps. Standardized symbols may not be used for this problem solving situations.

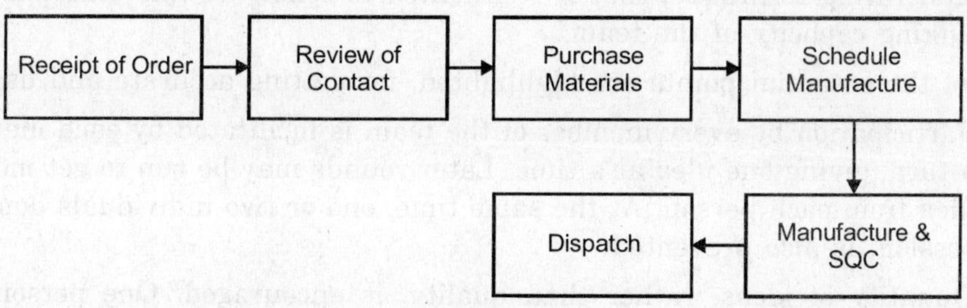

Fig. 3.2

3.3 CAUSE AND EFFECT DIAGRAM

The cause and effect diagram is a pictorial representation of lines and symbols designed to show meaningful relationship between an effect and its causes. This was developed by Dr. Kaoru Ishikawa and also referred to as Ishikawa diagram or a fishbone diagram.

These diagrams are used to investigate either a ' bad' effect or to take action to correct the causes or a 'good' effect and to learn those causes that are responsible. For every effect, there may be more than one cause. Figure 3.3. shows the cause and effect diagram, with the effect on the right extreme and the causes on the left. The effect is the quality characteristic, that needs improvement. Causes are sometimes broken down into the major causes of work methods, materials, measurement, human resource, equipment, and the environment.

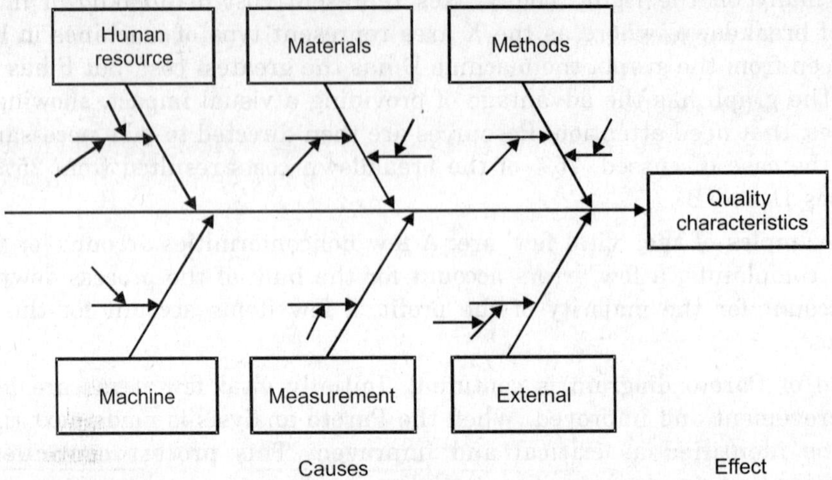

Fig. 3.3

Each major cause is further subdivided into several minor causes. For example, under work methods, we may have training, knowledge, ability, physical characteristics, etc. The cause and effect and effect diagrams, are the means of visualising all these major and minor causes.

The first step in the construction of a cause and effect diagram is, for the team to identify the effect or quality problem. The major causes are placed on the right side of the paper, and then minor causes are identified and placed on the diagram.

The minor causes are determined by the brain-storming technique. The brain-storming is an idea-generating technique, that is well suited to construct this diagram. It uses the creative thinking capacity of the team.

Some of the essential points are highlighted, for getting accurate and usable result:

1. Participation by every member of the team is facilitated by each member taking a turn, giving one idea at a time. Later rounds may be run to get more than one idea from each person. At the same time, one or two individuals dominating the session, is also prevented.
2. Quantity of ideas, rather than quality, is encouraged. One person's idea will trigger someone else's idea, and a chain reaction follows. Frequently, what may look as a trivial or 'dumb' idea, may lead to the best solution.
3. Criticism of an idea is not allowed. There should be freewheeling and exchange of information, that kindles the imagination. The evaluation of ideas is done, after all the ideas are placed on the diagram.
4. A prime factor of participation, is the visibility of the diagram. To provide space for all ideas on causes, A1 size paper may be pinned to a board for maximum visibility.
5. Focus on solving a problem, rather than discussing how it began. The team leader should ask questions, using the why, where, when, who, and how techniques.

6. After a few hours of incubation (the next day), another brain-storming session may be conducted. A copy of the ideas may be provided to the team members, after the first session. When no more ideas are generated, the brain-storming activity is stopped.

After constructing the cause and effect diagram, most likely causes are determined by studying the diagram, in another session. Team members may vote on one or more causes. The causes, with the most votes are circled, as shown in Fig. 3.4 and thus four or five major causes, are identified.

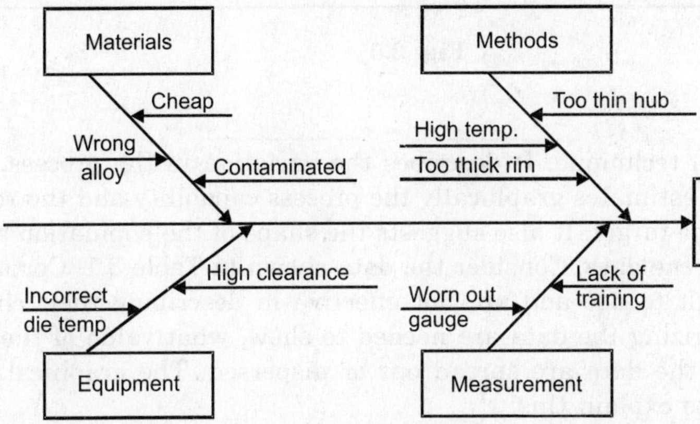

Fig. 3.4

Solutions are developed to correct the causes and improve the process. The possible solutions are decided by the consideration of cost, feasibility, resistance to change, other consequences, training needed, etc. The solutions are then tested and implemented. The diagrams are to be exhibited in key locations, to stimulate people with new ideas, upon facing new problems. The diagrams may be revised, as the improvements are made.

The cause and effect diagram has unlimited application in research, manufacturing, marketing, office operations, and service. The strongest asset of this method is the participation and contribution of everyone involved. These diagrams are useful to:

1. Analyse actual conditions for the product or service quality improvement, more efficient use of resources, and reduced costs.
2. Eliminate the conditions causing nonconformities and customer complaints.
3. Standardise the existing and proposed operations.
4. Educate and train personnel in decision-making and corrective-action activities.

3.4 CHECK SHEETS

The main aim of check sheets, is to ensure that the data is collected accurately by the persons. Figure 3.5 shows a check sheet for nonconformities in painting on a machined surface.

The check sheets are also designed to show location on the component, when necessary. A creative design of check sheet is quite useful. It should be user-friendly and, whenever required, include information on time and location.

Product: Mudgard Type of nonconformity	No. Inspected : 191 Tally	Total
Blister	卌 卌 ||	12
Drips	卌 卌 卌 卌 ||	23
Lighter coat	卌 ||	8
Thicker coat	卌 卌 卌 |||	34
Runs	卌 卌 卌 卌 |	21
Peelings	卌 卌 卌 |||	19
	Total	117

Fig. 3.5

3.5 HISTOGRAM

This is a statistical technique. It describes the variation in the process, as shown in Fig. 3.6. The histogram estimates graphically the process capability and the relationship to the specifications and the target. It also suggests the shape of the population and indicates, if there are any gaps in the data. Consider the data shown in Table 3.1. Certainly the data in this form are difficult to use and are not effective in describing their characteristics. Some means of summarizing the data are needed to show, what value of the data tend to cluster about and how the data are spread out or dispersed. The graphical or analytical methods may be used to explain this.

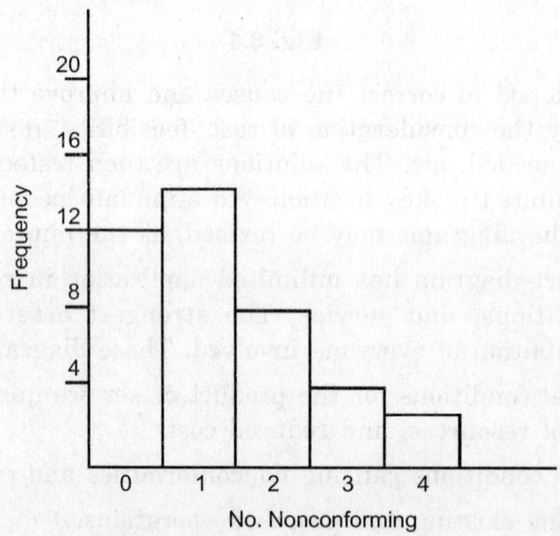

Fig. 3.6

Ungrouped Data

In the graphical technique, a picture of frequency distribution is plotted. It is a summary of how the data points or observations occur within each subdivision or intervals of observed values. In the analytical technique, data summary is made by computing a measure of the central tendency, such as average, median, and mode and a measure of the dispersion, such as range and standard deviation.

Referring to Table 3.1, the analyst using this tabular information would have difficulty in comprehending the meaning of the data. A better understanding can be obtained by tallying the frequency of each value as shown in Table 3.2.

Table 3.1 Number of defects in an assembly

3	0	1	2	4	0	2	1	3	1	2	0	1	2	1
0	4	2	2	0	1	0	1	2	1	0	4	1	0	1
1	0	3	2	1	0	3	1	2	3	1	0	3	1	0

Table 3.2 Tally of number of defects in an assembly

Number of non-conforming	Frequency
0	12
1	15
2	9
3	6
4	3

In the first step, an array is constructed, which is an arrangement of raw numerical data in ascending or descending order of magnitude. An array of ascending order from 0 to 4, is shown in the first column of the table. The next step is to tabulate how many times a particular value occurred, which is called, the frequency. This is shown in the second column of the table. Through Table 3.2, one can visualise the distribution of the data. This table is classified as a frequency distribution. The frequency distribution is a useful method of visualizing the data and is a statistical concept.

When a greater visual clarity is desired, frequency distributions are presented in graphical form called, histogram. A histogram consists of a set of rectangles that represent the frequency of the observed values, in each category. Figure 3.6 is a histogram for the data in Table 3.2.

Grouped Data

When the number of categories become large, the data are grouped into cells. In general, the number of cells should be between 5 and 20. As a guideline, one may use 5 to

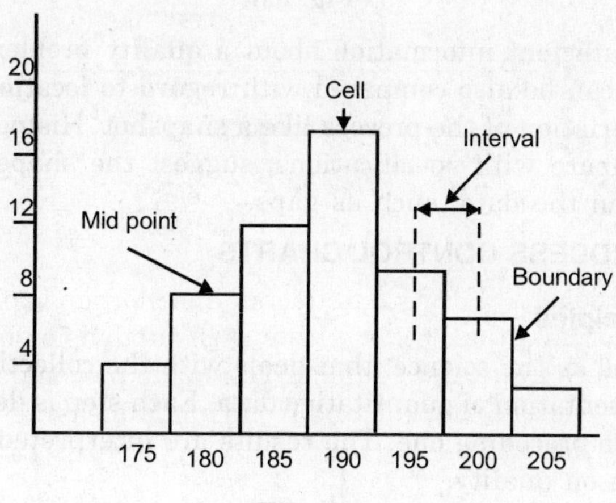

Fig. 3.7

9 cells when the number of observations is less than 100; use 8 to 17 cells when the number of observations is between 100 and 500; and use 15 to 20 cells when the number of observations is greater than 500. Figure 3.7 shows a histogram for grouped data of the quality characteristic, hardness. The interval is the distance between adjacent cell midpoints. Cell boundaries are halfway between the cell midpoints. If an odd cell interval is chosen, which in this case is five units, the midpoint value will be to the same degree of accuracy as the ungrouped data. This situation is desirable, since all values in the cell take on the midpoint value, when any additional calculations are made.

Histogram Shapes

The histograms have certain identifiable characteristics, as shown in Fig. 3.8. One characteristic of the distribution, is the symmetry or lack of symmetry of the data. Are the data equally distributed on each side of the center, or the data skewed to the right or to the left? Another characteristic, is peakedness or *kurtosis*, of the data. The third characteristic is the number of modes or peaks, in the data. There can be one mode, or two modes (bi-modal) or multiplc modes.

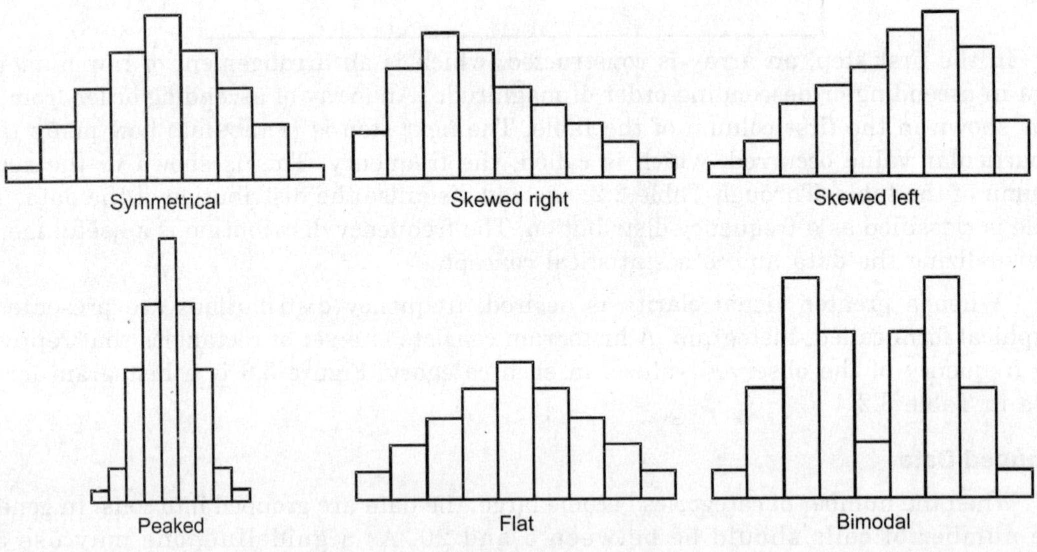

Fig. 3.8

Histograms give sufficient information about a quality problem to provide a basis for decision making. They can be also compared with regard to location, spread, and shape. A histogram shows the variation of the process like a snapshot. Histograms can determine the process capability, compare with specifications, suggest the shape of the population, and indicate discrepancies in the data, such as gaps.

3.6 STATISTICAL PROCESS CONTROL CHARTS

3.6.1 Statistical Principles

Statistics is defined as the science, that deals with the collection, tabulation, analysis, interpretation, and presentation of quantitative data. Each step is dependent on the accuracy and completeness of the preceding one. The results are interpreted and presented to assist in the decision making on quality.

Data that are collected for quality control purposes, are obtained by direct observations and are classified as either variables or attributes. Variables are those quality characteristics that are measurable, such as length in mm or weight in Newton. Attributes on the other hand, are those quality characteristics, that are classified as either conforming or not conforming to specifications, such as 'go-no go' gauge.

Analytical methods of describing a variation of data, have the advantage of allowing for comparisons between variations of data. They also allow for additional calculations and inferences. The two principal analytical methods of describing a variation of data, are the measures of central tendency and measures of dispersion.

Measures of Central Tendency

A measure of central tendency of a distribution is a numerical value that describes the central position of the data or how the data tend to build up in the center. There are three measures in common use in quality, (*a*) the average, (*b*) the median, and (*c*) the mode.

The average, is the sum of the observed values divided by the number of observations. It is the most common measure of the central tendency and is represented by the expression,

$$\text{The average } \overline{X} = \frac{\sum_{i=1}^{n} X_i}{n}$$

Another measure of central tendency is the median, Me, which is defined as the mid value of a series of ordered observations so that the number of items above it is equal to the number below it. When the number of observations is odd, the median is the midpoint of the values. If the ordered values are 5, 6, 8, 10, and 13 then the median is 8. When the number of observations are even, the median is the average of the two middle numbers. Thus the ordered values of 5, 6, 8, 10,13, and 16 has a median, that is the average of 8 and 10, which is 9.

The Mode, M, of a set of values, is the value that occurs with the greatest frequency. It is possible for the mode to be nonexistent, in a series of values or to have more than one value. For example, the series of values 40, 43, 45, 49, 52, and 58 does not have a mode; and the series of values 110, 113, 113, 113, 116, 120, 121, 123, 123, 123, 126, and 130 have two modes, namely 113 and 123. The series of values is called unimodal, if it has one mode, bimodal, if it has two modes, and multimodal, if it has more than two modes. When data are grouped into a frequency distribution, the midpoint of the cell with the highest frequency is the mode, because this point represents the highest point (greatest frequency) of the histogram.

The Average is the most commonly used measure of central tendency. It is used when the distribution is symmetrical or not appreciably skewed to the right or left and when a stable value is needed for inductive statistics. The median becomes the effective measure of the central tendency, when the distribution is positively (to the right) or negatively (to the left) skewed. The median is used when an exact midpoint of a distribution is desired. A control chart based on the median is user-friendly and excellent for monitoring quality. The mode is used when a quick and approximate measure of the central tendency is desired. The mode of a histogram is easily found by a visual examination.

Measures of Dispersion

A second tool of statistics consists of measures of dispersion, which describe how the data are spread out or scattered on each side of the central value. Both the measures are needed to describe a collection of data. The central tendency gives the 'variation of the mean' values and the dispersion gives the 'variation from the mean'. For example, the production of two identical departments may have the average of 750 components, but the department 1 has a high of 1000 and a low of 550, whereas the other department may have a high of 850 and a low of 600. The data for department 1 is spread out or dispersed farther from the average than that of the other department.

One of the dispersion measures is the Range, R. This is defined as the difference between the largest and smallest values of observation.

$$\text{Range,} \quad R = X_{max} - X_{min}$$

Another measure of dispersion is the Standard deviation. It is the numerical value that measures the spreading tendency of the data. A large standard deviation show a greater variability of the data, than does a small standard deviation.

$$\text{Sample standard deviation } s = \sqrt{\frac{\sum_{i=1}^{n}(X_i - \overline{X})^2}{n-1}}$$

In quality control practice, the range is a more common measure of dispersion. It is preferred, when the amount of data is too small or too scattered, to justify the calculation of a more precise measure of dispersion. It is suggested, that the range is used for sample size of up to 10. The standard deviation is used when a more precise measure is desired and when the sample size is more than 10. When the sample size is more than 30, it is considered as population and the word 'mean' (μ) is used to represent the average of the population.

Standard deviation of the population,

$$\sigma = \sqrt{\frac{\sum_{i=1}^{n}(X_i - \overline{X})^2}{n}}$$

Example: Find the average, median, mode, range, and standard deviation for the measured length of cylindrical pins. The data are 36.3, 38.2, 34.8, 36.0, 37.0, 35.9, 34.8, 36.6 mm

$$\overline{X} = \Sigma\, Xi/n = 36.2 \text{ mm}$$

Median = {34.8, 34.8, 35.9, 36.0, 36.3, 36.6, 37.0, 38.2} = 36.15 mm

Mode = 34.8 mm

R = 38.2 – 34.8 = 3.4 mm

$$s = \sqrt{\frac{\Sigma\,(X_i - 36.2)^2}{8-1}} = 1.13 \text{ mm}$$

A relationship exist between the standard deviation and the area under the normal curve, as shown in Table 3.3. One hundred percent of the items are included between the limits $-\infty$ to $+\infty$. These percentages hold true, irrespective of the shape of the normal curve. The fact that 99.73 % of the items are included between $\pm 3\sigma$, is the basis for variable control charts.

Table 3.3 Area under normal curve

Variation	Area under normal curve
$\pm 1\ \sigma$	68.26 %
$\pm 1.645\ \sigma$	90.00 %
$\pm 1.960\ \sigma$	95.00 %
$\pm 2\ \sigma$	95.45 %
$\pm 3\ \sigma$	99.73 %

3.6.2 Introduction to Control Charts

Variation

Variation concept is a law of nature, because no two natural items in any type of product, are the same. The variation may be small or big. Variation can be controlled only, if it can be measured. The variation in parts produced may occur in three different ways:

1. Variation within the piece. The hardness of the component may be different at either ends.
2. Piece to piece variation occurs among pieces produced at one time. The weight of three consecutive biscuits, produced from one machine could be different.
3. Time to time variation is understood by the difference in product, made at different times of the shift.

Variations are present in every process due to a combination of (*a*) the equipment, (*b*) materials, (*c*) environment, and (*d*) the operator. The source of variation in *equipment* includes the cumulative wear in the tool, machine vibration, positioning of work holding device, and hydraulic or electrical fluctuations. When all these variations are put together, there is a definite capability or precision within which the equipment operates. Even identical machines may have different capabilities. When scheduling the production of critical parts, this fact becomes an important consideration.

Another source of variation is the *material*. The quality characteristics such as hardness, tensile strength, shear strength, ductility, porosity, and moisture content may contribute to the variation in the final product.

The third source of variation is the *environment*. Temperature, humidity, illumination, radiation, particle size, and pressure may contribute to the variation in the product. In order to control environmental variations, products are reported to have been made in anechoic chamber or even in space capsules.

A fourth source of variation is the *operator*. This source includes the method by which the operator performs the operation. The physical and mental health of the operator may also contribute to the variation. A sprained ankle, a cut finger, a personal problem or headache, may make the operator's quality performance vary. His lack of understanding of the equipment controls or even the measuring instruments, due to poor training, may lead to frequent adjustments and so the variation in the output. In automated machines, this type of variation is minimal. Faulty inspection equipment, the incorrect handling of the instrument or wrong interpretation of a quality standard may also lead to the variation in the results.

3.6.3 Control Charts for Variables

3.6.3.1 Run Chart

A run chart is a simple chart used for analysing the process, in its initial stages of development. Plotting the data points is the first activity in the analysis of data. Without this run chart, calculation of average, standard deviation, etc., will lead to erroneous conclusions.

The typical run chart shown in Fig. 3.9, is called the average chart ($\overline{X}$ chart) and is used to record the variation in the average value of samples. The vertical axis of the graph is the variable, which in this case, is the weight measured in N. The horizontal axis is named as 'sub group number'. This identifies a particular sample consisting of a fixed number of observations (components). These subgroups are numbered and plotted in the order of manufacture and inspection. Averages are used on control charts rather than individual observations, because, the average values will indicate a change in variation much faster.

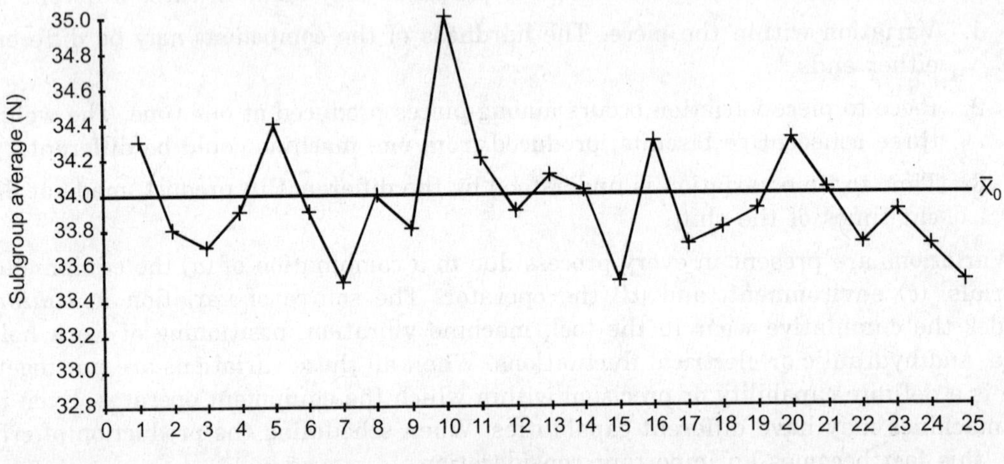

Fig. 3.9

The solid line in the center of the chart, can have three different interpretations, depending on the available data. First, it can be the average of the plotted points, which in this case of an $\overline{X}$ chart, is the average of the averages or 'X-double bar'. Second, it can be a standard or reference value, $\overline{X}_0$, based on prior data, or expected value. Third, it can be the population mean, μ, if that value is known.

3.6.3.2 Control Chart

The run chart has the tendency to show every variation in data as important. In order to indicate, when the observed variations are greater than that could be left to chance, the control chart method of presentation of data and analysis is used. This chart is a means of visualising the variations that occur in the central tendency and dispersion of a set of observations. It is a graphical record of a particular quality characteristic. It indicates whether or not the process is stable and within the statistical control limits. When the control limits are added, the run chart becomes a control chart, as shown in Fig. 3.10. The dashed lines, called the upper control and lower control limits are drawn to assist in judging the significance of the variation in the quality of the product. The control limits are established

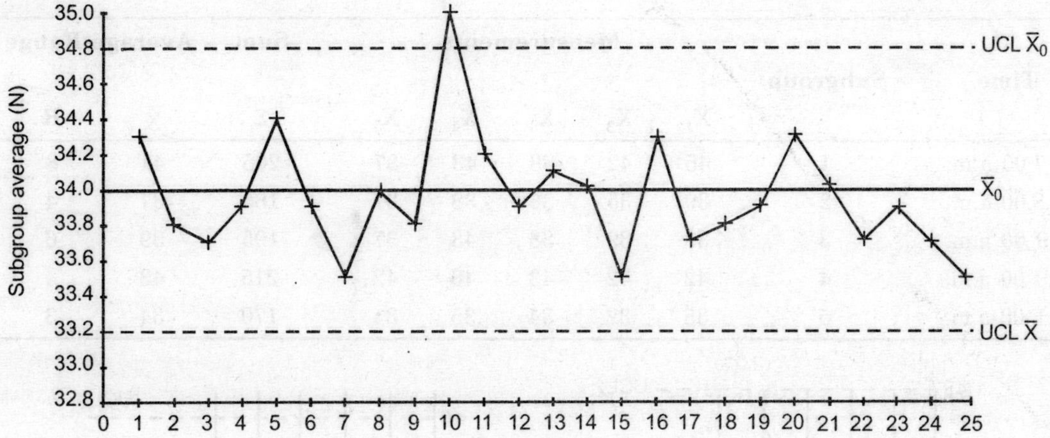

Fig. 3.10

at ± 3σ from the X_0 value, the central line. It is expected that more than 9973 times out of 10000 times, the subgroup values will lie within the control limits. When this situation occurs, the process is considered to be in control. When a subgroup value falls outside the control limits, the process is considered to be out of control, and a assignable cause for the variation is present. The subgroup number 10 in Fig. 3.10, is beyond the upper control limits, indicating that there has been a change in the stable nature of the process, causing the out-of-control point. So long as the sources of variation fluctuate in a natural manner, a stable pattern of many chance causes (random causes) of variation develops. *Chance causes* are inevitable, numerous, relatively less important and difficult to detect. But those causes of variation that are large in magnitude, and therefore readily identified, are classified as *Assignable causes*. When assignable causes for variation are present, the process is termed as out of 'control' or beyond the expected natural variation of the process.

This unnatural variation is the result of *assignable causes*. Many a times, corrective actions by operators, technicians, or maintenance workers are required. The natural variation is the result of *chance causes*, which require the action by the management in improving the quality. A majority of the quality problems are due to the management or the system and the minority, due to the operations.

3.6.3.3 Variable Charts

Normally, an $\overline{X}$ chart for the central tendency and a R chart for the dispersion are used together. An example of this problem is shown in Table 3.4 and Fig. 3.11.

Table 3.4 $\overline{X}$ and R chart—an example

Part No. 151238 **Quality characteristic: Length**
Date: 15 7 2004

Time	Subgroup	Measurements					Sum	Average	Range
		X_1	X_2	X_3	X_4	X_5	Σ	$\overline{X}$	R
7.00 a.m.	1	45	42	38	43	37	205	41	8
8.00 a.m.	2	39	35	36	38	37	185	37	4
9 00 a.m.	3	38	39	38	43	37	195	39	6
10 00 a.m.	4	42	42	43	46	42	215	43	4
11 00 a.m.	5	35	32	34	35	34	170	34	3

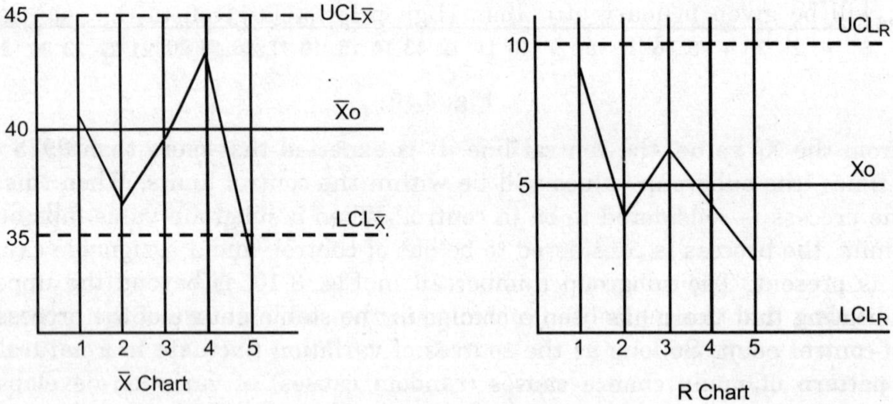

Fig. 3.11

The operator selects five components for testing and record the observations on the cylindrical pins, in the columns marked X_1, X_2, X_3, X_4, and X_5 respectively. The average of this subgroup is $\overline{X}$, and the range value of R is obtained as shown in Table 3.4. The operator marks these values on the $\overline{X}$ chart and R chart as shown in Fig. 3.11.

How frequently the operator shall inspect a product at a particular machine or work center is determined by the quality of the product. When the process is in control and no difficulties are encountered , fewer inspections may be sufficient. On the other hand, when the process is out of control or during start-up, more inspection may be needed. The inspection frequency is also determined by the amount of time that must be spent on non-inspection activities. In the case considered, the time between inspection is one hour.

At the next trial after an hour or so, the operator inspects the subgroup 2, as for the subgroup 1. This procedure continues further. It is found from the inspection that the fourth subgroup gave a value of 46 which is higher than the UCL. As the value 46, is an individual observation, it does not relate to the control limits. Therefore, this fact can be ignored. The subgroup 5, has an average of 34, which is lower than the lower control limit of 35. Therefore, the subgroup 5 is out of control and the operator will report this fact to the supervisor. The operator and the supervisor will the look for the assignable cause and if necessary, take the corrective action. This will be indicated in the control chart, to know when and where the trouble started. These charts are maintained by the operator or the quality personnel. Thus, these charts give the record of a specific quality characteristic and also the history of the process over time.

This control chart is used to improve the process quality, to determine the process capability, to determine when to leave the process alone and when to make adjustments, and to investigate causes of unacceptable or marginal quality. It is also used to make decisions on product or service specifications and decisions on the acceptability of a recently produced product or service.

The variable that is selected for these charts, must be a quality characteristic, that is measurable and expressed in numbers. The quality characteristics are usually mass, length, time, electric current, temperature, luminous intensity, or power, velocity, force, gravity, density, pressure and viscosity. The quality characteristics, that affect the function of the product, will be given primary attention. High priority is given to the selection of those characteristics, that give difficulty, in terms of manufacturing problems or cost. A Pareto analysis, may also be used to establish critical characteristics. Some inspection procedure may involve destructive testing of the components. Although a large number of variables make up a product or service, a careful selection of the quality characteristics is preferred.

3.6.3.4 Sub-group Size

The size of the sample or sub-group is arrived as follows:

1. As the subgroup size increases, the control limits become closer to the central value, and this makes the control chart more sensitive to small variations in the process average.
2. As the subgroup size increases, the cost of inspection per subgroup increases.
3. When the test is costly or destructive testing is involved or the component is costly, a small subgroup size of 2 or 3, is necessary and sufficient, because that will minimise the cost of testing plus the component.
4. For the sake of easy computation, five is the sample size normally chosen in industry.
5. From the statistics point of view, the distribution of the subgroup averages, $\overline{X}$'s, is nearly normal for subgroups of four or more, even when the samples are taken from a non-normal population, as per the central limit theorem.

There is no simple rule, to decide how frequently the sample should be chosen. It is suggested to take sample quite often in the initial stages and reduce the frequency when the data permit. According to the pre-control rule, if the process is adjusted every hour, sampling shall be done every 10 minutes; if the process is adjusted every 2 hours, sampling shall be done every 20 minutes and so on.

3.6.3.5 Example of Control Chart

There is a problem of assembling the hub of the pulley to the shaft, where the use of $\overline{X}$ chart and R chart is recommended. The width of the keyway, is the quality characteristic, to be controlled. Using a subgroup size of five, the inspector gets five subgroups every day. The results are recorded and shown in Table 3.5.

The 25 subgroups are necessary to construct the control chart. This is found necessary to get accurate estimation of the control limits, and simultaneously to save any further time in trials.

Table 3.5 Measurement of the keyway characteristic

All the dimensions in columns 2 to 6: 12 + (X/100) mm

Sub group Number	Measurements X_1	X_2	X_3	X_4	X_5	Average $\overline{X}$	Range R	Remarks
1	36	34	42	40	48	12.40	0.14	
2	34	41	39	36	45	12.39	0.11	
3	40	42	39	39	45	12.41	0.06	
4	43	38	49	39	51	12.44	0.13	
5	56	64	66	59	65	12.62	0.09	New inspector
.	..	..	..	..	..	...	...	
15	40	35	38	32	35	12.36	0.08	
16	43	45	48	49	50	12.47	0.07	
17	56	51	52	55	46	12.52	0.10	Poor material
..	..	..	..	..	..	...	...	
21	44	30	47	49	61	12.46	0.31	Damaged tool
..	..	..	..	..	..	...	...	
24	35	37	42	45	41	12.40	0.10	
25	36	38	41	38	37	12.38	0.05	
					Total	310.50	3.50	

The central values for the $\overline{X}$ and R charts are obtained as indicated before.

Assuming normal distribution for the data, trial control limits for the charts are established at ± 3σ from the central value, as follows:

$$UCL_X = \overline{\overline{X}} + 3\,\sigma_x \qquad UCL_R = \overline{R} + 3\,\sigma_R$$

$$LCL_X = \overline{\overline{X}} - 3\,\sigma_x \qquad LCL_R = \overline{R} - 3\,\sigma_R$$

where σ_x = population standard deviation of the subgroup averages.

σ_P = population standard deviation of the range.

In practice, the calculations are simplified by using the statistical constants along with $\overline{R}$, used as a measure of deviation. Then, the derived equations are obtained as follows:

$$UCL_X = \overline{\overline{X}} + A_2\overline{R} \qquad UCL_R = D_4\,\overline{R}$$

$$LCL_X = \overline{\overline{X}} - A_2\overline{R} \qquad LCL_R = D_3\,\overline{R}$$

Where, the factors A_2, D_3, and D_4 vary with the subgroup size and are given the standard statistical tables. The students are advised to refer Appendix I or the S.Q.C Data book[9,10] for obtaining these values. In the X chart, the control limits are symmetrical about the central line. But in case of the R chart, the lower control limit should be taken as zero, in case, the calculation indicates a negative value, because a negative range is impossible. Hence the value of D_3 for subgroup size of six or less, is taken as zero.

From Table 3.5, where the number of subgroups (sampled sets) is 25, the central values are obtained as

$$\bar{\bar{X}} = 12.42 \text{ mm} \qquad \bar{R} = 0.14 \text{ mm}$$

For a sample size of 5, $A_2 = 0.577 \quad D_3 = 0 \quad D_4 = 2.114$

and the trial control limits for the X chart are,

$$UCL_x = \bar{\bar{X}} + A_2\bar{R} \qquad LCL_x = \bar{\bar{X}} - A_2\bar{R}$$

$$= 12.42 + 0.577 \times 0.14 \qquad = 12.42 - 0.577 \times 0.14$$

$$= 12.50 \text{ mm} \qquad = 12.34 \text{ mm}$$

Trial control limits for the $\bar{R}$ chart are,

$$UCL_R = D_4\bar{R} \qquad LCL_R = D_3\bar{R}$$

$$= 2.114 \times 0.14 \qquad = 0$$

$$= 0.29 \text{ mm} \qquad = 0$$

The central values and the trial control limits for $\bar{X}$ and R charts for preliminary data are shown in Fig. 3.12.

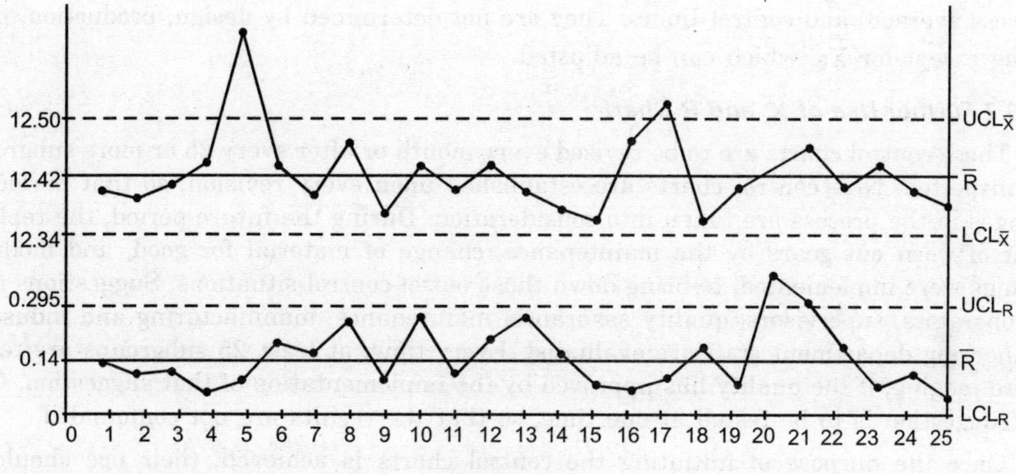

Fig. 3.12

3.6.3.6 Revised Central Values and Control Limits (Homogenization)

The out-of control points with assignable causes, are then removed to revise the central values and control limits. This process is called, homogenization. One of the out-of-control point at subgroup 20 on the R chart has an assignable cause and hence it is removed from the data.

The $\bar{X}$ chart is then analysed. Subgroups 5 and 17, have assignable cause, and hence these data are removed. Now the revised central values and control limits, are calculated with the remaining 22 subgroup data. The revised values of the characteristics are $\bar{X}_0 = 12.40$ mm and $\bar{R}_0 = 0.12$ mm.

This revised $\bar{X}$ chart and R chart, with their corresponding revised control limits, are shown in Fig. 3.13. This revised control charts are then referred, during inspection of future subgroups. To make the effective use of the control chart during production, this chart is displayed in a prominent place, which can be seen by the operators as well as supervisors.

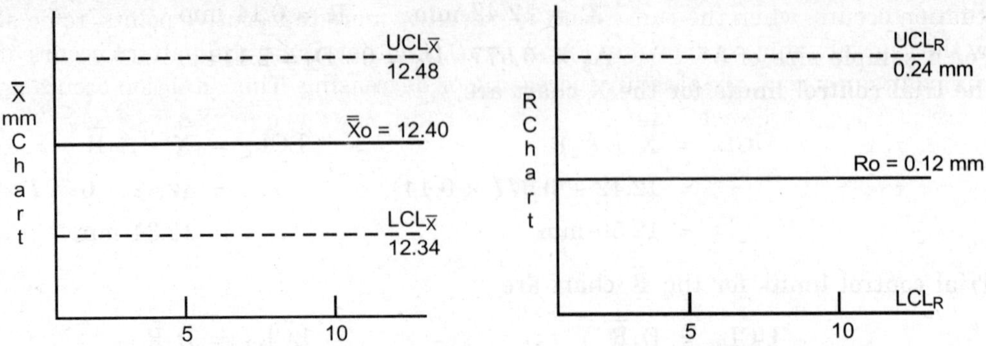

Fig. 3.13

It should be noted, that the adjustments to the process should be made while taking data. It is not necessary to run nonconforming material, while collecting data, because we are more interested in obtaining $\overline{R}_0$, and that is not affected by process (average) setting. The $\overline{\overline{X}}_0$ and $\overline{R}_0$ are independent. Further, it is the process that determines the central value (process average) and control limits. They are not determined by design, production, marketing except for $\overline{\overline{X}}_0$, which can be adjusted.

3.6.3.7 Further Use of $\overline{X}$ and R Chart

These control charts are to be revised every month or after every 25 or more subgroups are inspected. New control charts are established upon every revision, so that periodical changes in the process are taken into consideration. During the future period, the replacement of worn out gears by the maintenance, change of material for good, and modified toolings were implemented, to bring down those out-of-control situations. Suggestions from the operators, supervisors, quality assurance, maintenance, manufacturing and industrial engineering department staff are evaluated. Every time, at least 25 subgroups are tested before judging, if the quality has improved by the implementation of that suggestion. Only one suggestion is to be tested at one time, so that the results are not confounded.

Once the purpose of initiating the control charts is achieved, their use should be discontinued or the frequency of inspection be considerably reduced. The Median chart may be continued to monitor the quality. Attention should be directed toward the improvement of some other quality characteristic.

Advantages when the process is under control:

1. Fewer samples are needed to judge the quality, if the product is uniform. The cost of inspection is thus reduced to a minimum.
2. With the estimate of the process capability, or spread of the process (= 6σ), several reliable decisions relative to specifications can be made, such as product specifications, amount of scrap or rework, permitting interchangeability of components or using selective matching of components.
3. The customer can use the supplier's data and hence, test only a few samples as a check on the supplier's records. These charts are used as statistical evidence of the controlled process.

3.6.3.8 Out-of-control Process (Unnatural Patterns)

A process is considered out of control, even when the points fall inside the +3σ limits. This situation occurs, when the runs result in, seven or more consecutive points, to be above or below the central value, as shown in Fig. 3.14 (*a*). Another unnatural pattern occurs at (*b*), where six points in a row, are steadily increasing or decreasing. This situation occurs again, when there are two successive points in 1.5 to 3σ band, as shown in Fig. 3.14 (c).

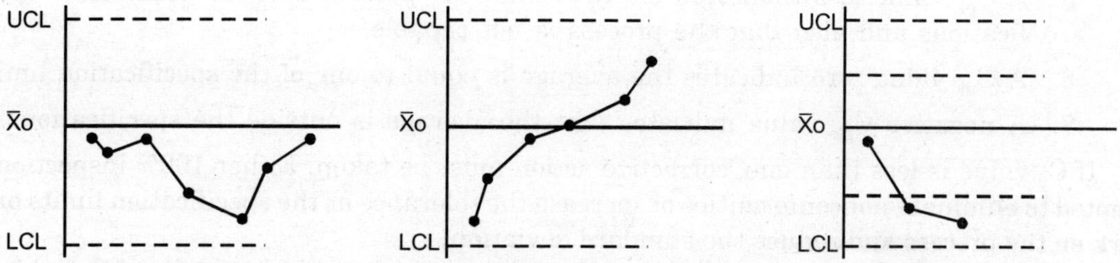

(*a*) Seven consecutive points above or below

(*b*) Six consecutive points increasing or decreasing

(*c*) Two consecutive points in outer quarter

Fig. 3.14 (*a*) (*b*) (*c*)

3.6.3.9 Process Capability

It should be noted that the control limits are for the averages, and specifications are the tolerable variation in the size of the component and hence for the individual values. The specification or tolerance limits are established by design engineers to meet particular function, whereas, the control limits and the process spread (process capability) are determined by the process, independent of the specifications. Thus the control charts cannot determine, if the process is meeting specifications or not. The process capability can be calculated only after the $\overline{X}$ and R charts have resulted in the optimal quality improvement. Once the process is in statistical control, the process capability is equal to 6σ where $\sigma = \overline{R}_0/d_2$ where d_2 is a statistical factor shown, in Appendix I or S.Q.C. data book.[9,10]

$$\text{Process capability index, } C_p = \frac{\text{USL} - \text{LSL}}{\text{Process capability}} = \frac{\text{Tolerance}}{6\sigma}$$

Where, USL and LSL are upper specification and lower specification limits, respectively.

If the capability index is greater than 1.00, the process is capable of meeting the specifications: If the index is less than 1.00, the process is not capable of meeting the specifications. In practice, the C_p value is chosen as 1.33 and a few industry, use 2.00. The larger the capability index , the better is the quality. The process capability index gives a measure of only, the precision (i.e., the closeness of the results) of the values obtained.

To measure the process performance in terms of the nominal or target value, a factor

$$C_{pk} = \frac{\text{Min}\{(\text{USL} - \overline{X}) \text{ or } (\overline{X} - \text{LSL})\}}{3\sigma} \text{ is also used.}$$

A C_{pk} value of 1.00 is the standard, and some organizations use, a value of 1.33. This index gives a measure of precision as well as the accuracy (i.e., the closeness to the target value) of the measured values.

The following points would be useful in the improvement of the process:

1. The C_p value does not change as the process average changes.
2. When the process is centered, $C_p = C_{pk}$.
3. C_{pk} is always equal to or less than C_p.
4. A C_{pk} value greater than 1.00 indicates that the process conforms to specifications.
5. A C_{pk} value less than 1.00 indicates that the process does not conform to specifications and also that the process is not capable.
6. A C_{pk} value zero indicates the average is equal to one of the specification limits.
7. A negative C_{pk} value indicates that the average is outside the specifications.

If C_p value is less than one, corrective action must be taken. Either 100% inspection is adopted to eliminate nonconformities or increase the tolerance or the specification limits or to work on the process and reduce the standard deviation.

Other control charts for variables

Certain other control charts for variables, which are used less, are listed in Table 3.6.

Table 3.6 Other types of control charts for variables

Type	Central line	Control limits	Remarks
$\bar{X}$ and s	$\bar{\bar{X}}$	$UCL_x = \bar{\bar{X}} + A_3\bar{s}$ $LCL_x = \bar{\bar{X}} - A_3\bar{s}$	Used when $n > 10$ and when data are collected automatically
	$\bar{s}$	$UCL_s = B_4\bar{s}$ $LCL_s = B_3\bar{s}$	
Median and Range	Me_{Me}	$UCL_{Me} = Me_{Me} + F_2R_{Me}$ $LCL_{Me} = Me_{Me} - F_2R_{Me}$	Used when process is in a maintenance mode and simple to calculate
	R_{Me}	$UCL_R = D_4\, R_{Me}$ $LCL_R = D_3\, R_{Me}$	
Moving average, MX and Moving range, MR	$\overline{MX}$	$UCL_x = \overline{MX} + A_2\, \overline{MR}$ $LCL_x = \overline{MX} - A_2\, \overline{MR}$	Used when only one observation is possible at a time
	$\overline{MR}$	$UCL_R = D_4\, \overline{MR}$ $LCL_R = D_3\, \overline{MR}$	

3.6.4 Control Charts for Attributes

An attribute is a quality characteristic that may conform or may not conform to specifications. Where measurement is not possible, the attribute can be color, scratches or defects or damage. Where measurement is possible, but not made to save time or cost, as in the case of using a 'go-no go' gauge and determining, if it conforms or does not conform to specifications.

A NON-CONFORMITY, is a departure of quality characteristic from its intended level or state, that occurs with a severity sufficient to cause an associated product or service not to meet a specification requirement. (A *Defect* is a departure of quality characteristic from its intended usage requirements.) Defect is the term used, when evaluation is in terms of usage and non-conformity is appropriate, for non-conformance to specifications.

A NONCONFORMING UNIT is used to denote a unit of product or service, containing at least one nonconformity. (*Defective* is the term used, when a unit of product or service is evaluated in terms of usage rather than conformance to specifications).

One of the major advantages of the attribute chart is, that, when a large number of variable quality characteristics are to be studied and controlled, the use of attribute chart can minimize the study, by providing overall quality information, at a fraction of the cost.

There are two different groups of control charts for attributes.

For nonconformities: A **c** chart, showing the count of nonconformities in an inspected unit, such as a gear assembly, a roll of paper or 10 m of cloth. Another closely related chart, is the **u** chart, which is for the count of nonconformities per unit.

For nonconforming units: A proportion **p** chart, showing the proportion of nonconforming in a sample or subgroup, the proportion being expressed, as a fraction or per cent. Another chart in this group, is for number of nonconforming (parts), **np** chart.

Objectives of the attribute charts: The attribute charts are used:

1. To determine the average quality level, as a benchmark.
2. To bring to the attention of the management, any changes in the average quality, if it is increasing or decreasing.
3. To improve the quality, as the chart tells whether the idea for quality improvement is appropriate or not appropriate.
4. To evaluate the quality performance of the operating and the management personnel. Supervisors and the executives can be evaluated, by chart of nonconforming units.
5. The attribute charts suggest the source of difficulty and the variable charts find the cause.
6. To determine acceptance criteria of a product before shipment to the customer. The attribute charts provide the information, whether or not to release an order.
7. The lower control limits of the attribute chart are of less significance.

3.6.4.1 The p Chart

The *p* chart can be used to control one quality characteristic or a group of quality characteristics of the same part or of the same type of parts or to control the entire product. The *p* chart can be drawn to measure the quality produced by a work center or by a department or by a shift or by an entire plant. It can be used to report the performance of an operator, group of operators, or management, as a means of evaluating their quality performance.

The subgroup size of the *p* chart may be, either variable or constant. Normally a constant subgroup size is preferred. But, when there are changes in mix or 100% automated inspection, the subgroup size changes. A minimum of 50, is suggested to start with.

Data are collected for at least 25 subgroups by audit or from the past records. Table 3.7 shows the results of the inspection from the wheel rim assembly department for the bicycle. The trial central value and the control limits are calculated, as per the formulas listed:

Table 3.7 An example for p chart

The sample size is constant, n = 250

Sub group no.	Number nonconfor-ming, np	proportion nonconfor-ming, p	Sub group no.	Number noncon-forming, np	proportion nonconfor-ming, p	Sub group no.	Number nonconfor-ming, np	proportion nonconfor-ming, p
1	4	0.016	10	3	0.012	19	7	0.028
2	7	0.028	11	6	0.024	20	3	0.012
3	5	0.020	12	5	0.020	21	2	0.008
4	3	0.012	13	4	0.016	22	3	0.012
5	2	0.008	14	3	0.012	23	7	0.028
6	19	0.076	15	2	0.008	24	6	0.024
7	6	0.024	16	6	0.024	25	4	0.016
8	5	0.020	17	5	0.020			
9	0	0.000	18	8	0.032			
					Total		125	

Average proportion nonconforming,

$$\overline{p} = \Sigma np/\Sigma n \text{ or } \Sigma n_d/\Sigma n$$

$$= 125/\ (25 \times 250) = 0.02$$

$$\text{UCL}_p = \overline{p} - 3\sqrt{\frac{\overline{p}\,(1-\overline{p})}{n}}$$

and

$$\text{LCL}_p = \overline{p} - 3\sqrt{\frac{\overline{p}\,(1-\overline{p})}{n}}$$

where n is the number inspected in a subgroup. The calculation is then obtained as follows:

$$\overline{p} = 0.02$$

$$\text{UCL}_p = 0.02 + 0.027 = 0.047$$

$$\text{LCL}_p = 0.02 - 0.027 = 0$$

i.e. UCL_{np} = 12 numbers

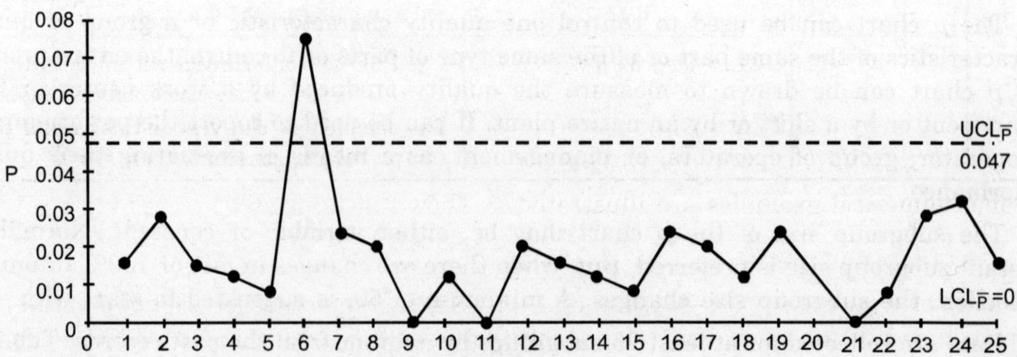

Fig. 3.15

The lower control limit if negative is taken to be zero, negative proportion of nonconforming is impossible. The central value, $\overline{p}$ and the control limits, are shown in Fig. 3.15, for the data obtained from Table 3.7. Then, the out-of-control points that have assignable causes, are discarded and the central values and control limits are revised. Subgroup 6 was out of control and had the assignable cause. Hence, that reading was removed. The revised central values and the control limits are then calculated and taken as standard.

The revised values are:

$$\overline{p} = 0.016$$
$$UCL_p = 0.037$$
$$LCL_p = 0$$

These values are used as process average and control limits for the next period. This procedure can be continued for the future months and checked, whether there is any further improvement in quality.

The process capability is the central line (value), for all attribute charts. If the central value is not satisfactory, the management is to initiate steps to provide resources and take corrective actions. When the plotted points lie outside the control limits, the operating personnel are usually responsible. A plotted point lies below the lower control limit due to exceptionally good quality. It should be investigated for the assignable cause, so that it is not due to an inspection error.

3.6.4.2 Other Control Charts for Attributes

Other types of control charts for attributes are listed in Table 3.8.

Table 3.8 Other types of control chart for attributes

Types	Central line	Control limits	Remarks
np	$\overline{np}$	$UCL = \overline{np} + 3\sqrt{\overline{np}(1-p)}$	Used for nonconforming units.
		$LCL = \overline{np} - 3\sqrt{\overline{np}(1-p)}$	The sample size must be constant
c	$\overline{c}$	$UCL = \overline{c} + 3\sqrt{\overline{c}}$	Used for nonconformities within a unit. The sample size is one inspec-
		$LCL = \overline{c} - 3\sqrt{\overline{c}}$	ted component (e.g. a carton of 5 blades)
u	$\overline{u}$	$UCL = \overline{u} + 3\sqrt{\overline{u}/k}$	Used for nonconformities within a unit. Here $\overline{u}$ is the count of nonconformities/unit.
		$LCL = \overline{u} - 3\sqrt{\overline{u}/k}$	The sample size can very in this case. If the sample size is constant, then $k = n$

Some numerical examples are illustrated as shown in Appendix I.

3.7 SCATTER DIAGRAMS

A simpler way to find, if a cause-and-effect relationship exists between two variables, is to plot a scatter diagram. The relationship between the cutting speed and tool life, is shown in Fig. 3.16. The cutting speed is plotted along the X axis and is the independent variable. The tool life is plotted along the Y axis and is the dependent variable or response. Other examples in this type of study are: automobile speed versus fuel kilo-meterage, training taken versus errors committed, breakdowns versus equipment age, etc.

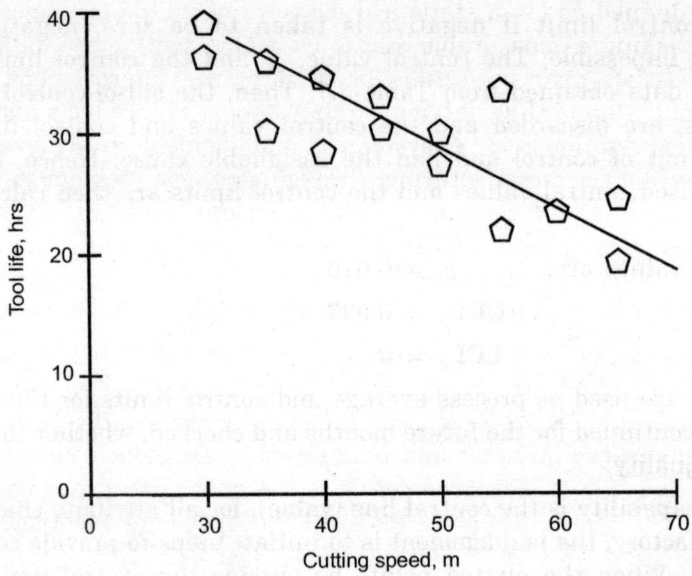

Fig. 3.16

The data are obtained from the trials and plotted as shown in Fig. 3.16. It is observed from the graph, that as the speed increases, the tool life decreases.

Figure 3.17 gives different patterns and their interpretation. In (*a*), a positive correlation exists between the two variables. At (*b*), there is a negative correlation and in (*c*) is an example of no correlation.

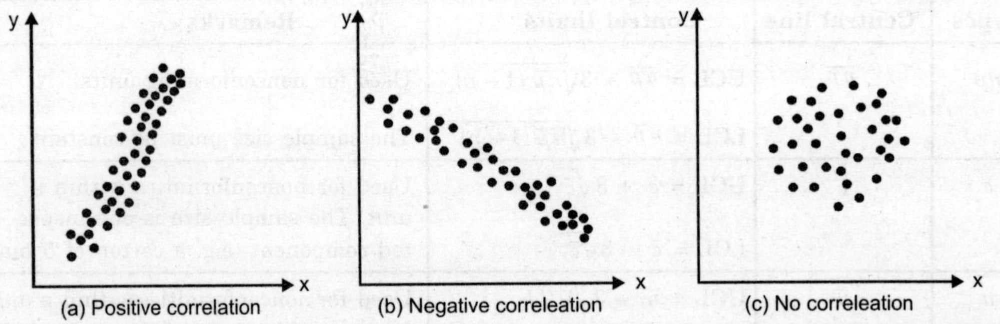

Fig. 3.17

A perfect correlation is indicated by points falling along a straight line. Using the least square method, the linear relationship can be obtained.

3.8 'SIX SIGMA' CONCEPTS

Moses, 3500 years ago, deployed the tribes of Israel 'to spy out the holy land and bring back a report'. The spies unanimously declared that the land was good, but cannot be approached, because of strong fortifications. At least two of them professed the faith that the land could be won at justifiable costs and occupied the land. —*BIBLICAL STORY*

Six sigma is defined as (1) A statistical measure of the performance of a process or a product, by establishing a measurable status on yield, defects per million opportunities, (2) A goal that reaches near perfection for performance improvement, by reducing the variation (very small standard deviations) so that almost all products and services meet or exceed customer expectations, (3) A system of management to achieve lasting business leadership and world class manufacturing, through strategic problem solving methods and the management philosophy focussed on eliminating mistakes, wastes, rework and scrap, and (4) A combination of technical skills (tools and methodologies) and soft skills (people skills, change management, and change in philosophy) It is a TQM process that uses the process capability analysis as a way of measuring progress.

'Six sigma' is highly effective in improving a company's operational efficiency, by raising productivity and lowering costs. It improves the design process, gets products to market faster with fewer defects, and thus reinforces the customer loyalty. In essence, 'Six sigma' is a total management commitment and philosophy of excellence, customer focus, process improvement and the rule of measurement. It is one of the great management innovations of past three decades and a highly powerful tool to boost the organisation's competitiveness. 'Six sigma' emphasizes the acquisition of clear voice of customers, and it transformation into critical quality characteristics, translation into actionable information and ultimate delivery of superior process or product or service.

In GE Plastics-Pacific, Six sigma led to reduce drastically product variation and increased plant capacity by 30 %, with no additional investment[18].

Success stories supporting the Six sigma concepts, of high return on investment, defect reduction, cycle time reduction, waste reduction and market share gain, and innovation, and customer satisfaction are plenty. The failures with 'Six sigma' have also been reported, but they are due to poorly mapped or poorly managed projects.

Table 3.9 is an extension of Table 3.3. We can see from Table 3.9, that, for $\pm 6\ \sigma$ variation, 99.9999998 % of the product or service will lie between the specification limits. *i.e.*, the non-conformance will be 0.002 part in one million or 2 per billion. The corresponding process capability index (C_p) is 2.0. Tab.3.9 shows the percentage conformance for various specifications, besides the non-conformance rate and process capability.

Table. 3.9 Non-conformance rate and process capability

Specification limits	Percent conformance	Non-conformance rate (ppm)	Process capability index Cp
$\pm 1\ \sigma$	68.7	317300	0.33
$\pm 2\ \sigma$	95.45	485500	0.67
$\pm 3\ \sigma$	99.73	2700	1.00
$\pm 4\ \sigma$	99.9937	63	1.33
$\pm 5\ \sigma$	99.999943	0.57	1.67
$\pm 6\ \sigma$	99.9999998	0.002	2.00

The objectives of 'Six sigma' may be listed as follows:

1. Decrease manufacturing and design cycle time

2. Enhance customer satisfaction and market position.
3. Decrease costs due to inventory, scrap and rework.
4. Cultivate new business and hold on to old business.
5. Increase profitability and share holder value. The goals of 'six sigma' are reached by starting with reduction of defects, and through yield improvement, improved customer satisfaction, and higher net income.

The essential ingredients (means) of 'Six sigma' are:

1. Genuine focus on the customer
2. Data and facts driven management
3. Process focus and improvement
4. Highly structured problem solving method
5. People involvement through team leaders, team selection, and training
6. Proactive management through committed leadership, effective quality council and selection of projects.

Implementation Steps:

1. Emphasising 'dpmo' as a standard metric that can be applied to all parts of an organisation-manufacturing, engineering, administration, and software.
2. Providing extensive training, followed by project team deployment to improve profitability, reduce non-value added activities and achieve reduction in cycle time
3. Focusing on corporate sponsor responsible for supporting team activities, helping to overcome resistance to change, obtain resources, and focus the teams on overall strategic objectives.
4. Creating highly qualified process improvement experts such as coach (master black belt), and team leaders (black belt) who can apply improvement tools and lead team members (green belt).
5. Ensuring that appropriate metrics are identified early in the process and that they focus on business results.
6. Setting the objectives for improvement.

If a given process fails to meet the objective, it is re-analyzed, altered and tested to find out if there are any improvements. If no improvement is found, the process is re-analyzed, altered and tested again. This cycle is repeated until one sees an improvement.

Once an improvement is found, it is documented and the knowledge is spread across other units in the company.

The five phases of 'six sigma' implementation are:

1. Define the (process) problem: Identification of the customers and their priorities, identification of the project based on business objectives, customer needs and feed back, and identification of the critical quality characteristics as considered by the customers.
2. Measure how you perform, determine how to measure the process, identify the key internal processes that influence the cost, time, and quality, and measure the defects currently generated relative to those processes.

3. Analyse where the problem starts, determine the most likely causes of defects, and Identify the key variables that are most likely to create process variations.
4. Improve the situation, by identification of the means to remove the causes of the defects, confirm the key variable and quantify their effects on the cost, time, and quality, identification of the maximum acceptable range of the key variable and a system for measuring the deviations of the variables, and modification of the process to stay within the acceptable range.
5. Control: Determine how to maintain the improvements, and put tools in place to ensure that the key variables remain within the acceptable ranges under the modified process.

'Six Sigma' methodology is also used in many business process management initiatives now a days. Besides manufacturing, these business process management initiatives include call centers, customer support, supply chain management and project management.

Example: One company is supplying engine spares with a promise of 15 days delivery time. Actually it could supply say, some lots in 10 days, some in 15 days and a few in 18 days, in the ordinary situation. But, with 'six sigma', the customer will receive the spares in 14 days, or 15 days or 16 days. The inconsistency (variation from the expected) is removed in the interaction with the customers.

Two types of applications are often cited. In the first application, it is used to remove variation in routine, simple, and repetitive internal processes such as *'supply of spares'* or as in despatch of accurate bills on the same day of every month in *'credit card processing'*. The second type of application is in the complex new products design and development projects such as spending several crores of rupees on new turbines or hybrid engines. 'Six sigma' can discover inconsistencies in the design stage itself.

According to Subir Chowdhary[4], the 'six sigma' represents not merely a statistical measure but also a management philosophy. It combines the *people power* with the *process power*.

The General Electric, Sony, Motorola and Polaroid are some of the organisations in the west who have succeeded through 'six sigma' implementation. In the Indian scene, the institutions namely BIS, DNV, TUV and TQMI have been acting as quality consultants. Organisations such as, TVS Lucas, Sundaram Brake lining, Sundaram Motors, Shriram Fibre, Rane, Shriram Pistons and WIPRO, have implemented this concept, succeeded, and also have obtained International Quality Awards for several years.

According to the recent report of RIL.,[18] the Six sigma initiative was implemented in 2004 to achieve Zero defect work culture. The team of Black belts spearheaded the cross-functional high impact projects in business, manufacturing and service functions. Their six sigma projects were rated as the top three by the Indian Statistical Institute, Bangalore and one 'six sigma' project had won an award by American Society for Quality Conference, Seattle in 2005.

3.9 CONVENTIONAL MANAGEMENT TOOLS

There are various methodologies for identification and idea formulation on the problem, through which subsequent solutions are developed and implemented. Some of such methods are presented below:

3.9.1 Why? Why? Analysis

It is a simple and effective tool. This approach focuses on the process (to reveal the causes), rather than the people. The steps, Why-Answer-Action will have be repeated many times, to obtain the causes. The two examples that follow show how the analysis proceeds to solve the issues.

Example 1: There was a delay in dispatch of the goods.

Why? Was there a delay in dispatch of goods?

Answer: Cutting tool failed, resulting in delay in manufacture. They were reused tools.

Why? The tools were re-used?

Answer: The ordered tools were not delivered

Why? The ordered tools were not delivered?

Answer: The supplier had some difficulty

Action: 1. Change the dispatch schedule, if ever the tools were not delivered or

2. Enter into contract with the same or other suppliers

Example 2: The piston did not run smoothly

Why? Did the piston not run smoothly?

Answer: The strainer got clogged

Action: Clean the strainer

Why? Did the strainer get clogged?

Answer: The lubricating oil was dirty

Action: Drain the lubricating oil and refill

Why? Did the oil get dirty?

Answer: Dirt entered the oil tank

Action: Protect the tank from oil entering

Why? Did dirt enter the oil tank?

Answer: The top cover found with a hole

Action: Plug the hole

Why? Did the cover have a hole?

Answer: An error occurred while repairing

Action: Standardise the repair work procedure

3.9.2 Five Ws and Two Hs?

Seek the answers to questions such as, What? Why? Where? When? Who? How? and How much? The causes reveal themselves and remedies appear nearer.

WHAT? To get the subject matter

1. What was done?
2. What is being done?
3. What should have been done?
4. What else is to be done?
5. What else should have been done?

WHY? To find the purpose / reason

1. Why did he do it?
2. Why it was done?
3. Why did he do it there?
4. Why did he do it then?
5. Why was it done that way?

WHERE? To zero-in on the location

1. Where to do it?
2. Where is it done?
3. Where should it be done?
4. Where else could it be done?
5. Where else should it be done?

WHEN? To establish the sequence

1. When to do it?
2. When was this done?
3. When should it be done?
4. When else it can be done?
5. When else it should be done?

WHO? To identify the person responsible

1. Who did it?
2. Who does it now?
3. Who is going to do it?
4. Who else can do it?
5. Who else should do it?

HOW? To get the details on method/procedure

1. How to do it?
2. How was it done?
3. How should it have been done?
4. How else it can be done?
5. How else should it have been done?

HOW MUCH? To estimate the cost of damage/time for normalcy

1. How much is the damage/loss?
2. How long the abnormal condition existed?
3. How much will be the cost/time to get back to normalcy?
4. How much cost/down time can be reduced?
5. How else cost/down time can be reduced?

3.9.3 Forced Field Analysis

Readers' attention is invited to the discussion in Chapter 2 on this topic.

3.9.4 Nominal Group Technique

This technique provides for ideas input from every one in the team and for effective decision making. For example, a team is to act on a current complaint from the customer. Every one in the team writes the problem on a paper, what they think is most important. They are listed in a chart and then, the team members are asked to rank, from most important to least important. The ranking are given a numerical value starting from, say, on a 10-to-1 scale. Points for each problem are totaled, and the ones with highest number of points, is considered to be the most important.

3.9.5 Brain-storming

Human mind is the perennial source of ideas and thoughts. Once the thinking is crystallised we will be able to express our ideas clearly by writing, speech, and actions. But the human mind is a complex phenomenon wherefrom, the ideas do not emerge due to lack of confidence, shyness, fears of the unknown, and traditions. But in many situations, funny, revolutionary, and unconventional ideas have facilitated solutions to complex problems.

The barriers to idea formulation are removed easily by collective thinking. If one gives out an idea be it feasible or non-sense, every other individual will be ignited with new ideas further in line or against or with deviations. The group dynamics break away the barriers to idea formulation. The team thinking thus promotes confidence, courage, and transparency, and also energizes the minds quicker towards constructive methods. The synergy works well. The brainstorming is one of the effective methods for analysis and for solving the problems.

1. Human thinking

Human thinking may be classified into the following five categories:

1. Analytical thinking
2. Lateral thinking
3. Creative thinking
4. Logical thinking and
5. Reverse thinking

1. In analytical thinking, we make use of our intellect (knowledge), through mathematics or definite relationships between the outcomes and the known input variables to obtain solutions. The learning curve, the growth limit model, the exponential model, linear or multi-linear or non-linear models are the results of this type of thinking.
2. In lateral thinking, the psychological features such as intuition, experience, common sense, tolerance, sacrifice, empathy, and mutual understanding are used to solve the problems.
3. In the case of creative thinking, traditions are kept aside. The questions such as, why? why not? and what else? have brought to light a score of new ideas, extended applications and identified solutions to many of the age-old problems.

   Examples:

   (*a*) When Newton saw the apple falling down, he started thinking why should it fall down and not go up! The result was the discovery of 'gravity'.

(*b*) When Einstein started questioning some natural phenomena, he propounded the revolutionary equation, $E = mc^2$.

(*c*) The Ice cream was served in porcelain cups for a long time. Being fragile, the container material had problems and was changed to plastic. But the plastic cups created more environmental problems because of their non-degradable nature. The creative thinking has given rise to the *wafer container*, which can also be eaten along with the ice cream! The disposal problem was solved once and for all.

(*d*) Another example is that of microoven. Creative thinking has given good-bye to the use of fuels such as coal or kerosene and reduced pollution in the household to a greater extent. The microwaves vibrate the molecules and heat them rather than conducting heat from a source.

4. In logical thinking, the deductive logic and inductive logic have assisted in finding the solutions to the problems. The analog models, extrapolation, interpolation, trend analysis, simulation study, analysis of consequences of pros and cons, the comparison of case studies and reports from under similar circumstances are adopted to arrive at solutions.
5. In the reverse thinking the ideas are constructive but extended in the negative direction or upside down and the consequences are extrapolated, experimented, and developed.

Typical examples are: (*a*) In the modern wet grinder design, the base stone rotates and the central shaft is guided at the center. This is different from the conventional grinder wherein the top shaft is rotated over the pit in the stationary bottom stone. (*b*) In the sewing machine, the needle stitches with the eye at the *tip* whereas in hand stitching the eye is at the *base*. (*c*) In the washing machine, top loading was risky and many women lost their hands while loading. The side loading on to the rotating drum has simplified the process and avoided any accidents.

2. Brainstorming methodology

People do not speak their minds, in general, because it is *easy* to do that way. The *agree*-culture seems to be favoured by many people for 'smooth sailing'. Some are even afraid that strange or wrong ideas will alienate other people. Such a human psychology has been found to exist even among the educated. The brainstorming method promotes active participation of people, as a catalyst to those people.

The method of brainstorming was the brainchild of Mr. Alex Osborn, an advertising executive and was subsequently developed by many others. The brainstorming is one of the effective techniques of eliciting new ideas from the group, raising them from *passive to active* and even as *proactive* group. This can be obtained by two methods:

(*a*) the structured or round robin method and

(*b*) the unstructured or free wheeling method.

In the unstructured method, the response is at random and some may not participate, but it elicits creative ideas certainly. In the structured method, every body is given a chance to project one's idea and they are simply recorded, no criticism or comment is offered or laughed at, even it is silly. The steps involved in the structured method of Brainstorming are as follows:

1. Choose a place and time to meet.
2. Announce the rules to follow.
3. Present the topic or problem and allow for incubation.
4. Assign a person to record the view as they are proposed.
5. Set the fire and begin the session.
6. All the ideas are welcome. No limit to ideas. But one idea is given by a person at a time, so that participation by all is ensured.
7. The raw ideas are simply recorded. No idea is ever criticized, commented upon or laughed at.
8. The ideas are listed, grouped, and evaluated by the team. Repetitions, if any, are removed.
9. The ways of setting right or solution to the existing problems are identified and listed
10. What and how the means to solutions may go wrong, are then identified and listed. In consequence, the countermeasures will also be listed.
11. The duration of each session may be from 20 to 30 minutes.
12. If needed many rounds may be run during the session.
13. Brainstorm again after a few hours or on the day next, to collect any residual ideas emerging from the team.

Four rules for the successful Brainstorming are listed as follows:

1. SUSPENSION OF JUDGMENT: The ideas are not evaluated as they are presented. Criticism or discussion of an idea is absolutely barred.
2. FREEWHEELING: As in dreaming, one moves from one bizarre situation to another with or without apparent link. One should not mind getting unusual, remote, wild, and silly ideas. In fact wilder the ideas, the better is the result.
3. QUALITY OF IDEAS: Quality implies measurement or evaluation. Never evaluate the idea. Stimulate as many ideas as possible from the group.
4. CROSS FERTILISATION OF IDEAS: One can build on other's ideas. The modification of an idea or combination with another idea is encouraged.

3.10 MANAGEMENT AND PLANNING TOOLS/NEW MANAGEMENT TOOLS

3.10.1 Affinity Diagram

This diagram permits the team to creatively generate large number of ideas and then group them logically for understanding and possible solutions.

In this procedure, the issue is stated in full, then brainstormed using short sentences, posted them for the team to see. The ideas are sorted into logical groups and finally brief headings for each group are identified. The affinity diagram encourages team creativity, break down barriers, promote breakthroughs and motivate ownership of the process. Figure 3.18 shows a typical example of this approach.

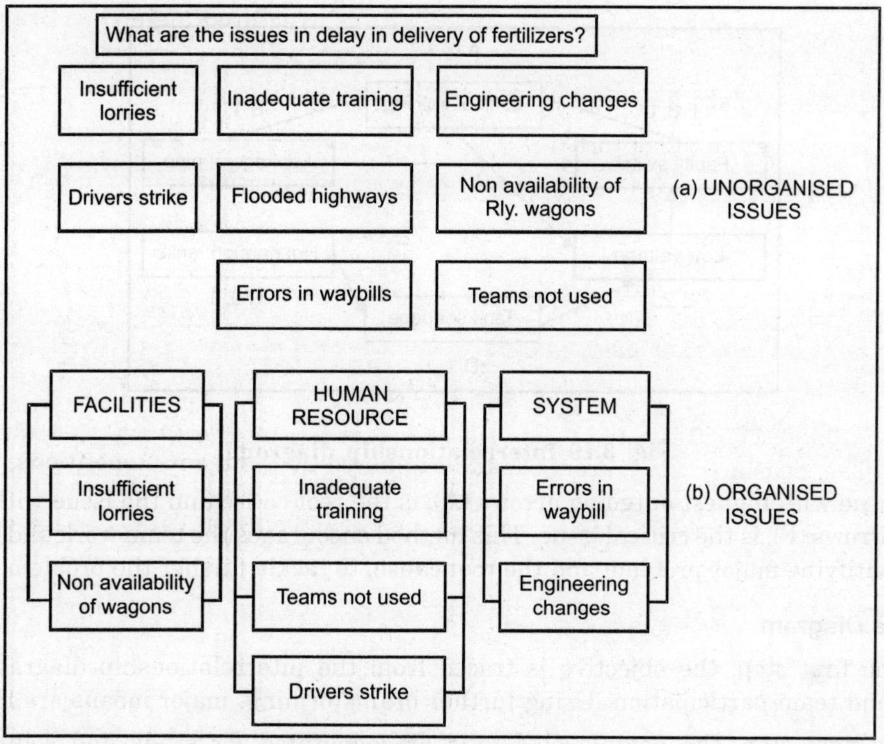

Fig. 3.18 Affinity diagram

3.10.2 Inter-relationship Diagram

This method is useful in clarifying the relationship in complex situations. The team will be able to classify the cause and effect relationship, so that the key elements can be used to solve the problems.

Steps:

1. The team agrees on the statement of the problem.
2. Different ideas or issues from other methods are initially listed and named with alphabets, A, B, etc.
3. Begin with the issue A, and evaluate the cause and effect relationship with B. If A is stronger, draw the arrow A to B, by a thick line. Each issue is compared with A, one by one. Draw thick arrows wherever strong influence is identified. In this example, only issues B, E and F have relationship with A. The first trial is now over.
4. Second iteration is to compare B with issues C, D, E and F. The third step is to compare C with other issues. The fourth is compare issue D with E and F. The fifth step is to compare issue E with F.
5. The diagram may be reviewed and revised, if necessary.
6. The incoming and outgoing arrows are recorded as indicated, above the rectangle block. The completed diagram is shown in Fig. 3.19.

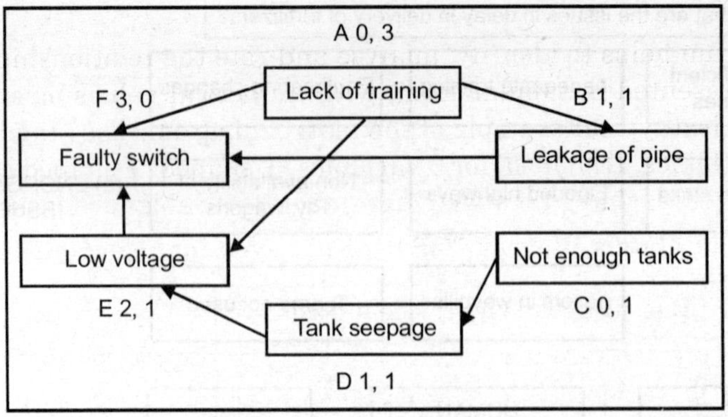

Fig. 3.19 Interrelationship diagram

The issue with highest outgoing arrows (A), is the root cause and the issue with highest incoming arrows (F), is the critical issue. This method encourages the team work and effectiveness in identifying major problem and the root cause, to tackle further the problem further.

3.10.3 Tree Diagram

In the first step, the objective is traced from the interrelationship diagram, brainstorming and team participation. Using further brainstorming, major means are identified.

In the next step, the next level details are generated for study and solution. The question, "What is need next?" is repeated to two three levels, to complete the diagram. The diagram may be reviewed to find, if any actions are ignored or the action will yield expected results. An example of this approach is shown in Fig. 3.20. The merit of this method is, that it encourages the team work and thoroughness.

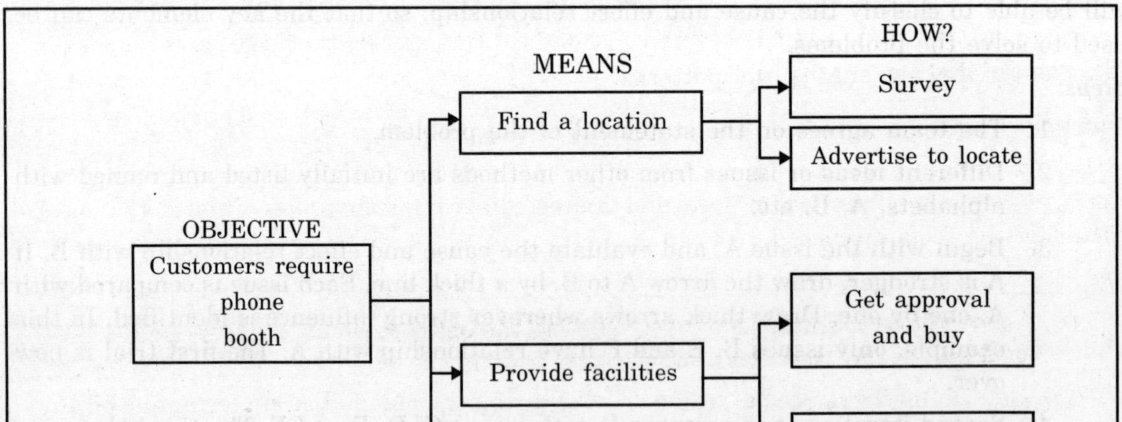

Fig. 3.20 Tree diagram

3.10.4 Matrix Diagram

The matrix diagram helps to identify, analyse and rate the relationship among the variables. Data can be presented in tabular form, with numerical values or otherwise. Quality function deployment, is a typical example of the matrix diagram. The standard formats that are used are: for 2 variables, L shaped; for 3 variables, T shaped, Y shaped and C shaped and for 4 variables, X shaped. L shaped matrix diagram for 2 variables are most frequently used.

Table 3.10 Matrix diagram for uses of seven management tools

Tool	Use of creativity	Analysis	Consensus	Action
Affinity diagram	O		O	Δ
Interrelationship diagram			O	Θ
Tree diagram		Θ		Θ
Prioritisation matrix			O	
Matrix diagram		O	Θ	O
Process decision program chart	Θ	Θ	Θ	O
Activity network diagram			Θ	O

(*Legend: Always* O *Frequently* Θ *Occasionally* Δ)

The seven management tools are presented in Table 3.10 as matrix diagram. The steps involved in its construction are:

(*a*) Select the appropriate format.

(*b*) Determine the relationship symbols. Numerical values may be added when necessary.

(*c*) Complete the matrix, by analysing each cell and insert appropriate symbol.

The matrix diagram approach encourages lateral thinking by the team, in terms of the relationships, their strengths and patterns.

3.10.5 Prioritization Matrix

In this method the issues, tasks, and characteristics are prioritized, based on weighted criteria, using a combination of tree and matrix diagram techniques. This is the most difficult, of the tools discussed.

Steps:

(*a*) Construct an L shaped matrix combining the options, which are then lowest level of detail of the tree diagram with the criteria.

(*b*) Determine the implementation criteria, using the nominal group technique or any other technique, with proper weightage criteria. Each team member submits the most important criteria on a piece of paper. They are listed on as flip chart and the team members submit the rank in another paper, ordering those listed criteria on the chart. Those criteria with greatest value are the most important. Three or four criteria are chosen.

(*c*) Prioritize the criteria using the NGT. Each team member weighs the criteria so the total weight equals 100%. The results are shown in Table 3.11 (*a*).

Table 3.11 (*a*) Weightage for different criteria

Criteria	Member A	Member J	Other members	Total	Weightage
Low cost	25	30	...	155	1.55
Easy to implement	35	30	...	210	2.10
Technology permits	20	15	...	100	1.00
Customer preference	20	25	...	110	1.10
	100	100			

(*d*) Using NGT, the options are ranked, in terms of importance by each criterion, the results are averaged, and rounded to the nearest integer.

(*e*) Compute the option importance score under each criterion, by multiplying the rank by the weightage of criteria. The details are shown in Table 3.11 (*b*). The options with the highest total, is to be implemented first.

Table 3.11 (b) Improvement of a process by consensus criteria method

Options	CRITERIA Low cost		Easy to implement		Technology permits		Customer preference	Total
1.Train supervisors	9 × 1.55	+	10 × 2.10	+	8 × 1.0	+	10 × 1.1	54.0
2.Purchase trucks	10 × 1.55	+	8 × 2.10	+	9 × 1.0	+	7 × 1.1	49.0
3.Have teams of 4 men	8 × 1.55	+	7 × 2.10	+	10 × 1.0	+	6 × 1.1	43.7
4.Training clerks	6 × 1.55	+	6 × 2.10	+	8 × 1.0	+	5 × 1.1	35.4

3.10.6 Process Decision Program Chart

The Process decision program chart avoids unexpected developments and identifies possible counter measures. Figure 3.21 shows an example of this technique.

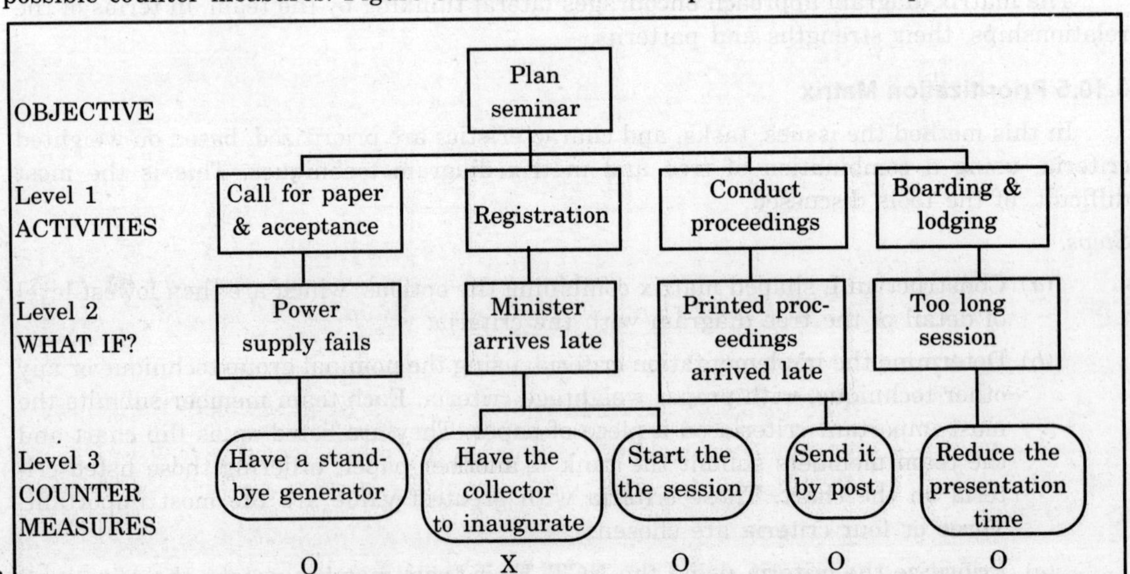

Fig. 3.21 PDPC for conducting the seminar

Initially the team states the objective, that is to plan a successful industrial seminar. Those activities are listed in the first level, which are, call for papers, screening and acceptance, registration, conduct proceedings and arranging Boarding and lodging facilities. The activity of conducting the proceedings is explained hereinafter. The team is brainstormed to determine what could go wrong with the seminar proceedings, and these are shown in Level 2, i.e., 'what if level'. Countermeasures are discussed and listed in the last level. Now the countermeasures are evaluated and the optimal ones are selected and marked O, and rejected ones are marked, X, as shown in the figure.

This method is preferred if the task is new or unique, complex, or potential failure has great risks. It provides a means to effectively minimize uncertainty in implementation stage.

3.10.7 Activity Network Diagram

PERT, CPM, and Arrow diagram are the typical variations of this diagram. They allow the team to schedule the project efficiently. The details such as the critical path, project completion time, simultaneous tasks, and precedence relationships are obtained from this diagram.

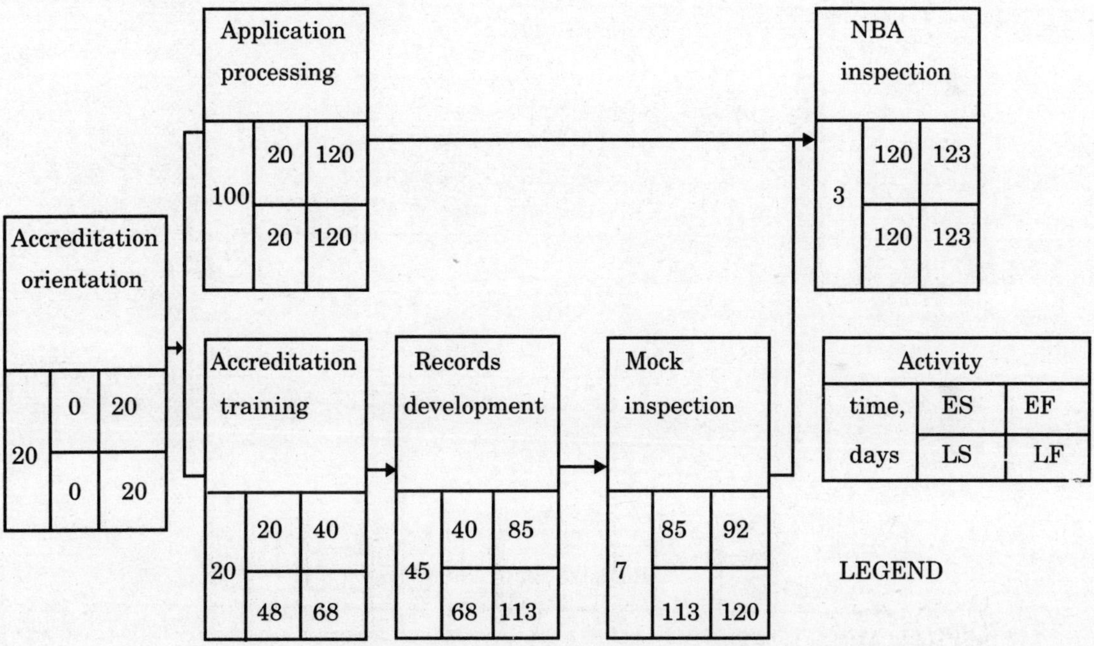

Fig. 3.22 Activity network diagram

Steps:

(*a*) The team brainstorms or documents all the activities to complete the project.

(*b*) The first task is identified and fixed on the extreme left of the board.

(*c*) The tasks done simultaneously, are placed in parallel.

(*d*) Steps (*b*) and (*c*) are repeated until all the tasks are located on the board in correct sequence, as shown in Fig. 3.22.

(*e*) Number all activities and draw the corresponding arrows. Activity times are recorded in the lower left box. It may be hours, days, weeks or months.

(*f*) Find the critical path, after completing the details of box in each activity.

The critical path is the path along which all the activities are completed in the minimum time. The advantages of this method are:

1. A realistic project execution time is determined.
2. Bottlenecks are identified and when necessary, corrective actions can be planned.
3. Focus is made on the activities lying in the critical path. Time-cost trade off can be worked out, to complete the project earlier, with optimum additional cost.

❑ ❑ ❑

CHAPTER 4

TQM Tools

4.1 BENCH MARKING

4.1.1 History

Bench marking is literally defined as reference or standard against which something can be measured or judged. Bench marking is not a new concept and everyone has bench marked in his or her personal and professional lives. But what is new may be the development of bench marking as a formal and systematic discipline. Bench marking was there since early 20th century and took a competitive look due to efforts of Robert Lamp of Xerox Corporation.

4.1.2 Introduction

It is a systematic and continual measurement process, comparing the performance of one's organization process against competition/business leaders available anywhere in the world to gain information, which in turn help the organization to improve its performance. The purpose of bench marking is to improve products and processes, delivery and service to meet the customer needs. The connection between business process and customer needs is critical to efficient bench marking.

4.1.3 Concept of Bench Marking

As shown in Fig 4.1, bench marking consists of measuring performance against best practices/performances studying how do they achieve performance levels and using the information, adopting them to their environment to achieve breakthrough performance.

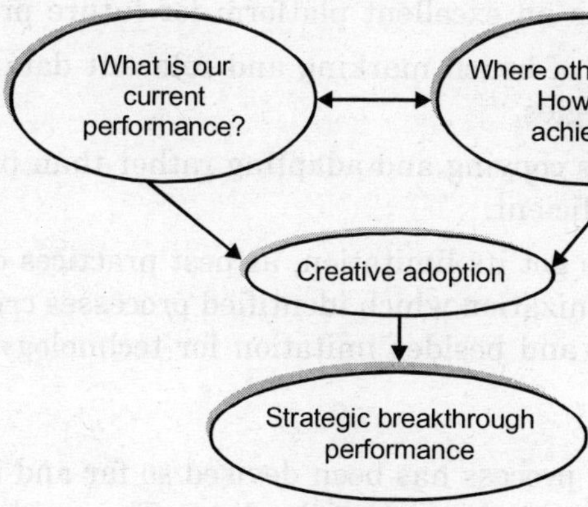

Fig. 4.1

The bench marking strategy concentrates on both best practices and measurements. Measurements are usually expressed as numerical values. First, measurement of best in class practices form the target and performance of the organization, planning to improve, will be plotted against best in class practice. Secondly, managers have to estimate the gap and why there is a performance gap. Then they have to understand the processes of best in class organization and their own processes to meet goal. In the improvement process, competition, product performance and customer satisfaction are considered. Therefore, bench marking is about setting the goal and objectives and improving the processes to meet them.

4.1.4 Reasons to Bench Mark

Bench marking is a tool to attain competitive and business advantage. It is a powerful and extremely effective when it is integrated with culture of organization. Thereby, it helps the organization to develop strengths and reduce weaknesses. The reasons needed are listed below.

1. Since bench marking has got the external orientation, it helps the organization to collect all information of the products of their organization and competitors completely. In case, if organization falls short of competitors, or any improvements are noted elsewhere, the process can inspire organization to compete.
2. Bench marking, in contrast with the traditional method of showing continual improvement, set the objectives, based on external information. This motivates the personnel to attain goals or objectives. What appeared to be impossible here is made possible in other's organization, inspire the personnel to achieve goal.
3. Bench marking testing procedures can test product samples, periodically throughout the year. The documentation of results helps to understand the extent of variability or assure the products are within limits, ensuring product quality consistently. This also helps to observe the competitors' reproducibility.
4. Bench marking testing provides a database that allows you to establish purchase specifications, which meet the requirements of process/product. Therefore, bench marking the incoming products helps to fix a set of specifications, which suppliers have to meet, producing consistent results.
5. The unbiased bench marking identify strengths and weakness of one's product with competitors, indicating position of their product in market place. This knowledge can serve as an excellent platform for future product development.
6. A thorough knowledge of bench marking and relevant data help organization to build marketing strategies.
7. Since bench marking is copying and adapting rather than prevention, it is found to be time and cost efficient.

However bench marking has got its limitation, as best practices or quality has no end but keep moving. Therefore, organization which identified processes critical to its objectives, have to be constantly innovated and besides imitation for technology breakthrough.

4.1.5 Bench Marking—Process

No standard bench marking process has been devised so far and it varies from organization to organization, according to their needs and culture. The number of stages and steps may vary. Therefore each organization has to customize its own model to fit with their overall approach to continuous improvement and background culture. Even though number of steps varies, the following six steps contain the core activities:

1. Decide what to benchmark.
2. Understand current performance.
3. Planning.
4. Observe others.
5. Learn from data.
6. Use the findings.

Step 1: Decide what to bench mark

This is the first step in benchmarking process to identify critical processes and success factors. These critical processes are ones, which support the company's mission and vision. Therefore only critical activities will be benchmarked to realize its vision. So it is necessary to:

- State the mission, purpose/goal of function or department
- Understand critical processes and how they are measured
- Decide what kind of data is needed and how will be collected
- Identify team members for this purpose
- List the customer needs, that are most important
- List the major customers by volume or value
- Identify areas to be benchmarked

Pareto analysis can be applied to find out vital a few than and trivial many. Cause and effect diagram and flow diagram are also used to trace the input and relevant activities.

Step 2: Understanding current performance

It is essential to understand the current performance and the scope to improve them. Several techniques like fish bone diagram and flow diagram are applied to this effect. Input and output have to be identified. Careful questioning is necessary to understand the climate and culture of the organization. To make this process effective, team members are actually process owners or who work in the process, where correction can be implemented. Then document the process and suitable quantification method is adopted. It is ensured that collection of information is sufficient for benchmark comparisons.

Step 3: Planning

The purpose of planning is to:

- Identify the bench mark candidate
- Type of public data to be collected
- Method of collection
- Establish numeric methods to be used

To identify appropriate benchmark partners, it is good to use the information available with the public and proper inquiry it can be identified. Based on approaches, bench marking can be classified as

(*i*) Internal benchmarking

(*ii*) Competitive benchmarking

(*iii*) Process benchmarking

(i) Internal Benchmarking

This is performed within one organization where similar activities were performed at same or different places. By this procedure, personnel are trained by copying the work and sound habits of the best performers. This procedure has shown good improvement in productivity. It is found to be advantageous, as the problem of confidentiality does not arise.

(ii) Competitive Benchmarking

It involves the investigation with the competitors' products, practices, and processes. Reverse engineering is applied to understand processes from end product to raw material. A few competitors share information and others do not. The data collection has to be done through public and third party like journals, product literature, consultants and experts. The organization also collects comparative data about its own product and its competitors at customer location also.

(iii) Process Benchmarking

It is sometimes known as generic or functional benchmarking. Here we consider the practices of identified business leaders and benchmarking is done against any specific activities. It can be done against any business sector that is doing this process. For example, airlines company, unhappy about a plane turn around time, has benchmarked against auto-receiving pit screws.

Some of the sources to identify benchmarking candidates are :

- Quality award winner (e.g., Malcom Baldrige Award).
- Business newspaper and magazine articles.
- Trade journal articles.
- Conference speeches.
- Industry and professional associations.
- Consultants and reports.

Step 4: Observe others

At this stage, after collection of information, benchmarking looks for :

- Description of how best processes are practiced.
- The effect of best practices.

Focus will be on the collected information. Collection methods have to be uniform to ensure appropriate data quality and accuracy. Time and cost of project is considered, since the target is always moving. Therefore robustness, must be built in to metrics and benchmarking, because things will change before project is complete.

Three techniques namely questionnaire, site visits and focus groups are used. Questionnaire is properly structured and carefully interpreted. Site visits provide opportunity to see processes practised by best in class workers. Before site visits are undertaken, internal operations should be fully understood and relevant information should have been acquired. This helps the team to debrief its findings for follow up activities. Care should be taken by team to follow "Benchmarking - code of conduct" to sustain bench marking process.

***Step 5:* Learning from data**

This stage involves :

- Summarize and interpret data.
- Analyse gap between your process and competitors.
- What is the gap? How much is it?
- Why there is a gap?
- Project where future gaps will be.
- Analyse things that was not on agenda.
- Develop key findings into new operational goals.

Bench marking studies can reveal three outcomes namely:

Negative gap: External processes are significantly better than internal process.

Positive gap: Shows our internal processes are better than our competitors.

Parity: Process performance may be approximately equal and requires further investigation to improve them. These gaps must be identified and quantified. Described by words and charts that each step can be understood and emulated. The level of detail must be sufficient for quantification to close it. 'Z' chart compares current productivity with the benchmark partner and rate of improvement needed to bridge the gap as shown in Fig. 4.2.

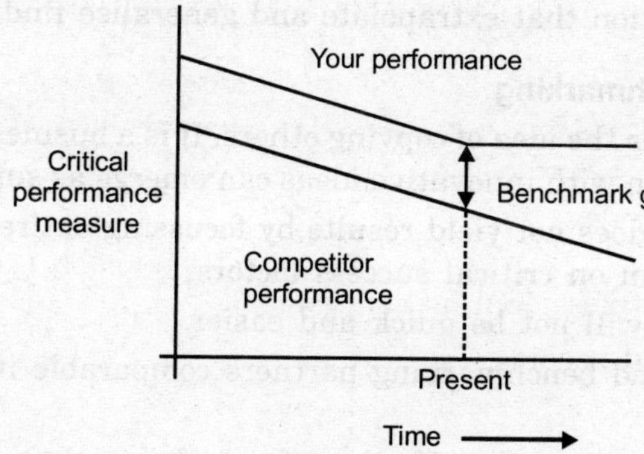

Fig. 4.2

To close the benchmark, strategic actions and operational process improvement have to be adopted as shown in Fig. 4.3. Strategic actions include restructuring or down sizing or reengineering. The qualitative observation may be used to develop an improved process.

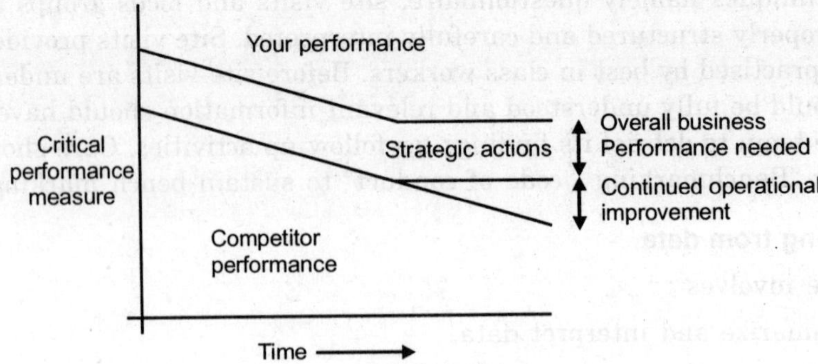

Fig. 4.3

***Step 6:* Using the findings**

To realise the benchmarking process, two groups have to agree on change namely the top management and owners of process. The key change management activities used are:

- Communicate the benchmark findings widely.
- involve a broad cross functional team of employees.
- Translate the findings to a few core principles.
- Provide necessary resources.
- Work down from principles to strategies to action plan.

Since benchmarking is a continuous process, process owner, stakeholders need to have a voice in the changes recommended. Before developing strategies, it is important to communicate with all who are involved in the change. A forum has to be provided to discuss the methodology, facts and findings from bench marking effort. It also includes commitment for change and expectations about changes. The best results are obtained when process owner fully participate in execution of action plan. The best results from benchmarking have come from organization that extrapolate and generalise findings into core principles.

4.1.6 Limitations of Benchmarking

- Benchmarking is the idea of copying others. It is a business philosophy for survival and organization with innovative ideas can emerge as superior in their market.
- Benchmarking does not yield results by focussing entirely on performance measures rather than on critical success factors.
- Benchmarking will not be quick and easier.
- Expecting to find benchmarking partners comparable in all respects to your organization.
- Benchmarking will not be effective, if it is focussed on processes with no opportunity for improvements.

4.2 QUALITY FUNCTION DEPLOYMENT (QFD)

The best and most sustainable innovation occurs where creativity and customer needs intersect. Good ideas don't just leap out of laboratories. They are called out by the clear voice of the customer and need to be reinforced with the right resources.

— James McNerney, Chairman and CEO, 3M, USA

4.2.1 History

The concept of quality function deployment was developed in the early 1970 in Japan. Yogi Akao and Shiguru Mageno were credited with the creation of this concept, specifically to Kobe Shipyard, Mitsubishi Heavy Industry Ltd., Japan. Subsequently these ideas were adopted by Japanese auto industries, specifically by Toyota around 1977. After a few years of rigorous study, and implementation, they were able to reduce around 61% start up costs. Due to energy crisis and economic problems, the QFD began to be adopted in the American auto industries in the mid 1980s. John Hausa and Dan Clausing of MIT were responsible for making this concept popular in USA. This concept can be applied to practically any manufacturing or service industry.

4.2.2 Introduction

QFD is a systematic and a planning tool to motivate business to success by integrating the quality related aspects of products and customer expectations and requirements. The expectations and requirements are termed as **voice of customer**. Voice of customer also includes stated and unstated customer needs or requirements. The purpose is to produce customer driven design for products / service organizations to have competitive edge in the business and make good profits or QFD deploys the voice of customer through the product's design, production, marketing, delivery and service. QFD attaches value to customer, which is the ratio of benefits received to the cost paid to the product. When products satisfy the customer requirement, value and sales goes up. When start up problems is reduced, the product development cycle will be reduced and reducing cost of the product. Increased sales and lower costs of product yield greater profits.

The voice of customer must be accurately defined. QFD translates them into engineering or technical characteristics and finally into design requirements (voice of engineer). This can be deployed through:

- Product planning.
- Product development.
- Process planning.
- Production planning.
- Service industries.

An organization which implements the QFD, gains an improved engineering knowledge, productivity and quality, reducing costs, cycle time and engineering changes. A prerequisite to QFD is market research. This helps to understand the customers' expectations and requirements. It is the process of understanding, the following:

What is the need of the customer?

How important are benefits?

How will competitors of this product meet the benefits?

The information of voice of customer is collected in a variety of ways: Direct discussion like interviews, surveys, focus groups, customer specification, observation, warranty data, field reports, trade shows, etc. The information can be solicited or unsolicited, quantitative and or qualitative, structured and or random in nature. The objective of QFD is to meet as many as customers' needs as possible.

The collected information has to be defined completely; otherwise the remaining process will become irrelevant. Since QFD aims to produce customer driven products, it becomes multi disciplinary or cross-functional team. The team comprises of members from marketing, design, engineering, sales, materials, and procurement. Time and communication are two very essential things that each team has to use to the fullest extent, since it is a process of collecting information related to the voice of customer, translating them into specification to design department, design specification to fabrication, specification to testing etc. Hence there is a possibility that the voice of customer will be lost and voice of organization may enter into the product design. Hence efficient inter-team communication is vital to run the project smoothly and remove unexpected problems. To facilitate this, team meetings have to be conducted and keep the members informed. Meeting may extend for either hours or days. Also a meeting format can be developed to measure how well a QFD process is working at each meeting and help the team focussed on a quality improvement goal. There are numerous methods like affinity diagram, inter relationship diagram and cause and effect diagram. These methods are used for sorting out the large amounts of information collected. The affinity diagram is found to be ideally suited for most QFD application.

From the collected information, conflicting customer requirements are identified early in the process and resolved. The team identifies and resolves issues in providing products, processes, services that satisfy more than customer requirements. Besides this, it is duty of team members to introduce a feature in the product that is not expected by customer but appreciate it. This is determined from the collected information. This is done to have competitive edge in the market. It also emphasis product-process alternatives and bottleneck identification and engineering. Bottlenecks is defined as technical, cost, and safety related limitation that has to be resolved successfully to achieve quality plan.

Early identification of these limitations helps to resolve them in time. This reduces the product or process development cycle time. This bottleneck engineering is a form of proactive quality work. QFD has also additional elements

- Technology deployment—related to product, process and techniques used in manufacturing processes.
- Reliability deployment—related to safety and long term product performance
- Cost deployment—business aspects of design, development, production, target costs, marketing process, product volume, etc.

4.2.3 Benefits of QFD

QFD was originally intended to reduce start up costs, but helped the organization to reduce cycle time of the product. US auto industry needed an average of five years to put a product on the market, whereas Honda was put into market in two years and a half, while Toyota did it in three years. This is due to the application of QFD.

The benefits are:

1. QFD meets or surpasses the customer satisfaction.
2. Helps management to plan its resources to improve the quality of product.
3. Early identification of bottlenecks in technology, and resolving them helps to release the product into market first.

4. Helps to develop a structured format about information gathered on customer needs, competitive product, and bottlenecks. Even a new employee can be fit into a particular project.
5. Identification of conflicting design requirements results in reduction in retooling, training and quality control measures. It reduces cycle time of product.
6. Since inputs are required from marketing, design, engineering and sales, horizontal communication channels has to be ensured. Otherwise, the voice of customer will be lost. This helps each department to know what others are doing. This promotes teamwork resulting in improved efficiency and productivity.
7. Since all information collected has been structured in right format, it helps organization to develop proper documentation. This acts a database for future design process identification. Also QFD is very flexible and new thing can be introduced and existing procedures can be changed.

4.2.4 House of Quality (HOQ)

This is an effective management tool that uses the voice of customer to drive design process or service, meets specified target values and match against how an organization will meet those requirements. The structure of QFD can be similar to framework of house as shown in Fig. 4.4.

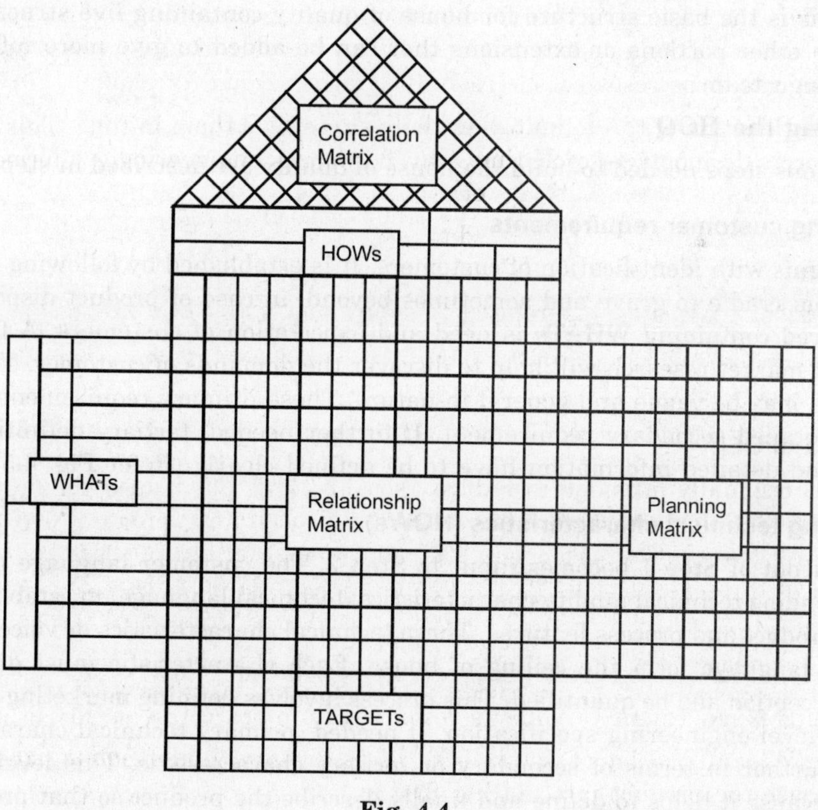

Fig. 4.4

The parts of house of quality are discussed as below:

1. Exterior walls of house indicate the voice of customers. The **left side** indicates the listing of **voice of customer** (or) what customer expects. Usually these are considered as **WHATs of house** listed and no order is followed. On **right exterior side** is prioritised customers' voice and **planning matrix**. It includes customers' bench marking, customer assessment, and target value, scale up factor and sales point.
2. Next one is the **upper section/ceiling** of house or **HOWs** of the house. This determines how each of customer's desires can be achieved. This is accomplished through engineering characteristics of products, design constraints and parameters. Basically each one of HOWs is technical characteristic that can be modified to achieve or to cause very little influence on WHATs of house.
3. Next, the relationship has to be determined between WHATs and HOWs. This is accomplished in **relationship matrix** in the **centre of house**.
4. The **roof of house** is the **interrelationship** between technical characteristics or HOWs of house. Trade off between similar or conflicting technical characteristics are identified.
5. The function of house prioritises technical characteristics. This is done, based on technical bench marking, design of technical difficulty and target value.
6. This is the basic structure for house of quality containing five structures. There are other portions or extensions that can be added to give more information to design team.

4.2.5 Building the HOQ

The various steps needed to build the house of quality are described in steps as follows:

Step 1: Listing customer requirements

QFD begins with identification of customers. It is established by following product and processes from cradle to grave and sometimes beyond, in case of product disposal. Then a list is prepared containing WHATs is need and expectation of customers. A fundamental knowledge of market research will help to discover the demands of customer. The customer requirements may be vague and general in nature. These primary requirements have to be defined as detailed secondary requirement. If further needed, tertiary definition is given. Organised and detailed information have to be defined clearly (Refer Fig. 4.5).

Step 2: Listing technical characteristics (HOWs)

Now, output of Step 1 becomes input to Step 2. The customer language is translated into corresponding technical quality characteristics (technical language) to establish technical targets for product and process features. These technical characteristics or voice of customer in technical language form the ceiling of house. Each characteristic must directly affect customer perception and be quantified. This process involves defining marketing specification into system level engineering specification. If needed, primary technical characteristic can be defined further in terms of secondary or tertiary characteristic. This level of detail is necessary because it helps to define and finally describe the product so that product can be developed, produced, delivered, sold, serviced, used and recycled or disposed properly. In many cases, a technical characteristic may affect more than one customer requirement and can even adversely affect another. Brainstorming is the suggested method for determining the required technical characteristics (Refer Fig. 4.6).

Step 3: Developing relationship matrix

(Between WHATs and HOWs)

This portion of the house is built by comparing customer requirements and technical characteristics and determines the interrelation between them. To avoid confusion, an L shaped matrix can be formed. (Refer Fig. 4.7). This makes the process simpler and does not need any experience. The relationship matrix depicts the degree of influence between each customer requirements to the technical characteristics both quantitatively and qualitatively. It is common to use symbols to represent the degree of influence between them (Refer Fig. 4.8).

- ● a solid circle represents strong relationship.
- o a single circle represents a medium relationship.
- Δ a triangle represents weak relationship.

If it is left blank, no relationship exists. To make it further simpler, symbols are replaced by numbers as below

- ● 9
- o 3
- Δ 1

This is useful to identify priority of characteristics, and determines trade off situations when conflicting characteristics are involved. After process is over, it is verified whether any column or row is left blank. If any row is left blank, then customer requirements are not met. Therefore additional technical characteristics have to be introduced. In case, if any column is left blank, then additional technical characteristics does not have any effect in any of customer requirements and can be removed from HOQ, after careful scrutiny.

Step 4: Developing correlation matrix (Between HOWs)

The roof of HOQ and correlation is used to represent the relationship between technical characteristics. It is in the form of a triangular table attached to technical characteristics as shown in Fig. 4.9. Symbols are used to describe the level of their inter relationship between them and they are given below:

- ● A solid circle indicates strong positive relationship.
- o A single circle indicates positive relationship.
- **X** A cross indicates strong negative relationship.
- ★ Star indicates negative relationship.

This gives the idea where the technical characteristics support each other and are in conflict. The conflicting technical characteristics indicate conflicting customer requirements and those are situations, where trade off has to be determined. If they are not identified and resolved, it leads to unfulfilled requirements. Trade off is defined as a situation where conflicting technical characteristics which affect customer requirements are handled. In this, a high level management decision is needed. For example, mileage and safety are two customer requirements of an automobile which are in conflict with each other in terms of weight reduction to increase mileage and adding safety gadgets to increase safety.

Step 5: Competitive assessments

It contains two parts, namely customer competitive assessments and technical competitive assessments.

(a) Customer Competitive Assessments

It is the portion of house attached to the right side of relationship matrix. This is done to see whether all customer requirements are met and to identify the areas for next design. Then by, comparing the competitors' product, based on the collection of customer perception and this information helps us to say where our product stands. Weightage is given to evaluate ranking of customer requirements by assigning numbers from 1 to 5. 1 indicates worst and 5 for best (Refer Fig. 4.10).

(b) Technical Competitive Assessments

This portion contains a block of rows added to the beneath of relationship matrix. This assessment is done for our product and competitors' product. This approach is helpful in assessing the gap between the products. This is done for every technical characteristic and ranking is done. A standard scale 1 to 5 is used. 1 stands for the worst, while 5 stands for the best (Refer Fig. 4.11). Technical characteristics and customer requirements that are strongly related should reflect strong relationship between two in their competitive assessment. If it is otherwise, a mistake in engineering judgement is occurred and should be corrected.

Step 6: Developing prioritised customer requirements

This portion is added to the right side of competitive assessment as shown in Fig. 4.12. It includes importance to customer, target value, scale up factor, sales point and absolute weight.

(a) Importance to the Customer requirements

The QFD team assigns number to each customer requirements. The range may be 1 to 10, 1 indicating least important and 10 indicates very important. The rating represents the relative importance of each customer requirements in terms of each other. This rating is useful for prioritising the customer requirements and helps to make trade off decisions.

(b) Target Value

Target value column is similar to customer competitive assessment. The range is 1–5 (1 for worst, 5 for best). This column decides; whether product remains to be unchanged, improve the existing product or a make product better than the competitor.

(c) Scale Up Factor

It is ratio of the target value to product rating given in the customer competitive assessment. It decides where product stands currently in the market. It also gives information about the target rating and determines whether the difference can be realized. Greater value indicates more efforts are needed to achieve the target.

(d) Sales Point

Its value lies between 1 and 2, with 2 being the highest. It tells how well customer requirements are sold. The aim is to promote best customer requirements that help in sale of the product. QFD team decides the value to be assigned.

(e) Absolute Weight

It is the product of importance to customer, scale up factor and sales point.

Absolute weight = (Importance to the customer requirements) × (Scale up factor) × (Sales point)

From summation of all absolute weights, ranking can be made in terms of percentage. This is used as a guide for planning phase of the product.

Step 7: Developing prioritised technical characteristics

This portion of house is attached to the bottom portion of the technical competitive assessments corresponding to the rows of technical characteristics. It contains degree of technical difficulty, target value, absolute and relative weights. Objective of this is to identify technical characteristics needed most to fulfil customer requirements and need improvement (Refer Fig. 4.13).

(a) Degree of Difficulty

QFD team identifies degree of difficulty of technical characteristics expressed in I row of technical characteristics. The number is assigned by QFD team ranging from 1 – 10 (one for least difficulty and 10 for very difficulty). The degree of technical difficulty is used to evaluate the ability to implement certain quality improvements.

(b) Target Value

This value is entered below the degree of difficulty. Each characteristic will be assigned a value and it is the objective of each characteristic to achieve this value in order to demonstrate customer requirements are satisfied or surpassed.

(c) Absolute Weight

This is done by assigning numbers (weights) to the symbols used in relationship matrix. The absolute weight for technical characteristics is calculated as follows:

$$a_j = \sum_{i=1}^{n} R_{ij} C_i$$

a_j – row vector of absolute weights for technical characteristics

R_{ij} – Numbers (weights) assigned to relationship matrix ($i = 1\ldots n$, $j = 1\ldots m$)

C_i – column vector of importance to customer requirements ($i = 1\ldots n$).

m – Number of technical characteristics

n – Number of customer requirements

(d) Relative Weight

Both relative and absolute and relative weight identify areas where efforts need to be focussed. Relative weight gives additional information on customer scale up factor and scale point. This relative weight gives the degree of importance for customer requirements.

$$b_j = \sum_{i=1}^{n} R_{ij} d_i$$

b – Row vector of relative weights for technical characteristics (j = 1... m).

d_i – column vector of absolute weights for customer requirements (i = 1... n).

The resources can be allocated to the areas where quality improvement has to be made. Each QFD can be tailor made to suit to their needs.

4.2.6 Example for HOQ

A publisher decides to print a textbook for the kids of the age group 4 to 6 years. The QFD principles are applied in steps below to build the house of quality. Even though the real customers are children, only the parents purchase the book, which will be useful to the kids.

Step 1:

The customer requirements for the purchase of book are attractive and easy to understand. These requirements are called primary requirements and detailed as secondary customer requirements. The secondary customer requirements under attractive are cost effectiveness, pleasing colours, more pictures and humorous mixed stories. For example, cost effectiveness. is included under 'attractive', but it does not come under it. Secondary customer requirements under 'easy to understand' are brief text and informative, as shown in Fig. 4.5.

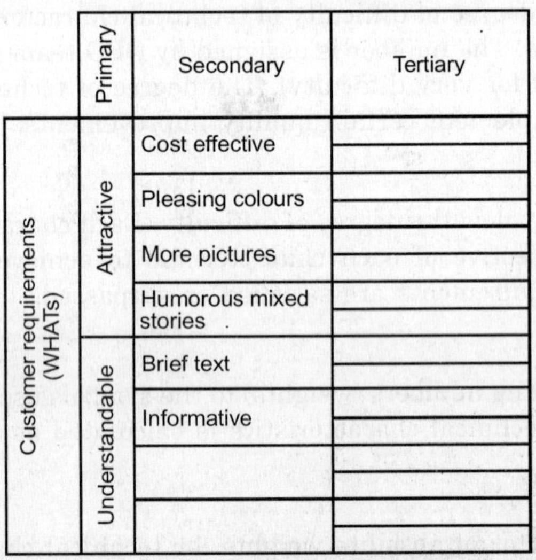

Fig. 4.5

Step 2:

To meet these customer requirements, corresponding technical characteristics are found out. Primary technical characteristics are collection of information and presentation of information. The secondary technical characteristics under collection of information are references, good artists and knowledgeable authors. The secondary technical characteristics under presentation of information are standard format, peer review, good printing and edited for clarity as illustrated in Fig. 4.6.

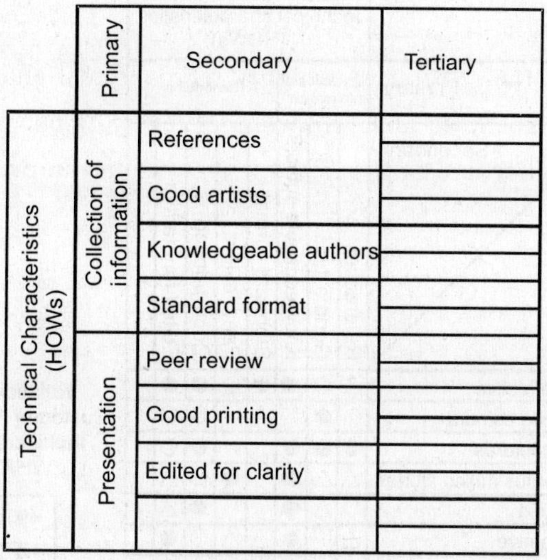

Fig. 4.6

Step 3:

The matrix is developed by connecting customer requirements and technical characteristics as L matrix as shown in Fig. 4.7.

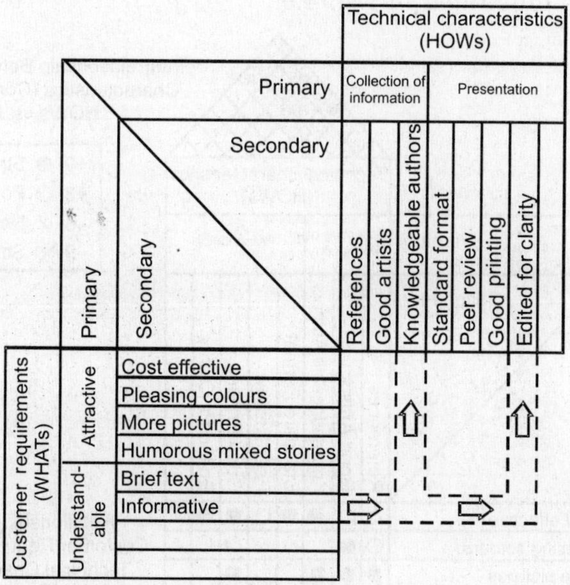

Fig 4.7

Step 4:

The relationship matrix is formed by symbols as discussed above. It indicates the degree of influence between customer requirements and technical characteristics as can be seen in Fig. 4.8.

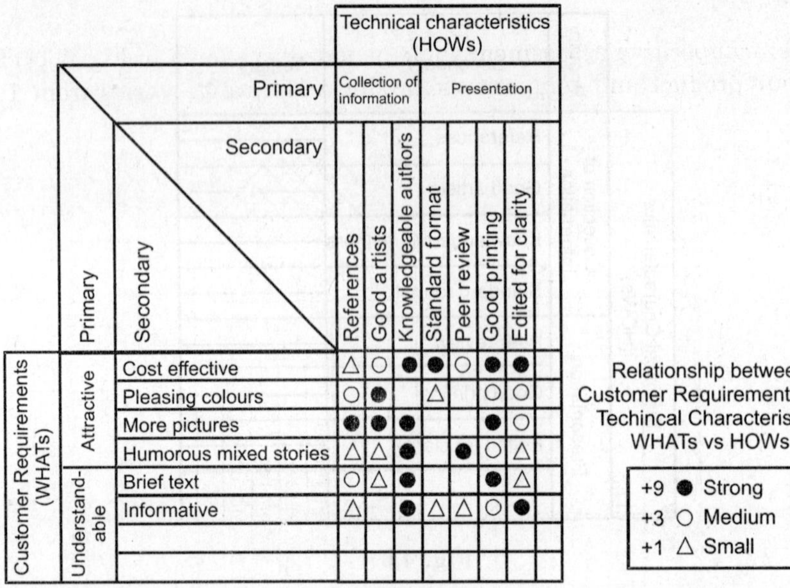

Fig. 4.8

Step 5:

The correlation matrix is formed at the top of HOQ indicating relation between technical characteristics, as illustrated in Fig. 4.9.

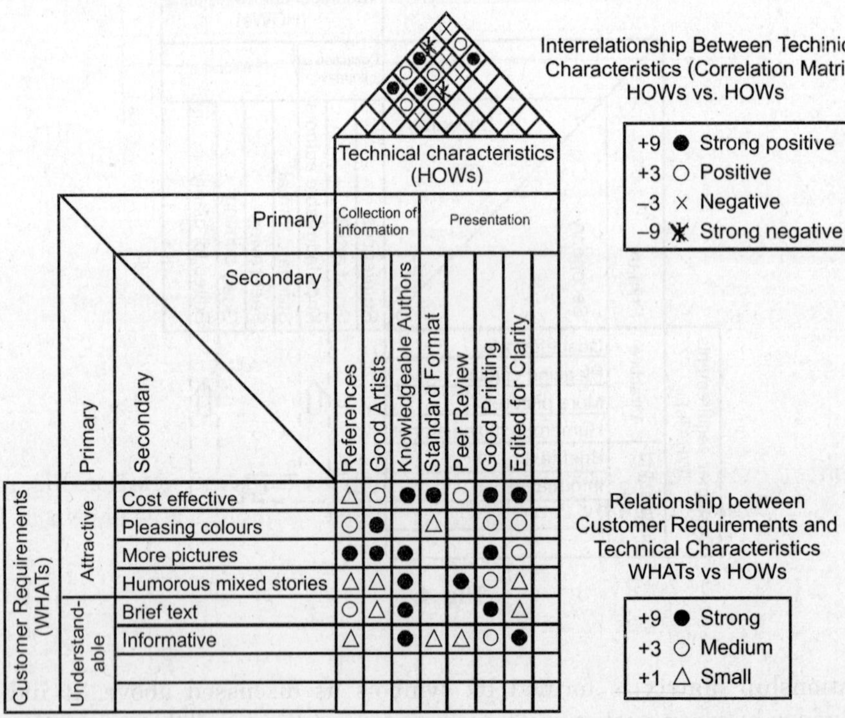

Fig 4.9

Step 6:

The customer competitive assessment table is added as shown in Fig. 4.10. Here rating is assigned for our product and competitors' product. The range varies from 1 to 5.

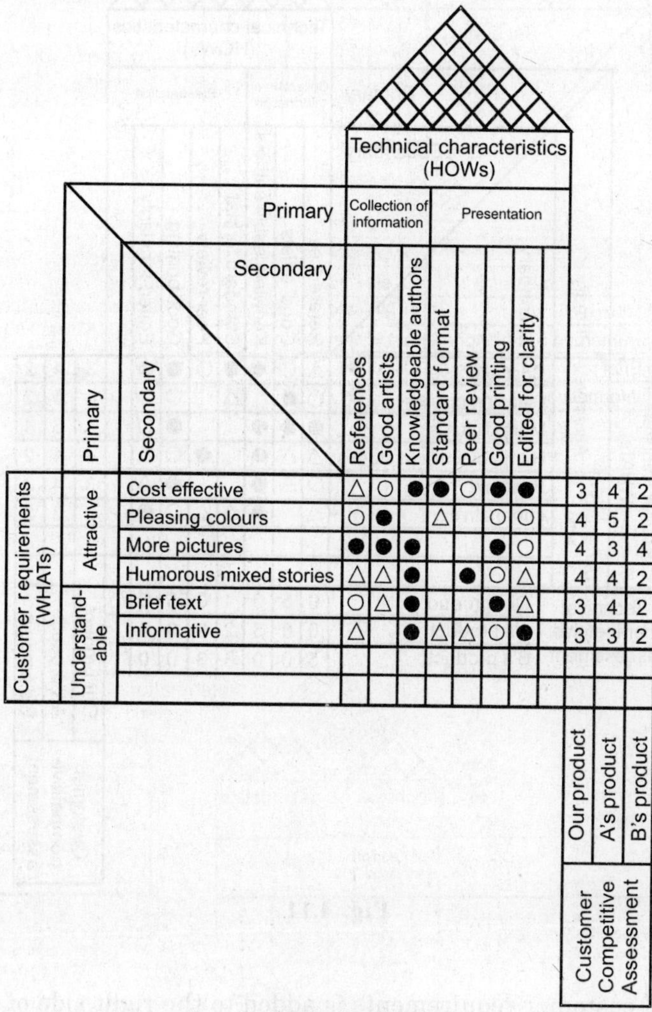

Fig. 4.10

Step 7:

The technical competitive assessment is added beneath the relationship matrix as shown in Fig. 4.11. This is done by converting test data as numerals as shown in Fig. 4.11.

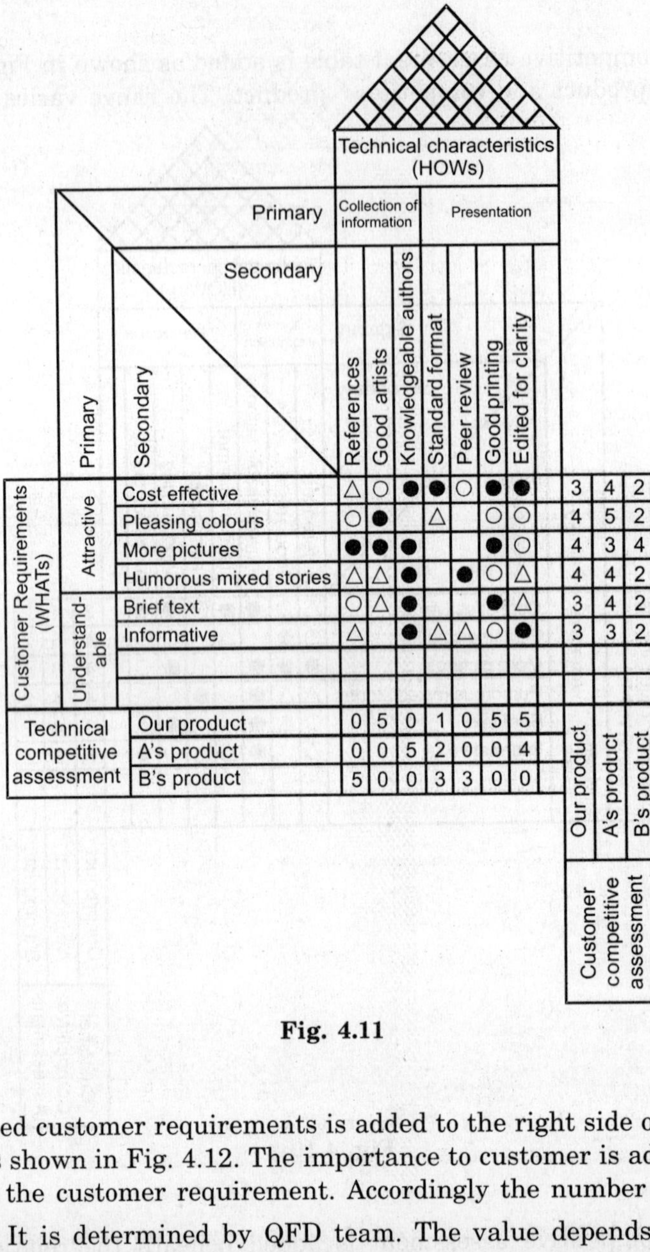

Fig. 4.11

Step 8:

Then prioritised customer requirements is added to the right side of customer competitive assessment as shown in Fig. 4.12. The importance to customer is added by determining the importance of the customer requirement. Accordingly the number is assigned.

Target value: It is determined by QFD team. The value depends upon, whether the product to be improved or exceed the competition or remain unchanged.

Scale up factor: It is the ratio of the target value to the product rating given in the customer competitive assessment.

For example, Cost effective, scale up factor = Target value/Product rating = 4/3 = 1.3.

Sales point: This is decided by QFD team and ranges between 1 and 2, 2 being the highest. If particular customer requirement promotes sales, then a higher value will be assigned. Otherwise 1 will be assigned.

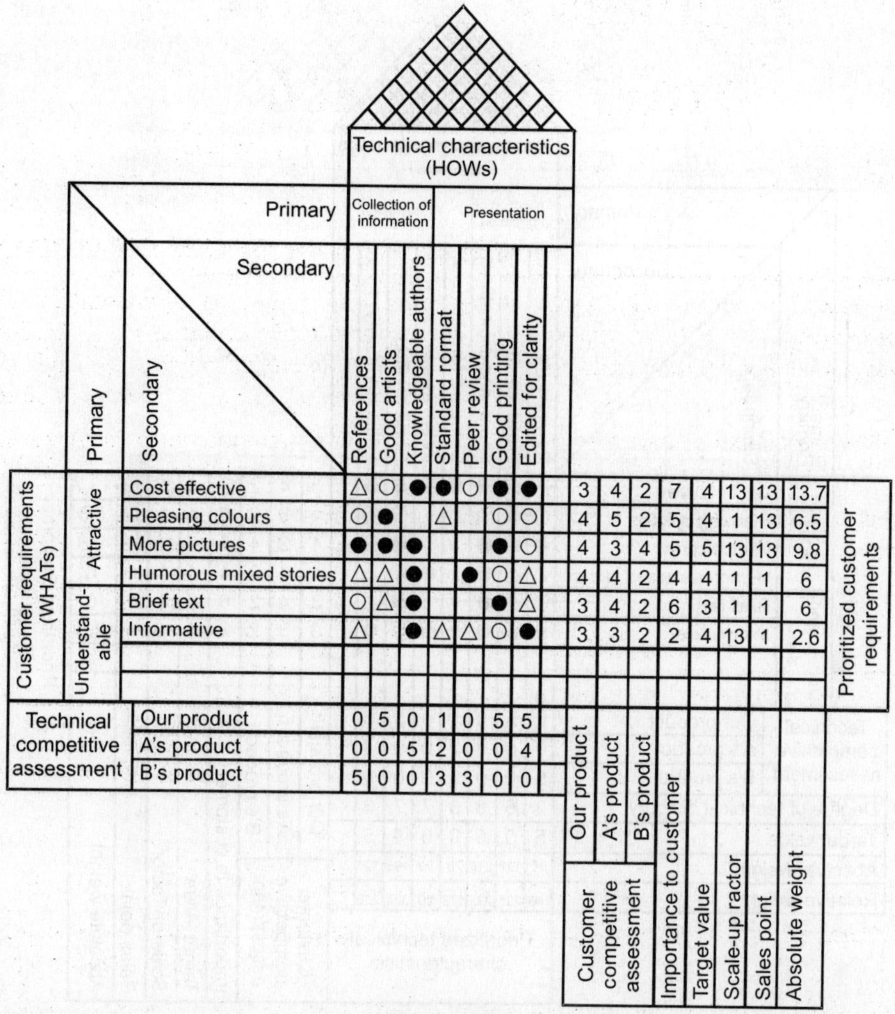

Fig. 4.12

Absolute weight: (Importance to customer) × (Scale up factor) × (Sales point)

For example, customer requirement *e.g.*, more pictures, absolute weight = 5 × 1.3 × 1.5 = 9.75

Step 9:

Finally prioritised technical characteristics is added to HOQ below technical competitive assessment as shown in Fig. 4.13.

Degree of difficulty: The value is assigned by QFD team and it indicates actual degree of difficulty involved in achieving technical characteristics.

Target value: It is done similar to the way; it is done for customer requirement.

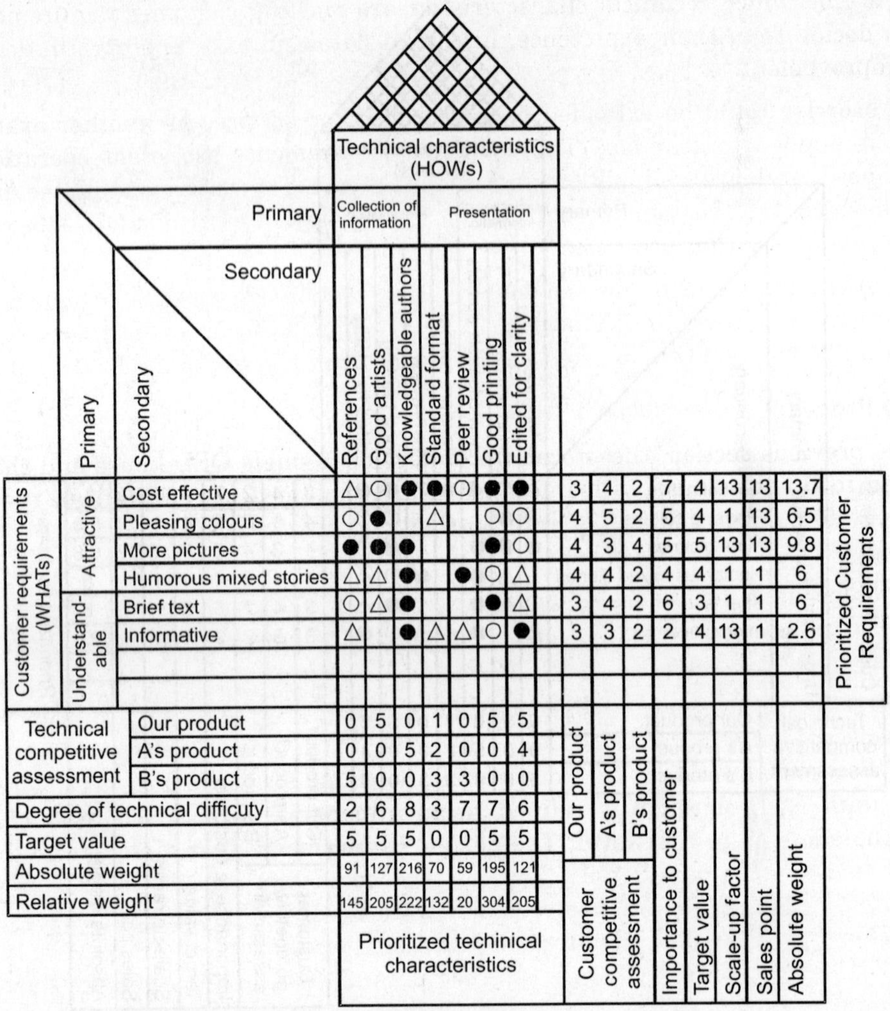

Fig. 4.13

Absolute weight: This is determined using

$$a_j = \sum_{i=1}^{n} R_{c_j} C_i \text{ (Explained earlier)}$$

e.g., for good presentation,

Absolute weight = 9 × 7 + 3 × 5 + 9 × 5 + 3 × 4 + 9 × 6 + 3 × 2 = 195

Relative weight: This is determined using the formula,

e.g., for good presentation,

Relative weight = (9 × 13.65) + (3 × 6.5) + (9 × 9.75) + (3 × 4) + (9 × 6) + (3 × 2.6)
= 304.

Step 10:

The greatest value of absolute weight and relative weight indicates the impact of technical characteristics on customer requirements. This can be organised into a parents diagram to find which technical characteristics are meeting customer requirements. QFD team can decide from their experience, historical data and take appropriate decisions for quality improvement.

This exercise could be extended to any product or service. As another example, this approach is applied to gear box. The customer requirements are silent operation, speed, accurate speed, and size, reliability and reasonable cost. The corresponding technical characteristics which meet customer requirements directly are number of teeth, lubricant, tooth thickness, manufacturing precision.

The QFD matrix can be formed and relation matrix can be established. It indicates both direction and strength of relationship. Next competitive assessment can be focussed and remaining steps can be followed as discussed in previous example.

4.2.7 QFD Process—Four Levels of HOQ

In the previous section, the procedure to develop a single QFD house and the steps to be followed to fill the house with information are explained. At each stage, the house of quality contains large amount of information. To obtain maximum benefit from this methodology.

All four levels of houses have to be listed. It is a labour-intensive process and takes more time in planning to reap a project, in terms of shorter development cycle and also meanings need for redesign.

The first house as shown in Fig. 4.14 is constructed by matching customer requirements against design requirements, i.e,. WHATs against HOWs to meet the intended needs. These HOWs became WHATs of in the second house as shown in Fig. 4.15. This process continues until each objective is refined to an automobile level. Each level of house is analysed the same as in first level. The design requirements from first quality house are translated into specific part details. The parts selected then become WHAT of the third matrix plotted against HOWs of the processes used to create parts. This is shown in third house as shown in Fig. 4.16. Finally the processes become WHAT of the last matrix as shown in Fig. 4.17. Where HOWs are process parameters to be controlled. Thus the cascaded matrices are used to fulfil the customer requirements to a set of process parameters to be controlled.

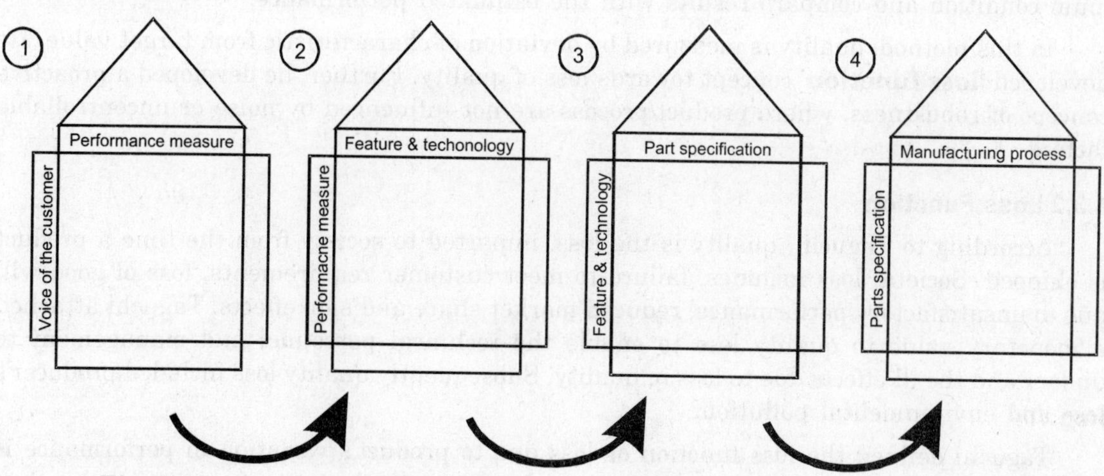

Fig. 4.14 **Fig. 4.15** **Fig. 4.16** **Fig. 4.17**

As seen above, QFD, Four levels of house is tedious and time consuming and became complex with size of matrix. In general cases, one specific house is sufficient, some cases require a second and varies from case to case.

Numerous examples can be cited by employing QFD techniques in developing a new product or improving the features of existing product.

4.3 TAGUCHI'S QUALITY ENGINEERING

4.3.1 Introduction

The design of experiments (DOE) found its roots in the UK and was developed during 1920s. R.A.Fisher in England who wanted to find out how much rain, sunshine, fertilizer and water to produce the best crop developed this concept. DOE combines the statistical techniques, study the effect of multiple variables simultaneously and determine factor combination for optimum result. Dr. Genichi Taguchi, a Japanese mechanical engineer, combined the engineering, statistical methods and experimental design principles with the economy of manufacturing. His philosophy was introduced in the major manufacturing industries to improve quality of product and process design in USA in 1980. Its objective is to design quality into every product and corresponding processes. Taguchi's technique is the off-line quality control method, where efforts are taken to build quality in upstream, i.e., from manufacturing to design phase.

Taguchi methodology is applied in five steps to obtain optimum results. The steps are discussed as follows:

(*i*) *Planning session:* Establish quality parameters or characteristics, factors, level, number of experiments, sample required. It is a team effort and all required parameters are found out through brainstorming.

(*ii*) *Designing and data collection:* Design and describe experiment to be conducted.

(*iii*) *Conducting experiment:* Conduct experiment as per trial descriptions.

(*iv*) *Analysis of results:* Perform complete analysis and determine the best design. Predict the expected performance with confidence. Establish required influence of factors.

(*v*) *Conforming improvements:* Run multiple samples using design prescribed by optimum condition and compare results with the estimated performance.

In this method, quality is measured by deviation of characteristic from target value. He developed **'loss function'** concept towards loss of quality. Further, he developed a proactive concept of robustness, where product/process are not influenced by noise or uncontrollable factors.

4.3.2 Loss Function

According to Taguchi, quality is the loss, imparted to society from the time a product is shipped. Societal loss includes, failure to meet customer requirements, loss of good will due to unsatisfactory performance, reduced market share and side effects. Taguchi attached a monetary value to quality loss to enable the technical personnel and management to understand the ill effects due to loss in quality. Subsequently quality loss included producer's loss and environmental pollution.

Taguchi defined the loss function or loss due to product's variation in performance is proportional to the square of the performance characteristic deviation from its target value.

The relationships between quality loss function and quality characteristic are shown in Figs. 4.18 and 4.19.

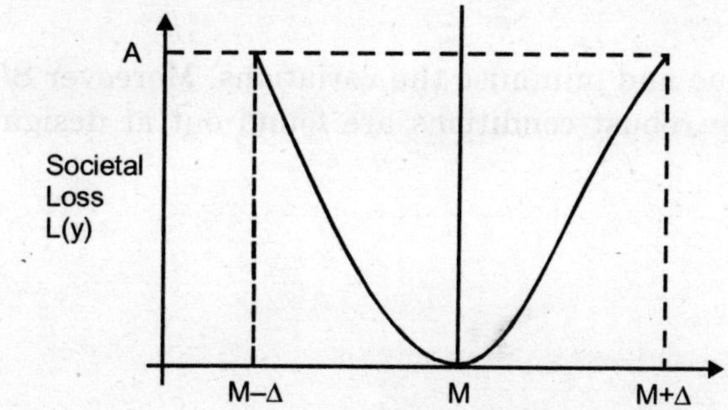

Fig. 4.18 Quadratic

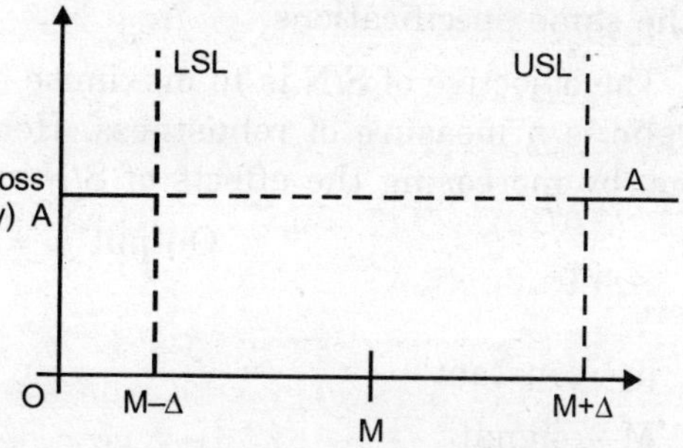

Fig. 4.19 Traditional

When the quality characteristic 'y' is at target value 'm', the loss is at minimum. Deviation of quality characteristic from target value in either direction, increases the losses in a quadratic manner. Loss function indicates that as long as quality characteristic is within certain specific limits, i.e., between upper specification limit (USL) and lower specification limit (LSL), no loss is incurred. It does not distinguish between quality characteristics at target and a value in between two limits. It may have an effect on performance variation but not on the quality. Taguchi's loss function is given by

$$L(y) = k\,(m - y)^2$$

where

k – quality loss coefficient

y – value of quality characteristic

m – target value

Constant 'k' can be evaluated and it is related to financial value of quality characteristics. Essentially, Taguchi defines three types of loss functions.

1. Small is better (e.g., defects, impurity levels)
2. Bigger is better (e.g., mileage, process yields)
3. Target is better (e.g., humidity level, outside and inside diameter)

Taguchi aims to achieve one of the three target based function with minimum variation.

4.3.3 Signal to Noise Ratio (S/N Ratio)

S/N ratio is another method to determine effectiveness of the product / process. It is a proactive strategy equivalent to reactive loss function. By measuring the output quality characteristic, the performance can be evaluated and the impact of design parameters can be studied. The performance contains both desirable and undesirable components in output quality characteristic measured. The desirable component is called signal and undesirable component is called noise.

There are three types of noises:

1. *External noise:* Variable of environment or conditions of use that disturb the product (e.g. Temperature, dust)

2. *Internal noise or deterioration noise:* Changes due to use or during storage.

3. *Unit to unit noise:* Differences exist between individual products that are produced to the same specifications.

The objective of S/N is to maximise its value and minimise the variations. Moreover S/N ratio is a measure of robustness. Hence the robust conditions are found out at design stage, by increasing the effects of S/N ratio.

$$\text{Output } y = \beta.\text{M}$$

where

β – constant

M – signal

Noise occurs due to controllable variables $x_1, x_2 \ldots x_m$

$x_1, x_2 \ldots x_m$ and error factors $z_1, z_2 \ldots z_m$

$$y = f\,(m_1, x_1, x_2 \ldots x_m, z_1, z_2 \ldots z_m)$$

$$\therefore\ y = \beta.\text{M} + [f\,(m_1, x_1, x_2 \ldots x_m, z_1, z_2 \ldots z_m)]$$

the first part in RHS is desirable component (signal) and second part is undesirable component (noise). Better design is achieved, by increasing the value of signal and reducing the value of noise.

The major S/N criteria, in engineering practice are:

1. Nominal the best.
2. Target the best.
3. Smaller than better.
4. Larger than better.
5. Classified attribute.
6. Dynamic.

4.3.4 Taguchi Robust Design

He focussed a design for quality by defining three design levels, as follows:

1. System Design (Primary)

Functional design focussed on related technology. It developed prototype using engineering and scientific knowledge. Customer requirement is taken into consideration at this stage.

2. Parametric Design (Secondary)

It involves both reducing cost and improving performance, without removing causes of variation. Here, optimal conditions are selected so that product is insensitive to noise variables.

3. Tolerance Design (Tertiary)

Here, this method is used to eliminate / reduce the variation by controlling causes, but at an increased cost. When statistical tolerances are beyond limits, then this concept is applied. It uses analysis of variance (ANOVA) to find out which factors contribute the total variability and the loss function. This enables one to decide on the trade off between quality and cost.

The Taguchi methodology has been built on traditional design of experimental methods to improve the design of product and process.

4.4 TOTAL PRODUCTIVE MAINTENANCE (TPM)

4.4.1 History

Total productive maintenance is a new concept, which integrates the maintenance activity in the manufacturing process. Earlier, the maintenance activity was regarded as a non-profit activity. Peak performance of any organization is possible only when current plant and equipment is at its highest productive level, with the cooperation of all areas of organization. This concept is traced back to the concept of productive maintenance originated in USA in late 1940s. The American based productive maintenance, was modified and enhanced to fit into industries in Japan in 1951. Nippondenso was the first company to introduce preventive maintenance in 1960 and it was the first company to obtain TPM certification. The company combined the features of the preventive maintenance and maintenance prevention, resulting in TPM. The aim of TPM is to maximize the plant and equipment effectiveness and achieve optimum life cycle cost of production equipment.

4.4.2 Introduction

TPM diagnoses symptoms of machine and accordingly decides the type of treatment to make it fit for use. Therefore it is also called as 'medical science' of machines. When the running machine breaks down, it does not make money, but it is costing our money also. On the other hand, the running machine makes money through making products, meeting deadlines and keeping customers happy. The companies which adopt JIT concepts demand perfect equipment maintenance. Hence machine breakdown cannot be tolerated. Similarly, company using lean manufacturing system, links all machines and processes. As excessive capacity is minimised, even when one machine stops, the whole productivity gets halted. Therefore, it is essential to devise a prevention strategy to completely eliminate breakdown of machines, besides speeding up repairs to reduce the down time.

The 16 major losses (Kobetsu Kaizen) occurring in industrial organisation have been identified as:

A. Equipment efficiency

1. Breakdown loss
2. Set up or adjustment loss
3. Cutting tool loss
4. Start up loss
5. Idling loss or minor stoppage
6. Speed loss (at low speeds)
7. Loss due to defect or rework
8. Down time loss

B. Human efficiency

1. Management loss
2. Operating motion loss

3. Line organisation loss
4. Logistics (infrastructure) loss
5. Measurement/adjustment loss

C. Ineffective use of resources

1. Energy/power loss
2. Tool, die or jig breakage loss
3. Yield (output) loss

The TPM is implemented along all the *three* directions listed above.

The TPM is team-based production maintenance and involves every level and function in the organisation from top management to the shop floor. The objectives of TPM as:

- Achieve zero defects, breakdown and zero accidents in all functional areas of organization.
- Encourages self-maintenance.
- Meeting deadlines, earning good will of the customer.
- Increase productivity and overall plant efficiency.
- Encourages input from all employees.
- Using small group activities for continual improvement.

Thus TPM combines maintenance techniques and involvement of machine operators who have got better knowledge on the condition of machines. Due to automation of machines, size of production operators is reduced, while size of maintenance personnel is increased. Appropriate training should be given to operators, which enable to detect, find and eliminate potential causes of trouble, before it manifests into system failure. This is the uniqueness of TPM. The TPM program aims to eliminate unplanned equipment and plant maintenance and sudden breakdowns. Care is taken to plan all maintenance activities without disturbing the production.

4.4.3 Types of Maintenance

1. Breakdown Maintenance

Repairing will be done after machine breaks down. This is permitted when equipment failure is not significant.

2. Preventive Maintenance

It includes both periodic maintenance and predictive maintenance. It may be a daily maintenance as in cleaning, oiling, inspection, tightening screws and parts etc or weekly or monthly or yearly to maintain the health of equipment.

3. Periodic Maintenance

Maintenance of equipment is done at certain time based interval and parts are replaced if necessary to avoid sudden failure.

4. Predictive (Diagnostic) Maintenance

The service life of parts used in the machine is determined before the failure, based on the data collected through diagnosis and statistical tools. Maintenance will be scheduled accordingly.

5. Corrective Maintenance

This method improves or modifies the equipment to prevent breakdowns or to make maintenance easier.

6. Maintenance Prevention

This method is used to design and install equipment that needs little or no maintenance.

4.4.4 Steps to Implement TPM in an Organization

TPM is an extension of TQM to maintain function. The first activity is to assess the current performance of equipment, breakdowns, accidents and overall plant efficiency and decide the starting point of TPM. No standard procedure has been developed to implement TPM. The following seven basic steps will form a framework to implement TPM in an organization. It can also be modified according to requirements of organization.

1. Management understanding concept.
2. Management introducing concept.
3. Training the employees.
4. Improvement needs.
5. Goal.
6. Developing plans.
7. Autonomous work groups.

Step 1: Management understanding the concept

Proper understanding, commitment and active involvement of the top management are needed. The management must accept the change and learn about TPM. This philosophy must be integrated with corporate culture, to gain competitive advantage. It needs dedication from management, a long-term support from top to bottom. As TPM is trying to tap unused resources, the brainpower and ability of employees, the management must allow people to make decisions.

Step 2: Management introducing the concept

Upon understanding the philosophy, it is the duty of top management to practice it. Initially it is communicated through announcements, letters to concerned individuals, publishing in the house magazine and display in the notice board. The operating and maintenance personnel are given more autonomy. Management must lead the way and make it known to the employees that it is serious in implementing the philosophy. This gives a positive direction to employees and gets response effectively.

Step 3: Training the employees

Training has to be given to the employees at all levels. It begins with senior management to first line supervisors. Some may need intensive teaching and some may need awareness program. In teaching process, not only the procedure of TPM but also 'why's should be explained. Training aims to have multi skilled employees whose morale is high and perform all required functions effectively and independently. Education is given to operators to upgrade their skills. It also includes providing required training environment for self-learning and training to remove employee fatigue and make work more enjoyable.

***Step 4:* Improvement needs**

Small groups, technicians and operators will identify the condition of machines and inform the volume and quality of service required for each machine to the management. Since equipment problems drain productivity, the following seven major (from among the 16) losses have to be measured and tracked.

1. Breakdown losses.
2. Set up and adjustment loss.
3. Idling and minor stoppages.
4. Reduced speed.
5. Non conformance and rework.
6. Start up.
7. Yield loss.

These losses have to be quantified and translated into equipment effectiveness and eradicated by adopting the following procedures

1. Install suitable equipment in the first place.
2. Daily maintenance.
3. Periodic inspection.
4. Restoration to correct from deterioration.

Besides this, safety is one of the basic principles of TPM. Safety principles highlight dangerous conditions and behaviour of machines to cause accidents.

Down time losses can be quantified as follows:

(i) Availability of machine: It is ratio of time a machine is available to the total time it should be available.

$$A = T/P \times 100$$

where,

A – Availability in percent

T – Operating time (P-D)

D – Down time

P – Planned operating time

(ii) Performance efficiency (PE): It is measured to find out reduced speed losses, i.e., how much actual cycle time is slower than design cycle time.

$$PE = (C \times N/T) \times 100$$

where

PE – Performance efficiency in percent

C – Theoretical cycle time

N – Processed quantity

(*iii*) *Rate of quality:* It refers to what is the percentage of good parts out of total produced. This is sometimes called yield and represent poor quality losses.

$$Q = (N - R/N) \times 100$$

where

Q – Rate of quality products

N – Processed quantity

R – Non-conformities

(*iv*) *Equipment effectiveness (EE):* Equipment effectiveness (EE) is product of three previous quantities *i.e.,*

$$EE = A \times PE \times Q$$

Normally, the target for improvement is 90% for overall equipment effectiveness and 80% for overall plant effectiveness.

***Step 5:* Goal**

This step begins with identification of needs and setting goals. The goals are time framed and based on prioritising the problems. To achieve the goal, TPM requires activities in *eight* key areas, such as listed:

1. Focussed improvement to make equipment more efficient.
2. Autonomous maintenance.
3. Planned maintenance.
4. Quality maintenance.
5. Early equipment management program.
6. Technical training.
7. Office TPM.
8. Safety, health and environment.

***Step 6:* Developing plans**

This step involves developing and implementing an overall plan of action. It includes:

- Training all employees.
- Formation of autonomous work groups.
- Use teams of maintenance and operators to work on troublesome problems.
- Change of team structure as processes and procedures are improved.

***Step 7:* Autonomous work groups**

It is a team consisting of maintenance crew and operators. The operators may be able to do routine maintenance and are trained by skilled maintenance personnel to do certain tasks like troubleshooting and set ups. This team is authorised to make decisions to keep machine fit for production. The objective of this group, is to reduce the occasions for maintenance activity. Another benefit is to free the skilled maintenance personnel to undertake major overhaul and assisting with trouble shooting problems that autonomous group is unable to do. *Autonomous work group* is a team consisting of maintenance personnel and operation. This team is given authority to make decision to keep machine fit enough for production. Here maintenance personnel act as consultants and offer training to workers to handle minor trouble shooting and set up, besides their routine maintenance.

4.5 FAILURE MODE AND EFFECT ANALYSIS (FMEA)

4.5.1 History

The products and processes that do not meet the customer requirements or fail to perform cannot be considered as good quality. Proactive strategies are adopted to focus on failure prevention. FMEA is one of the qualitative tools, which support proactive quality strategies. Successful implementation of FMEA requires relevant knowledge and insight as well as engineering judgement. FMEA concept has been there for long time. It was introduced in the late 1940s along with the introduction of military standards. It was encouraged in 1960s by aerospace companies. Then the use of FMEA was extended to automobile industries and other types of industries, understanding the value of this approach. In the last decade, it has undergone metamorphosis where focus was on severity, occurrence and detection rating.

4.5.2 Introduction

In the early 1980, the word "continual improvement" was introduced to the quality standards. Since then the concept is focussed on "prevention" than "appraisal". In this context, many concepts were introduced: the 6σ, lean manufacturing, QFD etc. FMEA is one such tool, adopted to improve the existing product or to develop a new product. This is done through identification, elimination, control or reduction of risk. It is the commitment of the organization for a variety of reasons, namely, customer demand, a part of continual improvement and competition. This concept identifies, what can go wrong? If so, what are the probability or frequency and effects on the performance? Hence, it is widely used to improve the reliability of product. Therefore FMEA is defined as a systematic tool to identify possible failure modes in the products / process, to understand failure mechanism (process that leads to failure), and effects of failure on the performance level and action plans for elimination or reduction of failure modes and documenting the whole procedure.

This approach helps us in the following ways :

- Prevention of failure.
- Elimination/reduction of waste.
- Increase of the reliability.

Traditionally, reliability techniques will be applied in the later stages of product development. Reliability is defined as the probability of product to perform as expected, under specified operating condition, for a given period of time and at a set of product performance characteristics. Safety is one of the critical parameters, when reliability testing is performed. Conventionally, engineers do the good job of evaluating the functions and form of products and processes in the design phase, but do not include reliability and quality in design phase. However, engineers rely on introducing factor of safety to make the design work and protect the end user from failure. A large safety factor will lead to over-designed product with reliability problems. The detection of failures at later stages does not help the organisation.

But this methodology is applied early in the development cycle in analysing the potential reliability problems of the product and enhances the reliability through design. Thus the early use of FMEA in design process helps engineers to produce safe, reliable and customer satisfying products. The data collected is used for future product improvement.

4.5.3 Types of FMEA

System FMEA – focuses on global system functions.

Design FMEA – focuses on components and subsystems.

Process FMEA – focuses on manufacturing and assembly process.

Service FMEA – focuses on service function.

Software FMEA – focuses on software function.

However for all purposes, all these types mentioned above can be categorised under design FMEA and process FMEA.

4.5.4 Design FMEA

It helps in design process by identifying and anticipating failure modes and ranking them according to their severity on the product performance. Then keep these design characteristics out of the system or at least minimize the resulting effects. Further, methods and procedures are to be developed to test product/process to validate them and ensure that it should not cause injury or affect the end user and surroundings. Thereby, design FMEA contributes to the reduction in developing time and cost of manufacturing.

4.5.5 Process FMEA

It is used to identify potential failure modes and rank them according to their severity and frequency. The prioritisation is done according to their customer requirements. It helps in identifying potential manufacturing or assembly causes in order to establish control or reduce occurrence and detection.

4.5.6 Procedure of FMEA

FMEA is a team approach. It is a cross functional management, where the team leader is responsible for coordinating all activities such as meeting time, place and frequency, corrective action and preventive action, follow up and developing and maintaining FMEA related documents. FMEA is a live document. Throughout the product development cycles, changes and updates will be introduced to the product and process. These changes have to be reviewed because they can also introduce new failure modes and therefore it is important to review and update changes. Following are the steps to conduct FMEA:

1. Product/process and its function must be understood, as all problems are not same. This is the most fundamental concept to be adopted in this methodology. This understanding helps the engineer to identify product/process function that fall within the intended and unintended users.
2. Block diagram of product/process has to be created and developed. The diagram shows the major components or process steps as blocks, identifies and shows their relations namely, input, function and output of the design. The diagram shows logi-

cal relationship of components and establishes a structure around which FMEA can be developed. The block diagram should always be included in the FMEA form.

3. Header on FMEA form has to be completed. FMEA form is discussed in detail subsequently. It includes part/process name, model date, revision date, responsibility, etc.
4. Thus the items/functions are listed logically in the FMEA form, based on the block diagram.
5. Then failure modes are identified. A failure mode is defined wherein component, subsystem, system, process, etc., could potentially fail to meet the design intent.
6. A failure mode in one component can cause failure in another component. Each failure should be listed in technical terms. Listing should be done component or process wise.
7. Then the effects of each failure mode have to be described. This is done as perceived by both internal and external customers. The examples of failure effect may include injury to user, environment, equipment, degraded performance etc. Then a numerical ranking is assigned to each failure. It depends upon the severity of the effect. Commonly, scale 1 is used to represent no effect and 10 to indicate very severe failure, affecting system of operation and user. By this, the failures can be prioritised and real big issues can be addressed first.
8. Then the causes of each failure mode have to be identified. A failure cause is defined as a design weakness that results in a failure. The potential causes for each failure mode should be identified and documented. The potential causes, for example, may be improper torque, contamination, excessive loading, etc.
9. Then the probability factor indicating the frequency of occurrence is considered. A numerical weightage can be assigned to each cause depending upon probability of occurrence. A standard scale is used, 1 indicates 'not likely' and 10 indicates 'inevitable'.
10. Current control mechanisms (Design and Process) have to be identified, which can prevent the cause of failure or detect failure, before it reaches customer. Accordingly, the team has to identify tests, analysis, monitoring and other techniques to detect failure. Previously undetected or unidentified failures may appear when a new product / process are introduced. Therefore FMEA should be updated and the required plans for the elimination of failures have to be drawn.
11. Assessment of detection rating has to be done. A numerical weightage can be assigned. Value 1 indicates, design control will certainly detect the potential cause, 10 indicates design control will not detect the cause or mechanism. A normal scale of 1 – 10 is used.
12. Risk Priority Number (RPN) is calculated and reviewed.

    $$\text{RPN} = \text{Severity} \times \text{Probability} \times \text{Detection}$$

    It is used to prioritise failure modes and viewed as a relative measure of the design risk.
13. Recommended actions have to be determined to address potential failures that have high RPN.
14. Responsibility and target completion date for these actions have to be assigned.

15. Revalidate each action by reassessing severity, probability and detection and review the revised new RPN. Check any further action is needed.

FMEA has to be updated as and when the design or process is modified or changed.

4.5.7 Pre-requirements for Conducting FMEA

1. Understanding the problem. All problems are not same.
2. Customer must be defined. Customer is not necessarily the end user. The worker doing second operation becomes a customer to the worker doing first operation.
3. Also the function, purpose and objective of what is to be accomplished must be known.
4. Team involved must be prevention oriented and always continual improvement factor should drive the FMEA.

4.5.8 Benefits of FMEA

1. Assists in finding out the best possible design and development options and providing high reliability and manufacturing part.
2. Provides a well-documented record, which includes improvements from corrective actions implemented, historical information useful in analysing product failures during manufacturing process and new ideas for improvement in similar design or process.
3. Design time or product development cycle time is reduced due to timely identification and correction of problems.
4. Improves quality, reliability and safety of product/service.
5. Improves company's reputation and competitive advantage including best in class value, defect free launch, cost effectiveness and quality performance.
6. Increases customer satisfaction.
7. List potential failures and identifies relative magnitude of their effects.
8. Improves organisational capability including best of class design, breakthrough technology and market value.
9. Establishes a superior work culture including right attitudes, efforts for continual improvement and team spirit.
10. Establishes a test program requirement to determine every failure mode and predict reliability value.

4.5.9 Stages of FMEA

Earlier, the pre requisites needed for conducting FMEA and steps to be followed during FMEA have been discussed in detail. These steps can be formed to four stages as given below.

Stage 1

It involves identifying possibilities and defines the scope. It includes function, possible failure mode, causes and effects of failure mode and detection/prevention of failure mode.

Stage 2

It measures the volume of risk involved from the failure modes identified. It includes the probability of cause and occurrence, severity of effect and effectiveness of control to prevent cause, assessment of Risk Priority Number (RPN).

Stage 3

It classifies severity of effects and solves high risk causes. This is done through the value of RPN. Based on RPN, it prioritises work, detailed action, assigning responsibility and target completion time to the team members and gets their consent.

Stage 4

It revalidates the above procedure, after corrective and preventive action is implemented. Checks whether target data and work is met. Review RPN and decide if any further action is needed.

4.5.10 Design/Process FMEA Document

The top portion of document is called header and mainly used for tracking the document. Expect the first column of work sheet, all other details remain the same. Header includes following :

Model No

It includes name and identification number of system, sub system or component in order to avoid confusion between similar components.

Prepared by

The details like name, telephone number, address of the personnel should be included in the space for clarification, if any.

Responsibility

The team in charge of design or process should be included in this space. It also includes the company or department of the person or group responsible for preparing the document.

It is a common work sheet that can be used both for both design FMEA and process FMEA. In design FMEA, following points are to be entered.

- Name and number of item.
- Listing the function of the item (system or sub system or component wise).
- Environment in which system operates.

In Process FMEA, descriptions of processes, listing of processes and complete purpose of processes have to be entered.

FMEA Team

The names of responsible individuals and departments that have authority to perform task should be included.

FMEA Date

The date of original FMEA compiled should be entered. In revision column latest revision data should be entered.

Potential Failure Mode

It lists the possible failure modes to meet design intent or process requirements. The beginning point is to collect information as listed in potential failure modes that caused failures in the past, concerned reports and brainstorming.

Table 4.1 FMEA work sheet

Design (or) Process FMEA

Model No. FMEA team members						Prepared by FMEA date (original)					Responsibility Date of revision					
Process / Product	Potential Cause of Failure	Potential Effect(s) of Failure	Severity	Class	Potential Cause(s)/ Mechanism(s) of Failure	Occurrence	Current Process Control	Detection	RPN	Recommended Actions	Responsibility and Target Completion Dates	Action Result				
												Action Taken	SEV	OCC	DET	RPN

In design FMEA, it may be methods in which item being analysed fail to meet design criteria or method may cause potential failure in the system. In process FMEA, the process could potentially fail to meet the requirements. Also, it can introduce potential failure modes in subsequent operation. Each potential failure mode for particular operation must be listed. The assumption made is that the failure could but not necessarily occur.

Potential Effects of Failure

It is defined as how a customer perceived the failure. The customer may include subsequent design/manufacturing operator and or the end customer. It must state the impact failure on personal safety and environment and break any product regulations. It also forecasts the effects of possible failure modes that have been listed earlier on the system, sub system or components. Some typical effects of failure may include noise, impaired operations, erratic operation, poor appearance, etc.

Severity

It is the assessment of seriousness of the effect of potential failure mode to the next component or the end user. It is applied to the effects of failure mode and to the potential failure. A value will be assigned depending upon the severity of the effects of failure. Severity is rated as 1–10 scale with a 1 being none and a 10 being very severe. The evaluation criteria is given in Table 4.2.

Table 4.2 System severity ranking

Effect	Severity of effect	Ranking
Hazardous without warning	Very high severity ranking when a potential failure mode affects safe system operation without warning.	10
Hazardous with warning	Very high severity ranking when a potential failure mode affects safe system operation with warning.	9
Very high	System inoperable with destructive failure without compromising safety.	8
High	System inoperable with equipment damage. Customer dissatisfied.	7
Moderate	System inoperable with minor damage. Customer feels discomfort.	6
Low	System inoperable without damage. Customer has some dissatisfaction.	5
Very low	System inoperable with significant degradation of performance. Noticed by most customers.	4
Minor	System inoperable with some degradation of performance. Noticed by average customers.	3
Very minor	System inoperable with minimal interference. Noticed by discriminating customers.	2
None	No effect.	1

Classification (CLASS)

This column is used to classify any special product/process characteristic for components, sub systems or system that may require additional process controls.

Potential Causes/Mechanism of Failure

Every potential failure cause and or mechanism must be stated completely and concisely. Proper cause identification requires some understanding of the failure mechanism based on process, mechanics. The cause will be known if we have identified the source or origin of potential failure. Then all the possible causes have to be examined and listed. The each of the listed causes has to be reviewed with equal weight. The cause and effect diagram, five Whys and fault tree analysis will be useful to identify possible causes of each failure and probability of failure.

Occurrence

It is the chance or probability that one of the specific causes/mechanism will occur. This has to be done for every cause and mechanism listed. The elimination or reduction in occurrence must come from any reasoning except for a direct change in design. Design change is only way by which reduction in the occurrence ranking can be affected. A scale of 1 to 10 is used to measure the severity criteria. The value 1 being the least chance of occurrence while 10 being highest chance of occurrence. The example is given in Table 4.3. Team has to work together to achieve consensus concerning ranking scores.

Table 4.3 Rankings of probability of failure

Probability of failure	Failure probability	Ranking
Very High: Failure is almost inevitable	> 1 in 2	10
	1 in 3	9
High: Repeated failures	1 in 8	8
	1 in 20	7
Moderate: Occasional failures	1 in 80	6
	1 in 400	5
	1 in 2,000	4
Low: Relatively few failures	1 in 15,000	3
	1 in 150,000	2
Remote: Failure is unlikely	< 3.4 in 1,000,000	1

Current Design Controls

It lists down all the methods of control for controlling the performance of product/process. Types of control methods vary with respect to different problems. The controls may include:

1. Measurement based control involving.

   Management review, Statistical process control techniques.

2. Documentation includes.

   Process flow diagrams, Product drawing, Specification, Process management plan and written procedures.

3. Design involving mistake proofing, Robust process design, Design out product/ process problems and design reviews.

4. Test and inspection.

5. Periodic check involves scheduled maintenance, Scheduled calibration, Training, operator calibration and audits.
6. Incentives includes measures associated with bonus, measures associated with penalty.

These methods are applied to :

(*a*) Prevent the cause or mechanism or failure mode effect from occurring (or) mitigates the rate of occurrence.

(*b*) Detect the cause and take appropriate action.

(*c*) Detect only failure.

Obviously, first type of design control is preferred, if possible. In order to achieve this, design control must become part of the design and severity rating will be changed in the subsequent documentation. If it is not possible to apply first control, second control is preferred. Third control does not help to reduce the occurrence rate of failure mode.

Detection

This column indicates the ability of design control / process control that can prevent or detect each of failure mechanisms. The probability that each control will effectively detect the failure is assigned a numeric value. The example is given in Tables 4.4 and 4.5. The evaluation criteria and ranking should be assigned based on the consensus of team and used throughout life of FMEA.

Table 4.4 Detection ranking table for design FMEA

Detection	Likelihood of detection by design control	Ranking
Cannot Detect	Design control cannot detect potential cause/mechanism and subsequent failure mode	10
Very Remote	Very Remote chance the design control will detect potential cause/mechanism and subsequent failure mode	9
Remote	Remote chance the design control will detect potential cause/mechanism and subsequent failure mode	8
Very Low	Very Low chance the design control will detect potential cause/mechanism and subsequent failure mode	7
Low	Low chance the design control will detect potential cause/mechanism and subsequent failure mode	6
Moderate	Moderate chance the design control will detect potential cause/mechanism and subsequent failure mode	5
Moderately High	Moderately high chance the design control will detect potential cause/mechanism and subsequent failure mode	4
High	High chance the design control will detect potential cause/mechanism and subsequent failure mode	3
Very High	Very high chance the design control will detect potential cause/mechanism and subsequent failure mode	2
Almost Certain	Design control will detect potential cause/mechanism and subsequent failure mode	1

Risk Priority Number (RPN)

It is the product of severity, occurrence and detection. i.e., RPN = (S) (O) (D). The product may be viewed and assessed and engineering judgement is used to detect, if work is acceptable. Values for the RPN can range from 1 to 1000 with 1 being smallest design risk possible. Then, rank the failure modes by RPN score from high to low. Based on RPN, appropriate actions can be prioritised. It does not mean failure with low RPN can be overlooked. Sometimes it can be disastrous. Therefore team members should give full attention on all failure modes and methods. All available methods should be exhausted to reduce RPN. The RPN interpretation is summarised in Table 4.6.

Table 4.5 Detection ranking table for process FMEA

Detection	Additional detection criteria	Rank
Cannot Detect	Absolute certainty of non-detection of defective product prior to shipment	10
Very Remote	Test/inspection probably will not detect defective product	9
Remote	Test/inspection will catch all but 25% of defective product	8
Very Low	Test/inspection will catch all but 10% of defective product	7
Low	Test/inspection will catch all but 1.00% of defective product	6
Moderate	Test/inspection will catch all but 0.25% of defective product	5
Moderately High	Test/inspection will catch all but 500 defects per million of defective product	4
High	Test/inspection will catch all but 60 defects per million of defective product	3
Very High	Test/inspection will catch all but 3.4 defects per million of defective product	2
Almost Certain	Test/inspection will catch all but 1 defects per billion of defective product	1

Table 4.6 RPN interpretation

RPN	Why	What to do
High	Due to probability of failure	Change design or process
High	Due to severity	Change design or process
High	Due to detection	Change process control/test method
Moderate	Due to detection	Consider improving present control/test method
Moderate	Due to probability of failure	Consider changing design or process
Moderate	Due to severity	Consider changing design or process
Low	All	Maintain present status

Recommended Action

Team examines the proposed corrective actions, giving priority to the top RPN and working in descending order of RPN. If no recommended actions are possible, 'None' has to be entered in the document for future reference. The purpose of action is to reduce or eliminate occurrence, improve control and improve containment by increasing the probability of detection. This action can include design of experiments, revised test plan, revised design, revised material selection and specification. This is done to reduce the rank in occurrence rating and severity rating.

Responsibility of Target Completion Dates

Individual or group has to assign the responsibility to carry out the recommended action and completion of target as scheduled. Before assigning the task, the expertise of members and availability to the task has to be matched.

Actions Taken

After action has been implemented, a brief description of the actual action and its effected date must be entered. This is useful for tracking the progress of plan. Then severity, occurrence and detecting ranking have to be re-estimated. Then, the new RPN have to be calculated and recorded in FMEA. The resulting RPN has to be evaluated and if necessary, appropriate actions have to be repeated. If no actions are taken, this section must be left blank.

4.5.11 Example of FMEA Document Preparation

As an example, FMEA approach is explained for a pressure cooker in Fig. 4.20. The failure modes in pressure cooker are identified and represented in block diagram for easy understanding of the concept. It is also shown in the FMEA documentation Table 4.7.

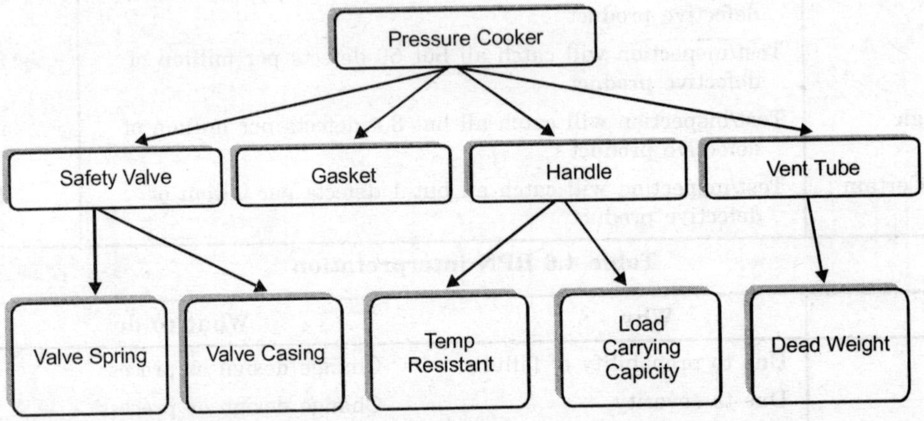

Fig. 4.20

Safety Features

Four safety features are provided. They are:

1. *Weight valve and vent tube:* Weight valve is used as pressure controller and time of the pressure cooking.
2. *Safety plug:* It has two functions, namely.
   (*i*) To work as a pressure indicator whether to open the lid or not.
   (*ii*) Acts as a fusible plug in case dead weight and gasket system fails to act.
3. *Gasket system:* If weight fails to act, gasket system acts to release pressure.
4. *Proper handle:* The handle is to lift the vessel including contents and it is to be heat resistant.

Other details like classification, potential causes of failure, etc., can be suitably made and RPN rating can be estimated. Accordingly actions are formulated and validated by the team. Then these actions are implemented to reduce the risks.

Table 4.7 FMEA work sheet

Design FMEA

Model No.					**Prepared by**					**Responsibility**						
FMEA team members					**FMEA date (original)**					**Date of revision**						
Process/ Product	Potential Cause of Failure	Potential Effect(s) of Failure	Severity	Class	Potential Cause(s)/ Mechanism(s) of Failure	Occurrence	Current Process Control	Detection	RPN	Recommended Actions	Responsibility and Target Completion Dates	Action Results				
												Action Taken	SEV	OCC	DET	RPN
Pressure Cooker	Failure of Deadweight and Vent tube	Very high. Safe use is not guaranteed	8			8		4	256							
	Failure of fusible plug	High causes e.g. Damage	7			5		4	140							
	Failure of Gasket	System operatble with some dissatisfactions	5			6		7	210							
	Failure of Handle	System opertable with some digradation of performance	4			3		2	24							

□□□

CHAPTER 5

Quality Systems

5.1 HISTORY OF QUALITY AND NEED OF A QUALITY SYSTEM

There is a fundamental and major shift in the way we view and approach the issue of quality towards customers. Before industrial revolution, the quality relied heavily on craftsman. It was an era of workmanship. After industrial revolution, the concept of mass production and interchangeability were introduced. The craftsmen became inspectors and standards were set. The gauges, tolerances and all above together, perhaps, laid the foundation of modern quality systems. It started with inspection to find and fix mistakes. The reactive strategy was followed.

Then quality control method was adopted, wherein statistical process control techniques played a major role. Here mistakes were detected and either modified or rejected. It is followed by quality assurance, where greater emphasis on design and production was made. The quality improvement took a further step by systematically identify and stop problems at source, if not possible, reduce these introduction of these factors into manufacturing. The recent technique is to build quality at design stage itself. The proactive strategy, which is based on cause and effect knowledge rather than historical data, is adopted.

Thus a quality system has become vital for the survival of an organisation. It adopts a strategy wherein quality is not decided at end; but it is process oriented. It is done systematically at every stage, right from procurement to product. To achieve quality improvement, the quality system must consist of required tools, techniques, methods and measures that help to plan, control and improve quality.

5.2 ISO—INTRODUCTION

ISO stands for International Organisation for Standards and abbreviated as ISO. The word ISO is derived from Greek, meaning equal. ISO was formed in the year 1947 with 25 members representing each from a Nation with headquarters at Geneva, Switzerland. Now, it consists of more than 148 countries. Each nation is represented by its National Standards Institute. For example, Bureau of Indian Standards (BIS) represents India, whereas American National Standard Institute (ANSI) represents the United States. It has a membership of over 170 National Standards Institutes from all over the world.

5.2.1 Need for ISO

Basically standards not only meet customer satisfaction but also raise the levels of quality, safety, reliability, efficiency and interchangeability at economical cost. After liberalisation, globalisation and privatisation policy, the international standardisation has become essential to have fair and free trade across the globe. ISO is the largest developer of standards. The technical committee of ISO, comprising of experts from industrial, technical and business sectors, is responsible for developing standards and put them into use. Others having relevant knowledge such as representatives from government agencies, testing laboratories, consumer association, environmentalists, academia, help the experts. The main objective of ISO is to develop standards, which have important economic and social implications. It not only helps the organisation (manufacturer/service, health or legal and other professional services) in solving fundamental problems in production and distribution but to the society in total. They provide government with a technical base for health, safety and environment legislation. ISO is a voluntary organisation occupying a pivotal position between public and private sectors in which unanimous opinion can be reached on solution so that both the requirements of business and needs of society are met. The ISO standards on quantities and units help us to conduct shipping and trade without chaos and confusion and help the world community to use scientific and technological development effectively. In addition, international standards help us to preserve the environment and make the planet habitable.

e.g., standardisation of dimensions of freight containers, standardisation of paper size, credit cards used in banking, grades of materials, etc., and finally establishment of safety standards that protect people. In general, international standards can contribute to the quality of life.

5.3 WHAT IS ISO 9000?

ISO Technical Committee (TC) 176 developed a series of international standards for quality systems, thus creating a revolution in the management of world wide quality in 1987 and subsequently interim revision was carried out in the years 1994, 2000 and 2008. These standards are termed as ISO 9000, a series of quality assurance methods to be practiced within the company. It is designed and intended to apply to virtually any product or service made by processes. A well designed, well implemented, rightly interpreted and carefully managed ISO 9000 quality system provides confidence that output of processes will meet customer expectations and requirements. It is aimed at providing confidence to all stakeholders of the company.

ISO 9000 became accepted reference internationally for quality management in business dealing. They are ISO 9000, 9001, 9002, 9003, 9004 and ISO 8402. Each standard contains specific guidelines pertaining to certain segment of quality related activities.

ISO 8402–quality management and quality assurance - vocabulary provides terminology used in other four standards.

ISO 9000–It is a guideline for selection and use of the standard on quality management, quality system elements and quality assurance. Also it provides road map; how a company can select and use a particular standard and among four standards in series.

ISO 9001–Quality assurance in design / development, production, installation and servicing where suppliers, capability is demonstrated through quality system to the buyers.

ISO 9002–Quality assurance in production, installation and servicing where suppliers' capability is demonstrated through quality system to the buyers.

ISO 9003–Quality assurance in final inspection and test.

In general, all the above three standards are applied in contractual situation and aimed at preventing non-conformity at each step. Here statistical quality control methods play a major role here.

ISO 9004–guidelines for quality management and quality system elements that is applied in non-contractual situation, i.e., it can develop good quality management system, implement them for internal use.

The quality system registration or ISO 9000 certification process involves the assessment of company's stated quality policy, its conformance of quality system to the standards. This process can be carried out by two party system or three party system. In two party system, customer audit the conformance of the system and found to be costlier. Now it is replaced by three party system if the third party or certification body found that system conforms to standard, certificate of registration will be issued to the supplier for a period of three years. The system is reviewed through surveillance audits semi annually and a complete reassessment after every three years because suppliers scope may change.

5.3.1 ISO 9001:2008 Series of Standards

Extensive surveys have been conducted on a worldwide basis to understand the experience and needs of all stakeholders of quality management system standards, resulting in 2000 versions of standard. Current revision has taken into account the previous experiences with QMS (1987 and 1994 revisions) and emerging insights into "generic management system".

'Generic' means that same standards can be applied to any organisation (large or small), product - including whether its product is actually a service in any sector of activity and whether it is enterprise, public administration or a government department. Management system refers to how organisations manage its processes or activities. Generic also specifies that it can be applied to any organisation and if it is desirous of implementing quality management systems, the required guidelines and regulations are available in ISO 9000.

The standards in the ISO 9000 family include the following:

ISO 9000:2005 – *QMS Fundamentals and vocabulary*

ISO 9001:2008 – *QMS - Requirements*

ISO 9004:2009 – *Managing for the sustained success of an organisation-A QM approach*

ISO 19011:2012 – *Guidelines for internal and external audits of QMS.*

ISO 9001:2008 sets out the criteria for a QMS and is the only standard in the family that can be certified to (although this is not a requirement). It can be used by any organisation, large or small, regardless of its field of activity. This standard is implemented by over one million companies and organisations in over 170 countries and 11,11,698 certificates have been issued by Nov. 2011. This standard basically re-narrates 2000 version. 2008 version introduced only clarifications to the existing requirements of 2000 version and some changes intended to improve consistency with ISO 24001:2004. There were *no new requirements*. For example, in ISO 9001:2008, a QMS being upgraded just needs to be checked to see if it is following the clarifications introduced in the amended version.

ISO 9001:2008 requires that a QMS in an organisation needs to demonstrate its ability to consistently provide product that meets customer and applicable statutory and regulatory requirements, and aims to enhance customer satisfaction through the effective application of the system, including processes for continual improvement of the system and the assurance of conformity to customer and applicable statutory and regulatory requirements. All requirements of ISO 9001:2008 are generic and are intended to be applicable to all organisations, regardless of type, size and product provided.

ISO 9004-2009 gives guidance on a wider range of objectives of a QMS than does 9001, particularly in managing for the sustained (long-term) success of an organisation. This is recommended as a guide for organisations whose top management wishes to extend the benefits of ISO 9001 in pursuit of systematic and continual improvement of organisation's overall performance. However, it is not intended for certification or contractual purposes.

ISO 19011:2012 covers the area of internal and external audits for QMS and EMS. 19011 provides guidance on the audit programs, the conduct of internal or external audits, and information on auditor competence. It provides an overview of how an audit programme should operate and how management system audits should take place. Effective audits ensure that an implemented QMS meets the requirements specified in ISO 9001.

5.4 MAJOR ELEMENTS IN ISO 9001:2008

Using the eight management principles as a foundation (discussed below), the standards are structured around four distinct process related modules as outlined below:

1. *Management responsibility*–requires top management commitment to create and maintain awareness of the importance of fulfilling customer requirements; establish the quality policy and the quality objectives and planning; establish a quality management system; perform management reviews and ensure availability of resources in time.
2. *Resource management*–requires that the organisation determines and provides the needed resources to establish and maintain the quality management system.
3. *Product realization*–requires an organisation to use outputs from quality planning and see that other processes are consistent to realize that required product and/or service. Their sequence and interaction must then be determined, planned and implemented.
4. *Measurement, analysis and improvement*–requires an organisation to define, plan and implement measurement, monitoring and analysis processes to ensure that the quality management system, processes, and products and / or services conform to requirements and continually improve the effectiveness of quality management system.

The model of a process based quality management system is shown in Fig. 5.1, illustrates the process linkages presented in Clauses 4 to 8. This illustration shows, that customers play a significant role in defining requirement as inputs. Monitoring of customer satisfaction requires the evaluation of information obtained through feedback from customer relating to quality perception, as to whether the organisation has met the customer requirements. The model shown covers all the requirements of this standard, but does not show processes at a detailed level.

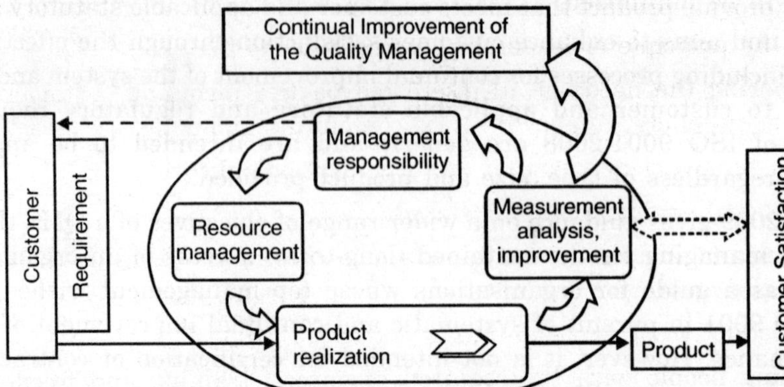

Fig. 5.1

5.5 QUALITY MANAGEMENT PRINCIPLES

The eight quality management principles are defined in ISO 9000:2005 and in ISO 9004:2009. They can be used by senior management as a framework to guide their organisations towards improved performance.

5.5.1 Principle 1 – Customer Focus

Organisations should understand current and future customer needs, meet customer requirements and strive to exceed customer expectations. The key benefits are (1) Increased revenue and market share obtained through flexible and fast responses to market opportunities, (2) Increased effectiveness in the use of the organisation's resources to enhance customer satisfaction and (3) Improved customer loyalty leading to repeat business.

Appling this principle of customer focus typically leads to:

- Researching and understanding customer needs and expectations
- Ensuring that the objectives of the organisation are linked to customer needs and expectations
- Communicating customer needs and expectations throughout the organisation
- Measuring customer satisfaction and acting on the results
- Systematically managing customer relationships
- Ensuring a balanced approach between satisfying customers and other interested parties (owners, employees, suppliers, financiers, local communities and society as a whole).

5.5.2 Principle 2 – Leadership

Leaders establish unity of purpose and direction of the organisation. They should create and maintain the internal environment in which people can become fully involved in achieving the organisation's objectives. The key benefits include: (1) People will understand and be motivated towards the organisation's goals and objectives, (2) Activities are evaluated, aligned and implemented in a unified way and (3) Miscommunication between levels of an organisation will be minimized.

Applying the principle of leadership typically leads to:

- Considering the needs of all interested parties including customers, owners, employees, suppliers, financiers, local communities and society as a whole
- Establishing a clear vision of the organisation's future
- Setting challenging goals and targets
- Creating and sustaining shared values, fairness and ethical role models at all levels of the organisation
- Establishing trust and eliminating fear
- Providing people with the required resources, training and freedom to act with responsibility and accountability
- Inspiring, encouraging and recognising people's contributions.

5.5.3 Principle 3 – Involvement of People

People at all levels are the essence of an organisation and their full involvement enables their abilities to be used for the organisation's benefit. The key benefits are: (1) Motivated, committed and involved people within the organisation, (2) Innovation and creativity in furthering the organisation's objectives, (3) People being accountable for their own performance and (4) People eager to participate and contribute to continual improvement.

Applying the principle of involvement of people typically leads to:

- People understanding the importance of their contribution and role in the organisation
- People identifying constraints to their performance
- People accepting ownership of problems and their responsibility for solving them
- People evaluating their performance against their personal goals and objectives
- People actively seeking opportunities to enhance their competence, knowledge and experience
- People freely sharing knowledge and experience
- People openly discussing problems and issues.

5.5.4 Principle 4 – Process Approach

A desired result is achieved more efficiently when activities and related resources are managed as a process. The key benefits include: (1) Lower costs and shorter cycle times through effective use of resources, (2) Improved, consistent and predictable results and (3) Focused and prioritized improvement opportunities.

Applying the principle of process approach typically leads to:

- Systematically defining the activities necessary to obtain a desired result
- Establishing clear responsibility and accountability for managing key activities

- Analysing and measuring of the capability of key activities
- Identifying the interfaces of key activities within and between the functions of the organisation
- Focusing on the factors – such as resources, methods, and materials – that will improve key activities of the organisation
- Evaluating risks, consequences and impacts of activities on customers, suppliers and other interested parties.

5.5.5 Principle 5 – System Approach to Management

Identifying, understanding and managing inter-related processes as a system contribute to the organisation's effectiveness and efficiency in achieving its objectives. The benefits are: (1) Integration and alignment of the processes that will best achieve the desired results, (2) Ability to focus effort on the key processes and (3) Providing confidence to interested parties as to the consistency, effectiveness and efficiency of the organisation.

Applying this principle typically leads to:

- Structuring a system to achieve the organisation's objectives in the most effective and efficient way
- Understanding the interdependencies between the processes of the system
- Structured approaches that harmonize and integrate processes
- Providing a better understanding of the roles and responsibilities necessary for achieving common objectives and thereby reducing cross-functional barriers
- Understanding organisational capabilities and establishing resource constraints prior to action
- Targeting and defining how specific activities within a system should operate
- Continually improving the system through measurement and evaluation.

5.5.6 Principle 6 – Continual Improvement

Continual improvement of the organisation's overall performance should be a permanent objective of the organisation. The key benefits include (1) Performance advantage through improved organisational capabilities, (2) Alignment of improvement activities at all levels to an organisation's strategic intent and (3) Flexibility to react quickly to opportunities.

Applying the principle of continual improvement typically leads to:

- Employing a consistent organisation-wide approach to continual improvement of the organisation's performance
- Providing people with training in the methods and tools of continual improvement
- Making continual improvement of products, processes and systems an objective for every individual in the organisation
- Establishing goals to guide, and measures to track, continual improvement
- Recognising and acknowledging improvements.

5.5.7 Principle 7 – Factual Approach to Decision Making

Effective decisions are based on the analysis of data and information. The key benefits are: (1) Informed decisions, (2) An increased ability to demonstrate the effectiveness of past decisions through reference to factual records and (3) Increased ability to review, challenge and change opinions and decisions.

Applying the principle of factual approach to decision making typically leads to:

- Ensuring that data and information are sufficiently accurate and reliable
- Making data accessible to those who need it
- Analysing data and information using valid methods
- Making decisions and taking action based on factual analysis, balanced with experience and intuition.

5.5.8 Principle 8 – Mutually Beneficial Supplier Relationships

An organisation and its suppliers are interdependent and a mutually beneficial relationship enhances the ability of both to create value. The key benefits are: (1) Increased ability to create value for both parties, (2) Flexibility and speed of joint responses to changing market or customer needs and expectations and (3) Optimisation of costs and resources.

Applying the principles of mutually beneficial supplier relationships typically leads to:

- Establishing relationships that balance short-term gains with long-term considerations
- Pooling of expertise and resources with partners
- Identifying and selecting key suppliers
- Clear and open communication
- Sharing information and future plans
- Establishing joint development and improvement activities
- Inspiring, encouraging and recognising improvements and achievements by suppliers.

The QM principles are applied in many different ways. The nature of the organisation and the specific challenges it faces will determine how to implement them.

5.6 ISO 9001:2008 QMS REQUIREMENTS

ISO 9001:2008 is generic in nature and concentrates on following three areas:

- Focus on Customer.
- Process oriented, where performance indicators are used to measure the effectiveness of process.
- Continual improvement.

Since it is generic in nature, any clauses that are not suitable to any organisation can be excluded and it should not affect the ability of organisation to meet customer requirements. The standards contain eight clauses, of which the first three clauses give the information about organisation, while last five clauses are the requirements that company has to meet. The numbering system (clauses) used in the standards is followed here, as

CL1. Scope

CL2. Normative reference

CL3. Terms and definitions

CL4. General Requirements

4.1 Develop your QMS

4.2 Documentation.

CL5. Management Requirements

5.1 Management commitment.

5.2 Customer focus.

5.3 Quality policy.

5.4 Planning.

5.5 Responsibility, authority and communication.

5.6 Management review.

CL6. Resource Requirements

6.1 Provide resources.

6.2 Human resources.

6.3 Infrastructure.

6.4 Work environment.

CL7. Realisation Requirements

7.1 Planning of product realisation.

7.2 Customer related processes.

7.3 Product design and development.

7.4 Purchasing.

7.5 Production and service provision.

7.6 Control of monitoring and measuring equipment.

CL8. Remedial Requirments

8.1 Establish monitoring and measurement.

8.2 Carry out monitoring and measurement.

8.3 Control of non-conforming product.

8.4 Analysis of data.

8.5 Improvement.

CL1. Scope

It is the requirement for any organisation to develop quality management system (QMS) in order to demonstrate its capabilities to meet the customer requirements. This purpose is achieved by evaluating performance of system and continually improving the system. The requirements of standard are applicable to any organisation of size, type and product.

CL2. Normative Reference

The required concepts and related definitions can be obtained from ISO 9000:2005 standards.

CL3. Terms and Definitions

Terms and definitions given in ISO 9000:2005 can be applied. Besides this, supply chain is defined as:

Supplier → Organisation → Customer

CL4. General Requirements

4.1 Develop your QMS

The organisation has to identify the requirements of customer and accordingly has to establish, document, implement and maintain QMS, as specified in the standard. Also QMS can be evaluated using performance indicators and work for continual improvement of system. It includes steps to:

1. Identify needed processes for QMS viz. management activities, provision of resources, product realisation and measurement.
2. Determine the sequence and interaction of processes for optimum results.
3. Determine the criteria and methods for effective operation and control of processes.
4. Ensure the availability of resources and information necessary to support operation and monitor process.
5. Monitor and analyse processes.
6. Implement action to achieve the desired results as planned and continual improvement of the processes.

The outsourced processes, if any, for any organisation, can be identified and included in QMS in order to maintain the quality of system.

4.2 Documentation

4.2.1 General

The standards enable the organisation to develop minimum documentation for effective planning, operation and control the processes. Also documentation has to result in continual improvement of QMS. A document is stated to have the following: Communication of information, Evidence of realisation and Sharing of knowledge.

1. *Communication of information:* It depends upon the nature of organisation's products and processes, type and size of organisation, competency of employees and complexity of processes. It also indicates degree of formality of communication system, level of communication skills and overall structure of organisation. Finally it has to satisfy the requirements of all interested parties, expectations of customers and must comply with statutory and regulating bodies.

2. *Evidence of realisation:* Evidence has to be provided to show the conformance of result that has been planned. "Say what you do, do what you say and prove it".

3. *Sharing of knowledge:* Disseminate and preserve organisation experiences.

The document media can be paper, magnetic, electronic, photographic, etc., and the standard allows the organisation to have its documentation in any form. Documentation of a organisation includes:

1. Statements of quality policy and quality objectives.

2. Quality manual.
3. Required documented procedures to achieve the objectives.
4. Needed documents for effective planning, and control of processes.
5. Required records in standard format.

4.2.2 Quality manual

It is a document specifying QMS of an organisation and it is based on organisation size, organisation complexity and culture. It has to include:

1. Scope of QMS, including details of and justification for any exclusion.
2. Documented procedures established for QMS or reference to them.
3. Description of interaction between processes.

4.2.3 Control of documents

The management representative (refer clause 5.5.2) is the authorised person to control all documents related to quality system. The MR along with the core team has to establish, document, implement and maintain the document proceedings as required in Clauses 4.2.3, 4.2.4, 8.2.2, 8.3, 8.5.2 and 8.5.3. It also defines the control needed for:

1. Approval of documents prior to use.
2. Review update and re-approve as and when necessary.
3. Identifying current revised status and valuable for use.
4. Identifying records that are legible and retrievable.
5. Identifying documents of external origin.
6. Prompt removal of obsolete documents and identify to retain them for any legal reasons.

4.2.4 Control of records

Organisation is free to develop records that may be needed to demonstrate conforming of their processes, products and QMS. They should be legible, easily identifiable and retrievable. The documented procedures are the evidence of conformity containing corrective action and preventive action (CAPA) and have to be defined with control needed for the identification, storage, protection, retention time and disposition of records.

CL5. Management Requirements

5.1 Management commitment

Top management refers to an individual or a group of people who can direct and control an organisation. It is the commitment of top management to demonstrate its capability in all possible ways to the development, implement and continual improvement of the QMS. This is achieved by:

1. Identifying and meeting requirement of customers and all stake holders.
2. Compliance to statutory and regulatory bodies.
3. Establishing quality policy and quality objectives.
4. Conducting periodic management reviews.
5. Providing adequate resources in time.

5.2 Customer focus

The top management has to ensure that customer requirements are determined and met with the aim of enhancing customer satisfaction (or) it has to strive constantly and satisfy or surpass customer requirements.

5.3 Quality policy

It consists of overall intentions and directions of organisation related to quality. It is the highest document, which shows the commitment of the top management to meet all requirements. Top Management shall ensure that quality policy has to be:

1. Appropriate to organisation's mission.
2. Includes a commitment for continual improvement of QMS.
3. Provides a frame work for establishing and revising quality objectives.
4. Communicated and understood throughout the organisation.
5. Reviewed for continuing stability.

5.4 Planning

Quality objectives: It is the responsibility of top management to establish quality objectives to meet product or service requirement and also at relevant function or department levels and/or at individual levels also. This is to ensure that everyone in the organisation has to exercise responsibility to achieve the objectives.

It consist of :

1. Statements or targets aimed and related to quality and in quantitative (measurable) terms.
2. Need to be constant with quality policy.
3. Commitment to continual improvement.

QMS Planning: This can be accomplished as presented in clause; by specifying necessary operational processes and resources necessary to fullfil objectives. In addition, the integrity of QMS is maintained wherever changes are planned and introduced. This emphasises that top management to plan consistently in order to improve the effectiveness of processes stated.

5.5 Responsibility, Authority and Communication

5.5.1 Responsibility and authority

Top management has to ensure that responsibility and authority of all people working in an organisation have to be defined and communicated within the organisation. Authorities and interrelationships can be shown in organisational chart.

5.5.2 Management representative (MR)

The top management has to appoint a member preferably from management as Management Representative. He has to contribute effectively for the improvement of QMS. Besides his normal responsibilities, he has to:

1. Ensure that processes needed for QMS are established, implemented and maintained.

2. Report to top management on the performance of QMS and any scope for improvement.
3. Promote awareness of customers requirements throughout the organisation.

5.5.3 Internal communications

It is the duty of top management to ensure the appropriate channels are established within the organisation and the communication takes place with respect to QMS. This can be reviewed from time to time, according to effectiveness, available technology and suitable conditions. Communication is a two-way traffic, and therefore, the direction from top to bottom and flow of information from department to higher levels should be clear and effectively convey the message.

5.6 Management Review

5.6.1 General

The top management has to review the QMS at planned internal (may be once in six months) to ensure its continuing suitability, adequacy and effectiveness. This review includes assessing opportunity for improvement and need for changes in QMS, including quality policy and quality objectives. Records of management review have to be developed and maintained.

5.6.2 Review input

The input to the review include information on:

(*a*) Results of internal and surveillance audits.
(*b*) Customer feed back.
(*c*) Process performance and product conformity.
(*d*) Status of corrective and preventive performance.
(*e*) Follow up actions from previous management reviews.
(*f*) Changes that could affect the QMS.
(*g*) Recommendation for improvements.

5.6.3 Review output

Normally, the output of management review can be used as input to improve the processes. The output from management review includes any decisions and actions related to the follwing:

(*a*) Improvement of the effectiveness of QMS and its processes,
(*b*) Improvement of product related to customer requirements, and
(*c*) Required resources.

CL6. Resource Requirements

6.1 Provide resources

It is the requirement of any organisation to provide resources:

1. To implement and maintain QMS.
2. Continually improve the effectiveness of QMS.
3. To improve customer satisfaction.

6.2 Human resources

General: The organisation has to ensure that personnel performing work, that has direct effect on quality of product or services, is having enough competencies on the basis of formal education, training skills and experience. It is to be noted that it includes people who manage the activities related to quality other than who work.

Competence, Awareness and Training: The competency can be defined as the demonstrated ability to apply knowledge and skills. The organisation has to identify the required competency for accomplishing activity in terms of education, training, skills and experience. If there is any gap, training may be arranged. It includes fresh and existing employees. Therefore organisation has to:

1. Determine the required competency for each activity for their working personnel, which affects the quality.
2. Meet the gap by conducting training programs viz. on job training or hiring persons etc.
3. Evaluate the effectiveness of training programmes, before and after conducting it.
4. Ensure that personnel are aware of relevance and importance of their activities and how they contribute to achievement of quality objectives.
5. Maintain records of education, training imparted, skills and experience.

6.3 Infrastructure

The organisation must determine and provide the infrastructure needed to achieve conformity to product/service requirement. It includes:

1. Buildings, work space and associated utilities (according to their requirement).
2. Process equipment (hardware and software).
3. Supporting services.

6.4 Work environment

The organisation has to determine and provide necessary work environment that has an effect on quality and maintain the same to achieve conforming to product requirements.

CL7. Realisation Requirements

7.1 Planning of product realisation

The organisation shall plan and develop the processes needed for product realisation. The planning of product realisation processes include all processes complying with requirements, as desired by organisation for successful realisation of products. This procedure starts with enquiry and ends with delivery of the product. In this regard, the organisation shall determine following as appropriate:

1. Quality objectives and requirement for the product, project or contract.
2. Need to establish processes, documents and provide resources and facilities required for the product.
3. Verification and validation activities and the criteria for product acceptance.
4. Need for records to provide conformance to process and product specifications.

7.2 Customer related processes

7.2.1 Determination of requirements related to product

The organisation has to identify the unique requirements of its customers. It includes:

(*a*) Requirements specified by customer explicitly and implied in terms of its product itself and its delivery. This includes requirements for delivery and post delivery activities like after sales servicing, technical support, etc.

(*b*) Requirements not stated by the customer, but necessary for organisation to understand.

(*c*) Statutory (written law) and regulatory (requirements issued by independent government bodies established by legislative act) related to product.

(*d*) Any additional requirements determined by the organisation.

7.2.2 Review of requirements related to the product

The organisation shall review the requirements related to the product and necessary procedures should be established and maintained by coordinating related activities. This review has to be conducted prior to the organisation's commitment to supply a product to the customer. It ensures that:

(*a*) Requirement of product are sufficiently defined and documented.

(*b*) Any differences between the contract or order requirements and those expressed earlier, are resolved.

(*c*) The ability of organisation to meet the defined requirements when there is no documented statement produced by customer.

It is the duty of organisation to understand the requirements before acceptance. When product or design function is changed, it has to be amended in the contract and relevant documents must be amended. The concerned personnel must be made aware of changed requirements. The review activity varies tremendously, according to nature of product produced by the organisation. In the review process, all the concerned functions have to be involved and all aspects of the review has to be appropriately recorded.

7.2.3 Customer communication

The organisation has to determine and implement effective arrangements for communicating with customers, in relation to:

(*a*) Product information (includes operating manuals, data sheets, etc.).

(*b*) Enquiries, contracts or order handling, including amendments.

(*c*) Customer feed back including complaints.

7.3 Product design and development

7.3.1 Design and development planning

The organisation shall plan and control the design and development of the product. This process includes inputs, resources, outputs, reviews, verification and validation. In this regard, the organisation has to determine:

(*a*) Design and development stages.

(*b*) Review, verification and validation appropriate to each design and development stage.

(*c*) The responsibilities and authorities required for design and development.

Organisation has to manage efficiently the interfaces involved in design and development by ensuring effective communication and clear assignment of responsibility. Only the current information has to be produced. This is important for the complex and large projects carried out over a long period of time.

7.3.2 Design and development inputs

Inputs relating to product requirements have to be determined and recorded. It includes:

(*i*) Functional and performance requirements.

(*ii*) Required statutory and regulatory requirements.

(*iii*) Applicable information derived from previous similar design.

(*iv*) Other requirements essential for design and development.

These inputs are reviewed for adequacy and have to be unambiguous, complete and do not conflict with each other.

7.3.3. Design and development outputs

Design and development may exist in various forms. These outputs must be able to check against inputs as specified in design and development. It has to be approved before product is released. Design and development outputs have:

(*i*) To meet input requirements for design and development.

(*ii*) Provide appropriate information for purchasing production and service provision.

(*iii*) Contain or provide reference product acceptance criteria.

(*iv*) Specify the changes of product that are essential for its safe and proper use.

7.3.4 Design and development review

The purpose is to conduct systematic reviews of design and development at planned intervals. In the review, all the functions/departments connected with the design and development stages are included. The records of the review results and subsequent necessary actions taken are maintained and recorded. This review includes:

(*i*) Whether the results of design and development are able to meet the requirements and

(*ii*) Identification of problem if any and propose necessary actions.

7.3.5 Design and development verification

This process of verification is to ensure that design and development outputs have met corresponding input requirements. It also includes comparison of new design, if any. Records of results of verification and necessary actions, if any, have to be maintained.

7.3.6 Design and development validation

This process has to be performed in order to demonstrate the capability of the product to meet the requirements for intended use or application. If possible, validation can be completed prior to delivery or implementation of a product. These records of results of validation and also subsequent follow up actions are to be maintained.

7.3.7 Control of design and development changes

Design and development changes have to be identified and recorded. The changes have to be reviewed, verified, validated as appropriate and must be approved before implementation. The review of design and development changes must include evaluation of the effect of the changes on constituent parts and products already delivered. Records of subsequent actions have to be maintained.

7.4 Purchasing

7.4.1 Establish control of your purchasing process

This includes the following steps:

(*i*) Establish criteria that you can use to control suppliers.

(*ii*) Evaluate your suppliers' ability to supply products that meet your organisation's requirements..

(*iii*) Select suppliers who are capable of supplying products that meet your organisation's specific requirements.

(*iv*) Ensure that the purchased products meet the specified purchase requirements.

7.4.2 Specify your purchasing requirements

Describe your purchase requirements. Make sure that purchase requirements are adequately specified before you discuss them with suppliers.

7.4.3 Verification of Purchased Product

The organisation has to establish and implement inspection and other activities necessary for ensuring that the purchased product meets the stated requirements of a product. The organisation shall also state, if required, verification at the supplier/sub contractor sites. The information also contains arrangement for verification and method of product release. Verification activity may also include self-certification of supplier, test certificates by independent agents or second or third party assessments.

7.5 Production and service provision

7.5.1 Control of production and service provision

The organisation has to plan and carry out production and service provision under controlled conditions. Controlled condition includes:

(*i*) The availability of information that describes the characteristics of product.

(*ii*) The availability of necessary work instruction.

(*iii*) Use of appropriate equipments.

(*iv*) Availability and use of monitoring and measuring devices.

(*v*) Implementation of monitoring and measurement.

(*vi*) Implementation of release/approval, delivery and post delivery processes.

7.5.2 Validation of processes for production and service provision

The organisation has to validate any processes for production and service provision. In this regard, a procedure has to be established so that the resulting output cannot be verified by subsequent monitoring or measurement. This arrangement helps the organisation to avoid deficiencies/defects because it becomes apparent when the product is in use or service has been delivered. This validation demonstrates the ability of processes to achieve planned results. Such validation is referred as process qualification. This includes:

(*i*) Defined criteria for review and approval of processes (includes inputs, controls, resources, outputs, parameters and operating characteristics).

(*ii*) Approval of equipments and qualified personnel.

(*iii*) Use of specific methods and procedures (includes tolerances, measurement, testing, analysis, etc.).

(*iv*) Requirement of records.

(*v*) Revalidation of processes (at periodic intervals; if not specified, once in a year).

7.5.3 Identification and traceability

The organisation has to establish procedures for the unique identity of the product, at any stage, till product realisation. The product status with respect to monitoring and measurements has to be identified along with product identification. The organisation has to control and record the unique identification of product, where traceability is required.

7.5.4 Customer property

Organisation has to take care of customer property, when it is under the control of organisation or being used by it. The customer property may include materials or components supplied, inspection equipments, tools, jigs, fixtures, packaging materials or intellectual property namely software, specifications, drawings, instructions, etc.

7.5.5 Preservation of product

The company has the responsibility to preserve the conformity of product during internal processing (in house/contractors site) and delivery to the desired destinations. The preservation includes the identification, handling, packaging, storage and protection of the products. Constituent parts and sub-assemblies of product have also to be preserved.

7.6 Control of monitoring and measuring equipments

Organisation has to determine the monitoring and measurements required to be undertaken and corresponding devices needed to provide evidence of conformity of products or services to the requirements as determined at the beginning of product realization. The company has to establish processes to ensure that monitoring and the measurements can be carried out in a manner consistent with the requirements of monitoring and measuring.

In order to ensure valid results, measuring equipment has to be:

(*i*) Calibrated or verified at specified intervals or prior to use. This is compared against international or national measurement standards. If no such standard exists, basis used for calibration or verification should be recorded.

(*ii*) Adjusted or readjusted as found necessary.

(*iii*) Identified to enable the calibration status to be determined.

(*iv*) Safeguarded from adjustments or changes that would invalidate the measurement results.

(*v*) Protected from damages and deterioration during handling, maintenance and storage.

Moreover, the organisation has to review or assess the equipments. If it does not conform to the requirements, then previous measuring results have to be validated and whole process is recorded. This enables the organisation to take appropriate action on equipments and any products affected. Records of results of calibration and verification have to be maintained.

CL8. Remedial Requirements

8.1 Establish monitoring and measurement process

The organisation has to identify, plan and implement monitoring, measuring, analysis and improving methodologies to the product, process and in total QMS itself. It is necessary to:

1. Demonstrate conformity of product.
2. Ensure conformity of QMS.
3. Continually improve the effectiveness of QMS.

It is the organisation's responsibility to determine appropriate methodologies for monitoring, measuring and the use of statistical techniques.

8.2 Carry-out monitoring and measurement

8.2.1 Customer satisfaction

It is the responsibility of the organisation to adopt proactive methods to determine the level of customer satisfaction and it is directly connected with feedback and performance indicator of QMS, employed in the organisation. Therefore, the organisation has to monitor information related to customer perception and ensure it has met customer requirements. To achieve this, the organisation can adopt any methodology but it should be meaningful.

8.2.2 Internal Audit

The organisation has to conduct the internal audits at planned intervals to conform the compliance of system to the requirements of ISO Standards and QMS requirements established by organisation. The internal audits must also demonstrate that QMS is effectively implemented and maintained. The management representative of the organisation has to plan schedule, scope and frequency of internal quality audits in a year, coordinate the activity and report the results of internal audit to top management for necessary actions. The plan of program is done based on the status and importance of processes and functions/departments to be audited, besides the results of previous audits.

Qualified auditors should carry out audits with objective of finding facts and not faults. The documented procedure has to be followed and maintained defining responsibility and requirements of planning and conducting the audits and reporting results. The corresponding records have to be maintained. The audit also covers office of MR and top management to detect non-conformities, if any, and identify the causes. It also includes follow up procedure to verify actions taken and reporting verification results.

8.2.3 Monitoring and measurement of processes

The organisation has to apply suitable methods for monitoring the processes and measurement of the QMS processes. These methods have to demonstrate the ability of the processes to achieve planned results. The ability of process depends upon reliability and repeatability of process, and timeliness in a process, competency of personnel involved and the other constraints related to equipments and material availability. When planned results are not met, corrective actions have to be taken to ensure conformity of product.

8.2.4 Monitoring and measurement of product

The organisation has to establish the practice of monitoring and measuring the characteristics of products and to verify whether the product requirements have been met. This has to be done at appropriate stages of product realisation process. The evidence of conformity with the acceptance criteria has to be maintained. The records shall indicate persons authorising the release of product. The product release must not be undertaken until all planned arrangements (measurement activities) are completed to the satisfaction and approved by a person of relevant authority, and if necessary, with the approval of customer.

8.3 Control of non-conforming product

The objective of this clause is to prevent use or delivery of product to customer, which does not conform to requirements. In this regard, the controls related responsibilities and authority to deal with non-conforming products should be defined in documented procedures. In this connection, organisation has to

1. Take action to eliminate the detected non conformity.
2. Authorise its use, release or acceptance under concession by relevant authority.
3. Take action to make use of it or alternative application other than its originally intended use.

Records of nature of non-conformities, their root cause analysis and subsequent actions taken including concessions obtained must be maintained. When a non-conforming product is corrected, it has to be subjected to re-verification to demonstrate conformity to the requirements. When a non-conforming product is detected after delivery or use, the organisation has to take action appropriate to the potential effects of non-conformity.

8.4 Analysis of data

The organisation has to determine, collect and analyse appropriate data to demonstrate the suitability and efficiency of the QMS and to evaluate the scope of continual improvement in QMS. The data generated from monitoring and measurement processes and collected from other relevant sources are used as inputs for analysis.

The analysis of data can provide information relating to :

1. Customer satisfaction.
2. Conformity to product requirements.
3. Characteristics and trends of processes and products including opportunities for preventive action.
4. Suppliers/service providers.

8.5 Improvements and remedial actions

8.5.1 Continual improvement

The organisation has to adopt proactive approach to continually improve the efficiency of QMS through the use of quality policy, quality objectives, audit results, analysis of data, corrective actions and preventive actions and the management review.

8.5.2 Corrective action

The organisation has to identify the root causes and take action to eliminate the cause of non-conformities, in order to prevent such recurrences. The corrective actions appropriate to the impact of non-conformities must be taken. In this regard, documented procedures have to be established to define requirements for:

1. Reviewing non conformities (including customer complaints).
2. Determining the cause of non conformities.
3. Evaluating the need for action to ensure that non conformity do not recur.
4. Determining and implementing the actions needed.
5. Records and results of actions taken and.
6. Reviewing corrective actions taken.

8.5.3 Preventive action

The organisation has to adopt proactive strategy, which anticipates possible causes of potential non-conformities in order to prevent their recurrences. The documented procedure has to be established to this effect which define requirement for:

1. determining potential non-conformities and their causes.
2. evaluating the need for action to prevent occurrence of non-conformity.
3. determining and implementing the actions needed.
4. records of results of actions taken.
5. reviewing preventive actions. (ISO 9001:2008 Clauses completed)

5.7 IMPLEMENTATION OF ISO 9001:2008

Everyone in the organisation has to be involved in the implementation of quality system (QS). The responsibility will be defined for every individual in the organisation, including top management. The necessary steps to be followed in order to implement QMS in any organisation are given below:

1. Top Management Commitment

First, top management must be willing to implement a quality system that will either meet or exceed ISO 9000 standards. The fullest support of the management has to be intended in the implementation process. Because it is the responsibility of top management to provide the required resources in time, to achieve the certification process. Besides this, certain responsibilities will be assigned to them in the standards.

2. Appointment of Management Representative

Next step is to appoint the management representative (MR). The MR can be selected preferably from top management for effective implementation and maintenance of quality standard. MR is responsible for coordinating all activities involved in implementation, documentation and maintenance of quality standard. MR is the source of guidance to all personnel involved in the process, both external and internal.

3. Awareness Program

It is essential to conduct short awareness program for all employees working in the organisation. It helps everyone to understand the quality system and how it affects day-to-day work and potential benefits.

4. Appoint a Task Force/Core Team for Implementation

After the awareness program, it is made to understand the intention of organisation to implement a quality system. Then, a task force or implementation team is formed, drawing members from all departments/functions at all levels. Each function has got equal representation. Then the team has to identify the processes, input and output, sequence and interaction. The team can be divided into committee to meet five clauses of standards.

5. Training

MR has to undergo lead auditor training for effective understanding, interpretation and implementation of quality standard. Besides MR, members of task force, supervisor and internal audit team must be trained. The leaders can take training from the consultant and in turn, they can train other employees of organisation.

6. Time Schedule

The time duration required for any organisation may vary depending on size and type of organisation and extent of its existing quality system. Normally it takes six months to eighteen months.

7. Selection of Process Owners

The implementation team identifies the processes in the organisation and selects the owners for each process. Owner has to identify input, output and the responsibility of process. The person responsible for the process may be at organisational/functional level.

8. Review of Existing System

The existing procedures, work methods, processes involved, instructions have to be reviewed and compared with ISO standards and to determine what is available and what is needed to complete the system. This analysis is done to fill gaps and performed by process owners and their teams assisted by external consultant.

9. Writing Documents

This includes preparing general quality policy, quality manual, defining responsibility of every individual of organisation, various processes involved, to maintain quality of specific functions. Then the quality objectives have to be prepared which is the performance indicator for reaching quality policy. The realisation programs with time schedule are to be prepared for realizing the quality objectives. Care must be taken in documentation procedure. It should not be over documentation or complex.

10. Installation of New System

Integrate policies, procedures, and realisation programs into routine working of organisation and it may be documented.

11. Internal Audit

This is necessary to check if the system is working effectively and producing the required information to the management. For this, the trained people should be used in audit team. The internal audit also helps to apply corrections wherever necessary.

12. Management Review

This is done to review the effectiveness of QMS in achieving stated quality objectives. The top management has to participate in the management review.

13. Pre Assessment

This is optional but a recommended procedure.

14. Registration

This process includes three parts, namely:

1. Identifying a system/certification agency (includes reputation of agency, accreditation and familiarity with Industry/Organisation, cost and lead time.)
2. Submitting an application along with quality manual for review.
3. Registration/Agency certification audit. The duration of audit will take 1 - 3 days and depends on system and complexity of organisation.

Some of the drawbacks in successful implementation are :

1. Using a generic document program or copying documents from another organisation.
2. Over documentation or complex in nature.
3. Using external agency/consultant, not involving employees.
4. Continuing documentation to text rather than other types of media.
5. Neglecting top management.
6. Developing a system that does not represent reality.

5.8 ISO—DOCUMENTATION

The prime aim of adopting ISO in any organisation is to satisfy the requirements of all stakeholders of the organisation. This is achieved by meeting or surpassing quality level of product/service as stated and efforts for continual improvement. To accomplish this, documentation is required to be developed in any organisation. The documentation may include quality policy, quality manual, system processes and procedures, records, etc. The documentation provides guideline for internal quality management and helps organisation for continual improvement and its success.

Documentation begins with the collection of all established procedures, policies, and records for supplying product/service to the customers. Implementation team will review the documents collected and attempts will be made to fit into quality management system process.

If it is accurate and up to date, it will be used. If it is necessary, the documents can be modified and unwanted parts can be rejected. The developed system documentation will be at four levels, as shown in Fig. 5.2.

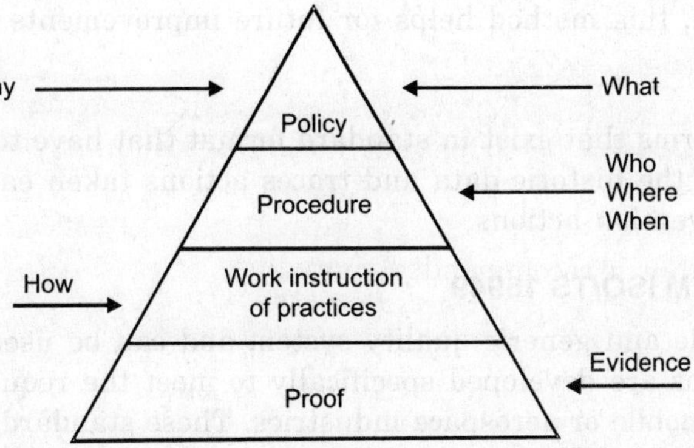

Fig. 5.2

The documentation moves from the one level to another in downward direction. Writing the documents is easy in the implementation process but putting policies and procedures to work well, will be most difficult. Therefore, more people have to be involved for satisfactory function of the organisation. It has to be ensured that all the departments/functions have due representation not only from management but also quality areas. The implementation team will split into smaller teams of 2-3 members who will be made responsible/owners for each process. The team has to write policies and procedures for the process. The team may also be assigned to develop other relevant records and forms. The team will review the documentation, make necessary changes like either clarification or modification or entire revision. Finally all documents will be formatted in order to have simple and effective control over documents. During this entire process, a consultant may be needed to facilitate the team's activities. If system is properly structured, change in one end will affect levels below it but not affect above. The four levels of documentation have been discussed now.

Policy

This is the first level of documentation. The organisation defines its overall intentions and directions. It also defines, why to do and what will be done. Statements used in the quality policy will be short, practical and easy to understand and usually requires one page or less.

Procedure

This is the second level of documentation and is more detailed than policies. It describes the method to be followed, perform the stated policies to ensure the quality of system. It defines who should perform the task, when it will be done and where the document is made available (location) to show task is performed. Procedures are applied to all areas within organisation and should be easy for understanding.

Work Instructions

These documents are most detailed in nature and describe how a job has to be done. These instructions may be in the form of a drawing, photograph, video or routing sheet or a sample for conformity. Normally the person who does the task, write the work instructions. This gives a pride of ownership and encourages him to involve in the process. Besides employee participation, this method helps for future improvements.

Records

Records are the forms that exist in standard format that have to be filled out. Records help us to understand the historic data and traces actions taken earlier. This helps us to take corrective or prevention actions.

5.9 QUALITY SYSTEM ISO/TS 16949

ISO 9000 is simple and generic quality system and can be used in any organisation. However, other systems are developed specifically to meet the requirements of particular industry such as automobile or aerospace industries. These standards are sector specific as company has customers in different industries to meet each sector's requirements. QS is also one of the sector specific standards to meet the requirements of automobile industries. The three big US auto makers Chrysler, Ford and General Motors had developed this standard in 1994, defining their fundamental quality requirements from their suppliers of production; servicing and new materials. The standard has been approved by Asian automakers. This system uses ISO 9001 as mainframe work and modified for continuous improvement, emphasising defective prevention and reduction of variation and waste in the supply chain. There are three levels in the standard:

1. ISO 9001 requirements.
2. Sector specific requirements.
3. Company specific requirements.

QS 9000 is now replaced by ISO/TS 16949.16949:2009 is an interpretation agreed upon by American and European automotive manufacturers; this version is based on 9001:2008. The emphasis on a process approach is stronger than in 9001:2008. This contains the full text of ISO 9001:2008 and automotive industry-specific requirements.

5.10 ISO 2004:2009 MANAGING FOR THE SUSTAINED SUCCESS OF AN ORGANISATION-A QM APPROACH

2004:2009 gives guidance on a wider range of objectives of a QMS than 9001, especially in managing for the sustained success of an organisation. It is recommended as a guide for top management who wish to extend the benefits of ISO 9001 in pursuit of systematic and continual improvement of organisation's overall performance. However, it is not intended for certification or contractual purposes. A brief summary of the clauses as per the standard is as follows:

CL 4. Success Management

4.1 Quality management approach

1. *Adopt* a Quality Management approach
2. *Establish* a QMS based on the eight QM Principles (discussed in # 5.5)
3. *Use* your QMS to make sure that resources are used efficiently.

4.2 Sustained corporate success

4.2.1 Meet the needs and expectations of interested parties in the following steps:

1. *Identify* all the relevant interested parties.
2. *Assess* the potential impact interested parties could have on the performance of your organisation.
3. *Figure* out how you're going to meet the changing needs and expectations of your interested parties.
4. *Meet* the long range needs and expectations of your organisation's interested parties.
5. *Establish and maintain* contact with your organisation's interested parties.
6. *Monitor* your organisation's business environment.

4.2.2 Analyse your organisation's business environment as follows:

1. *Identify* both short-term and emerging risks.
2. *Establish* appropriate processes to achieve your organisation's general strategy.
3. *Develop* a long-term planning perspective.
4. *Anticipate* your organisation's future resource needs.
5. *Assess* your organisation's compliance.
6. *Assess* compliance with current plans.
7. *Assess* compliance with current procedures.
8. *Establish* processes for innovation and continual improvement.

4.3 Business environment

Monitor your organisation's changing business environment

Use your environmental monitoring methods to identify the risks related to the changing needs and expectations of interested parties. *Assess* your organisation's interested party risks and *manage* your organisation's interested party risks.

4.4 Interested parties

Meet the needs and expectations of interested parties. *Meet* the needs and expectations of customers, employees, suppliers, partners, owners and of society. *Balance* the needs and expectations of interested parties.

CL 5 Strategic Management

5.1 General corporate orientation

Establish

1. A *mission* for your organisation, making sure that it is clearly understood, accepted and supported,
2. A *vision* for your organisation, making sure that it is clearly understood, accepted and supported and
3. *Values* for your organisation, making sure that they are clearly understood, accepted and supported.

5.2 Strategy and Policy Formulation

5.2.1 Establish a process to develop your strategy and policies

Develop plans and provide resources to support your strategy and policy development process. *Analyse* your organisation's strategic needs and unique policy requirements.

Establish a strategy and policies to ensure your mission, vision, and values are accepted and supported by all the interested parties.

5.2.2 Establish a process to review and update strategy and policies

Develop plans and provide resources to support your strategy and policy review and revision process.

5.2.3 Establish a process to monitor your business environment

Develop plans and provide resources to support your environmental monitoring and analysis process.*Monitor* your organisation's business environment and *analyse* that.

5.2.4 Establish a process to identify the needs of interested parties

Develop plans and provide resources to support your interested party needs assessment process.*Identify* the needs and expectations of interested parties.

Establish a process to identify the outputs that you require so that you are able to meet the needs and expectations of interested parties and *analyse* their needs and expectations.

5.2.5 Establish a process to assess your capabilities and resources

Develop plans and provide resources to support your capability and resource assessment process and *analyse* your current capabilities and resources.

5.2.6 Establish a process to identify future technology needs

Develop plans and provide resources to support your new technology assessment process and *analyse* your future technology needs.

5.2.7 Establish a process to identify future resource needs

Develop plans and provide resources to support your future resource assessment process and *analyse* your future resource needs.

5.3 Strategy and policy deployment

5.3.1 Implementing strategy and policies

Implement your organisation's strategy and policies as in following steps:

1. *Establish* processes and practices to translate your strategy and policies into measurable objectives.
2. *Establish* and maintain processes and practices needed to achieve your objectives. and
3. *Evaluate* strategic risks and develop counter measures.

5.3.2 Managing processes and practices

1. *Ensure* that processes and practices are efficient and effective, through communication with interested parties in order to check whether or not your processes and practices are efficient and effective.
2. *Assess* and understand your current performance and evaluate the efficiency and effectiveness of your processes and practices.
3. *Control* your processes and practices to ensure that they are efficient and effective.
4. *Provide* resources to support processes and practices.
5. *Develop* objectives that are designed to ensure that processes and practices are efficient and effective.
6. *Ensure* that process results (outputs) are consistent with your organisation's strategy.

5.3.3 Deploying strategy and policies

Identify your organisation's process relationships, by *describing* the sequence and interaction of your processes.

Use your process descriptions to support process review activities. *Use* the process descriptions

1. To show the relationship between organisational structures, systems, and processes.
2. To identify potential process interaction problems
3. To help prioritize changes and prove improvement activities.
4. As a framework for setting objectives at all organisational levels.
5. To figure out how to deploy the strategy and policies. *Implement* the organisation's strategy and policies.

5.4 Strategy and policy communication

Establish an effective communication process. *Communicate* with your interested parties, by communicating both vertically and horizontally and by tailoring your communications to meet differing needs. *Communicate* your strategy and policies, by establishing a feedback mechanism and by a feedback review cycle. Address changes in your business environment.

CL 6. Resource Management

6.1 General resource management

1. *Identify* the resources you need to achieve your objectives.
2. *Develop* resource management policies and methods.
3. *Establish* resource management processes.
4. *Ensure* that resources are used efficiently and effectively.
5. *Review* resource availability and suitability.

6.2 Financial resource management

1. *Provide* for the financial resources your organisation needs.
2. *Provide* for resources to support current operations and also future operations.
3. *Establish* processes to allocate financial resources.
4. *Make* sure that financial resources are used to achieve the organisation's objectives.

6.3 Human resource management

6.3.1 Management of people

1. *Make sure* that your organisation's vision, values, and environment support the active involvement of your people, by establishing a shared vision and values and by establishing a supportive work environment.
2. *Ensure* that your organisation's people are managed efficiently and effectively.
3. *Establish* an effective management approach.
4. *Establish* processes that empower the people.

6.3.2 Competence of people

Establish and maintain a people development plan and involvement of people.

Help the organisation's people to understand how significant their job responsibilities are and how important their activities are. Ensure that people understand how their work activities create and deliver value to customers.

Take steps to motivate and involve your people, by

1. Establishing a career planning system
2. Creating a knowledge sharing process
3. Introducing a recognition and reward system
4. Providing mentoring and coaching opportunities
5. Establishing a skills qualification system
6. Monitoring the needs of your people.

6.4 External resource management

6.4.1 Establishing mutually beneficial relationships

Establish mutually beneficial partnership agreements with partners and suppliers.

Establish agreements with product suppliers, service providers, technology suppliers, with financial institutions, governmental and non-governmental organisations and with other relevant interested parties. *Develop* mutually beneficial relationships with your partners and your suppliers.*Consider* providing partners and suppliers with resources and helping partners and suppliers to improve.

6.4.2 Selecting and evaluating suppliers and partners

Establish processes to:

1. Manage your partners and suppliers.
2. To identify partners and suppliers.
3. To select partners and suppliers.
4. *Establish* processes to evaluate partners and suppliers.

Use your processes to manage your partners and suppliers:

1. To ensure that supplier products and partner resources meet your organisation's needs and expectations.
2. To continually strengthen your relationship with partners and suppliers.
3. To continually improve your partner and supplier capabilities.

6.5 Infrastructure and resource management

Plan the development of your infrastructure. *Provide* an efficient and effective infrastructure.

Manage the infrastructure efficiently and effectively. *Assess* the performance of the infrastructure.

6.6 Work resource management

Establish a suitable work environment which:

1. Encourages your people to achieve their potential
2. Maximizes efficiency and minimizes waste
3. Which is safe, secure, and supportive
4. Uses ergonomic methods and follows ergonomic principles
5. Considers and respects psychological factors
6. Complies with all applicable standards and requirements.

Manage your organisation's work environment so as to:

1. Achieve, maintain, and sustain your organisation's on-going success.
2. Encourage and support your organisation's people.
3. Show visitors that you encourage productivity and creativity, and support the well-being of workers.

6.7 Inteligence resource management

6.7.1 Managing your business intelligence

Establish appropriate processes for knowledge management, information management and technology management.

6.7.2 Knowledge resource management

Assess how current knowledge base is being managed. *Consider* how your organisation obtains knowledge. *Acquire* the knowledge that your organisation needs. Distribute and communicate your knowledge.

6.7.3 Information resource management

Establish processes:

1. To gather reliable and useful data.
2. To convert data into information.
3. To manage information and data.

6.7.4 Technology resource management

Consider using technology to enhance your performance. *Establish* technology assessment processes. *Consider:*

1. The availability and use of energy and natural resources.
2. Integrating environmental protection into product design.
3. Trying to minimize your impact on the environment.

CL 7. Process Measurement

7.1 Using A Process Approach

Adopt a *process approach* to management by:

1. Establishing unique processes that address your needs.
2. Creating a network of interconnected processes.
3. Detailing your organisation's network of processes.

Use a *systems approach* to manage processes by:

1. Understanding your processes and process interactions.
2. Managing your processes as an integrated system.
3. Reviewing your organisation's processes.
4. Ensuring that your processes are efficient and effective.
5. By taking suitable steps to improve your processes.

7.2 Process Planning and Control

Identify the functions that your organisation needs. *Plan* the development of your organisation's processes. *Develop* your organisation's unique processes. *Control* how your processes function.

7.3 Process Responsibility and Authority

Appoint a process manager for each process. Give the process manager the authority and responsibility to manage his / her process. *Ensure* that the role of process manager is recognized and respected as well, throughout your organisation.

CL8. Evaluation Management

8.1 General approach to evaluation

Monitor your organisation's performance → *Measure* → *Analyze* → *Review* the organisation's performance.

8.2 Monitoring your organisation and it's environment

Establish processes for monitoring, collecting, and managing information about your organisation and its business environment.

Use your monitoring processes to collect information about your organisation and it's business environment. *Collect* information about:

(*a*) The needs of interested parties,

(*b*) Your strengths and weaknesses,

(*c*) Your opportunities and threats,

(*d*) Your process capabilities,

(*e*) Regulatory requirements,

(*f*) Products and services,

(*g*) Your business markets,

(*h*) Your labour markets,

(*i*) Technologies and

(*j*) Trends.

8.3 Measuring Organisational Performance

8.3.1 General approach to assessing progress

Assess your progress by measuring your actual achievements against the results you plan to achieve. *Use* a measurement and analysis process to monitor your actual achievements against the results you plan to achieve. *Select* appropriate and practical methods for collecting information and monitoring key performance indicators.

8.3.2 Defining key performance indicators

Identify factors that are critical to your organisation's success. *Select* your organisation's key performance indicators (KPI). *Implement* KPIs throughout your organisation.

Use your KPIs to measure performance.

8.3.3 Conducting internal audits

Select internal auditors.*Plan* internal audits. *Carry*out internal audits. *Prepare* internal audit reports. *Use* audit results to improve performance. *Verify* the effectiveness of your remedial actions.

8.3.4 Performing maturity self-assessments

Carry out comprehensive and systematic assessments of your organisation's maturity.

Use your self-assessment results and reports to help achieve and sustain organisational success.

Communicate self-assessment results and reports.

8.3.5 Using benchmarking to improve performance

Figure out what type of benchmarking you need to carry out.*Establish* and maintain a benchmarking methodology. *Apply* your organisation's benchmarking methodology. *Use* benchmarking results to improve performance.

8.4 Analysing Your Organisational Environment

Analyse the information you gathered while monitoring your organisation's business environment. *Maintain* information about your business environment. *Use* your environmental analysis to make fact based decisions about your strategy and policies.

8.5 Reviewing Performance Information

(*a*) *Establish* a management review process.

(*b*) *Collect* available information (inputs).

(*c*) *Collect* internal audit information.

(*d*) *Collect* self-assessment information.

(*e*) *Collect* benchmarking information.

(*f*) *Collect* risk assessment information.

(*g*) *Collect* customer feedback information.

(*h*) *Collect* environmental information.

(*i*) *Perform* periodic management reviews at planned intervals.

(*j*) *Generate* management review results and reports (outputs).

(*k*) *Evaluate* your organisation's achievements.

(*l*) *Discover* trends that affect your organisation.

(*m*) *Identify* opportunities that could be pursued.

(*n*) *Assess* previous improvement projects.

(*o*) *Use* results to make decisions and achieve sustained success.

CL 9. Change Management

9.1 Managing Change

1. *Achieve* sustained success by managing change.
2. *Achieve* success by managing improvements.
3. *Achieve* success by managing innovations.
4. *Achieve* success by managing learning.
5. *Encourage* learning, innovation, and improvement.

6. *Encourage* people to learn about products.
7. *Encourage* people to learn about processes, about technology, about infrastructure, their work environment, about organisational structures, management systems and interested parties.

9.2 Managing Improvements

Define continual improvement objectives. *Establish* a continual improvement process. *Make* continual improvement part of your culture.

9.3 Managing Innovation

9.3.1 General approach to innovation

Identify your innovation needs and requirements. *Establish* an innovation process whenever innovation is needed. *Provide* related resources to support innovation.

9.3.2 Exploring your innovation needs

Explore the needs for:

(*a*) Technological innovation,

(*b*) Product innovation,

(*c*) Process innovation,

(*d*) Organisational innovation and

(*e*) Systemic innovation.

9.3.3 Planning and prioritising innovations

Establish a process to plan and prioritize innovations. *Use* your innovation planning process to plan your innovations.

9.3.4 Factors that affect an innovation process

Manage and control your innovation processes. *Consider* how urgent the need for innovation is whenever you think about whether or not an innovation process should be established or whether or not it should be maintained.

Consider the impact your innovation objectives would have whenever you think about whether or not an innovation process should be established or whether or not it should be maintained.

9.3.5 Planning innovation and managing risk

Assess your organisation's risks whenever you plan to carry out innovation activities. *Prepare* preventive actions to mitigate your risks.

9.4 Managing Learning

Encourage improvement and innovation by supporting continuous learning. *Achieve* sustained success by making sure that organisation learns continuously. *Support* learning by collecting information and by gaining insights. *Achieve* sustained success by encouraging your people to learn continuously. Support personal learning initiatives. *Encourage* interpersonal networking. *Maintain* suitable learning systems. *Recognize* improvements in competence. *Acknowledge* and appreciate *creativity*. (ISO 9004:2009 completed)

5.11 INTERNAL AUDITING

When QMS is implemented in the organisation, internal audit is conducted in the organisation. The purpose of this activity is to check whether system is followed and expected results are obtained. The audit has to be done once in six months or at least once in a year depending on need. The audit can be defined as systematic and independent examination to determine whether quality activities and related results conform to planned arrangements and to check whether these planned arrangements are implemented effectively to achieve required objectives.

In short, auditing is the process of finding out strengths and weaknesses of a quality system.

5.11.1 Objectives of Audit

1. To apply corrective action to avoid repetition and deviation if any.
2. To follow up on non-conformance from previous audits.
3. To determine whether organisation follows documented QMS.
4. Steps for continual improvement in QMS.
5. Provide opportunity to improve quality system.

5.11.2 Auditor

The auditor is the qualified person who conducts all or any portion of quality system audit. Normally auditor looks for objective evidence, which includes records, files, other relevant information, statement of facts, etc. The auditor should be objective, honest and impartial. He/She pursues the policy, "believe but verify". He/She should be competent enough to apply knowledge and skills in the auditing process. The qualification of auditor includes education, training, experience, management capabilities and communication skills. The focus of the auditor is always as follows:

1. Process and effectiveness.
2. Focus on customer (includes feedback/complaints).
3. Continual improvement.
4. Resource planning and utilisation.
5. Measurement and monitoring and analysis.

The personal attributes of auditors are:

(*a*) Positive attributes

- Ability to listen.
- Ability to collect information.
- Good at taking notes.
- Tact and sense of proportion.
- Concentrate completely on audit process.
- Arrives at generally acceptable solution.
- Remain true to conclusion.
- Able to organise and conduct an audit.

(*b*) Negative attributes

- Easy to influence.
- Lazy.
- Argumentative.
- Biased.
- Immediately jumps to conclusion.

(*c*) Pre-requisites for auditors: Able to identify

- Understand competition and demand of product in the market.
- Stakeholders of organisation and their requirement.
- Target of organisation.
- Business standards they adopt
- Critical success factors.
- National and international regulations, codes and statutory bodies as applicable to the standards to the main document manuals.

(*d*) Desirable qualities of auditors

- Ethical conduct.
- Fair presentation.
- Due professional commitment.
- Independence.
- Evidence based approach.

5.11.3 Procedure of Quality Auditing

Planning is the first step to conduct quality audit successfully in organisation. This includes selection of auditors, decision on the activity or department to be audited or auditee, required documents, time duration. The audit plan shows the period over which all areas of organisation is audited. The audit plan also includes earlier audits, non-conformities if any, corrective action and follow up action, if any. The auditee represents organisation/department to be audited. The checklists also prepared are also the part of audit plan. It makes the audit more efficient and gives auditor the control of process. The advantages of checklists are:

1. Guidance to auditor.
2. Good help for fresher.
3. Speed up the audit.
4. Helps in documenting results of all enquiries.
5. Contains extensive and probing questions in conducting an organised audit.

Audit itself has three parts, opening/pre audit meeting, audit and closing meeting. Opening meeting includes discussion on audit process and schedule and previous audits are reviewed. The minutes of the meeting will be recorded and list of attendees has to be recorded in minutes.

Audit includes review of documents and checking how quality system is being implemented and maintained. A key person or supervisor of the organisation usually accompanies the auditor to the areas to be audited. It also includes probing and questioning auditee/

people working in area and look for factual evidence. This includes verification of records, whether relevant procedures are available with auditee. The purpose of the audit is not only the compliance of system and but also to change or modify, if necessary. It ensures the continual improvement and increased customer satisfaction.

Auditing is done with mutual trust existing between auditor and auditee. The auditor should keep respect on auditee and a conducive environment has to be created. Auditor has to ask questions in a variety of ways to make auditee understand the system. It is the responsibility of auditor to explain the significance of particular question. If he found auditee is stressed, a break can be given. The audit activity includes listening, verifying and working at documented evidence. The listening of auditor helps the supervisor/auditee to speak about the process and gather information first. It is then verified for compliance through records.

The questions can be opened, closed or clarifying. Open question: "what are the files maintained in the department?" This makes the auditee to come forward with the list of files maintained in this section. This helps us to get more information, opinion / explanation in the process, reasons behind the process. In this, auditor may get undesirable information also. Closed question is one which gives answer yes or no. It provides facts or evidence and reduces misunderstanding. However, it looks like interrogation. For example, is this document controlled? Clarifying questions help to obtain further information to avoid misunderstanding and helps auditee to relax. In the above process, auditor is encouraged to ask open question, and occasionally closed and clarifying questions. The argumentative, offensive questions which give misleading answers are to be avoided. The audit findings, audit conclusion and audit report reflect accurately audit activities. It is written in detail and includes conforming and non conforming items. In case of non-conformities, a non-conformity report (NCR) will be developed. NCR is a non fulfilment of requirement. The NCR may be related to:

1. Process measurement.
2. Continual measurement.
3. Resource related non conformance.

NCR includes the following details:

1. Where it is observed?
2. Objective evidence and as a basis for non conformance.
3. Name of person involved/precise document reference/element title and identification number.
4. Auditor's name and date.
5. Clear and right description of the non-conformity.

In the closing meeting, the lead auditor/team leader presents the summary of whole audit process with supporting evidence. The audit report contains:

1. Title sheet containing audit, date, areas audited and names of audit team, and statement that audit is sample with signature of lead auditor.
2. Details of NCR.
3. Procedures/suggestion for corrective action and follow up.

5.12 ENVIRONMENTAL MANAGEMENT SYSTEM (EMS)

Introduction

Based on the recommendations of the Strategic Advisory Group on the Environment, in 1992, the committee TC207 was formed. The objective of TC207 is to develop standards for environmental management system, which was identified as ISO 14000. This is similar ISO 9000 standards, aimed at the process rather than a performance of product/service. TC207 has established six sub committees namely, environmental management system, environmental auditing, environmental performance evaluation, environmental labelling, life cycle assessment and environmental aspects in products and standards. The environmental management system is part of a comprehensive management system that helps the organisation for environmental management against internally accepted criteria. The registration process closely resembles those involved with ISO 9000 related quality standard.

5.13 ISO 14000 SERIES STANDARDS

ISO 14000 document is named as EMS—General guidelines, on principles, systems and supporting techniques. It gives the general outlines on how to initiate, implement, improve and sustain the system. By following ISO 14001:2004 standards, a base to balance and integrate economic and environment interests is provided. ISO 14000 series focus on two areas and accordingly divided as, organisation evaluation standards and product evaluation standards. In addition, ISO 14050 covers terms and definitions that are common to both areas. ISO 14000 series has been described briefly as follows.

5.13.1 Organisational Evaluation Standards

These standards are as shown in Fig. 5.3 and consist of three categories: Environmental Management System (EMS), Environmental Auditing (EA), and Environmental Performance Evaluation (EPE).

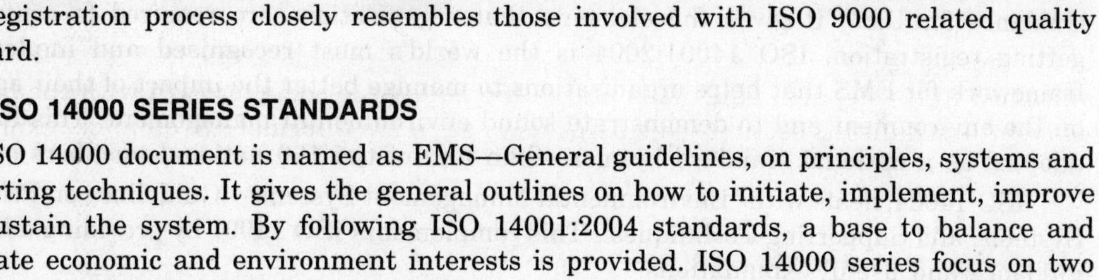

Fig. 5.3

These standards are under development and as shown in Fig. 5.4. They consist of three categories: Environmental Aspects in Product Standards, Environmental Labelling, and Life-Cycle Assessment (LCA).

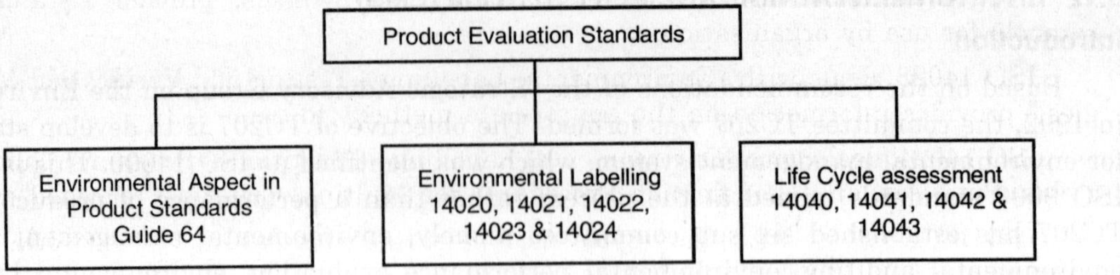

Fig. 5.4

ISO 14001:2004, deals with "Environmental Management Systems—Specifications with Guidance for Use". It gives the elements that organisations are required to conform for getting registration. ISO 14001:2004 is the world's most recognised and implemented framework for EMS that helps organisations to manage better the impact of their activities on the environment and to demonstrate sound environmental management. This has been adopted as a national standard by more than half of the 160 national members of ISO.

ISO 14004, deals with "Environmental Management Systems—Guidelines on Principles, Systems, and Supporting Techniques". This complements ISO 14001 by providing additional guidance and useful explanations.

ISO 14010, deals with "Guidelines for Environmental Auditing—General Principles on Environmental Auditing". It discusses about internal or external auditing.

ISO 14011, deals with "Qualification Criteria for Environmental Auditing—Audit Procedures—Auditing of Environmental Management Systems". This auditing standard is equally useful for EMS and QMS. It provides guidance on principles of auditing, managing audit programs, the conduct of audits and on the competence of auditors.

ISO 14012, deals with "Qualification Criteria for Environmental Auditors Performing Environmental Management System Audits", covering information about auditor qualifications, training, etc.

ISO 14031: "Guidelines on Environmental Performance Evaluation", provides guidance to organisation on evaluating its environmental performance. It also addresses the selection of suitable performance indicators, so that they can be assessed against criteria set by management. This information can be used as a basis for internal and external reporting on environmental performance. Communication on the environmental aspects of products and services is an important way to use market forces to influence environmental improvement.

5.13.2 Product Evaluation Standards

ISO Guide 64, deals with "Environmental Aspects in Product Standards."

ISO 14020, deals with "Environmental Labelling—Basic Principles for All Environmental Labelling." 14020 series addresses different approaches to environmental labels and declarations, including eco-labels (seals of approval), self-declared environmental claims, and quantified environmental information about products and services.

ISO 14021, deals with "Environmental Labelling—Self-Declaration of Environmental Claims: Terms and Definitions."

ISO 14022, deals with "Environmental Labelling—Symbols," provides a standard set of symbols for use by organisations.

ISO 14023, deals with "Environmental Labelling—Testing and Verification Methodologies," provides information on the appropriate methods to use.

ISO 14024, deals with "Environmental Labelling—Practitioner Programs: Guiding Principles, Practices, and Certification Procedures for Multiple Criteria Programs."

ISO 14040, deals with "Life-Cycle Assessment—Principles and Framework."

ISO 14001 addresses not only the environmental aspects of an organisation's processes, but also of its *products and services* by developing additional tools in addressing such aspects. Life-cycle assessment (LCA) is a tool for identifying and evaluating the environmental aspects of products and services from the cradle to the grave (from extraction of resource inputs to eventual disposal of the product or its waste) 14040 gives guidelines on the principles and conduct of LCA studies that provide an organisation with information on how to reduce the overall environmental impact of its products and services.

ISO 14041, deals with "Life-Cycle Assessment—Goals and Definitions/Scope and Inventory Analysis."

ISO 14042, deals with "Life-Cycle Assessment—Impact Assessment."

ISO 14043, deals with "Life-Cycle Assessment—Improvement Assessment."

ISO 14063, "Environmental communication guidelines and examples", helps companies to make the important link to external stakeholders.

ISO 14064 points 1, 2 and 3 are international greenhouse gas (GHG) accounting and verification standards which provide a set of clear and verifiable requirements to support organisations and proponents of GHG emission reduction projects.

ISO 14065 complements 14064 by specifying requirements to accredit or recognise organisational bodies that undertake GHG validation or verification using 14064.

5.14 ENVIRONMENTAL AND ECONOMIC BENEFITS

The ISO 14000 family of standards provides management tools for organisations to manage their environmental aspects and assess their environmental performance. Together, these tools can provide significant tangible economic benefits, including the following:

1. Reduced raw material/resource use
2. Reduced energy consumption
3. Improved process efficiency
4. Reduced waste generation and disposal costs
5. Utilization of recoverable resources.

With each of these economic benefits are distinct environmental benefits too. This is the contribution by 14000 series to the environmental and economic components of sustainable development.

5.15 THE PDCA CYCLE

The 14000 family is designed to be implemented according to the same PDCA cycle underlying all ISO management systems standards. Table 5.1 classifies the 14000 family according to their optimal place in the PDCA cycle.

Table 5.1 The ISO 14000 family and the PDCA cycle

Plan	*Do*	*Check*	*Act*
E M S implementation	*Conduct life cycle assessment & manage environmental aspects*	*Conduct audits and evaluate environmental performance*	*Communicate and use environmental declarations & claims*
ISO 14050:2009 EM vocabulary and framework	ISO 14040:2006 EM LCA Principles- Assessment of sites and organisations	ISO 14015:2001 EM Environmental and declarations	ISO 14020:2000 Environmental labels & General principles
ISO 14001:2004 EMS - Requirements with guidance for use evaluation-guidelines	ISO 14044:2006 EM LCA requirements and guidelines Declared Envl claims	ISO 14031:1999 EM Environmental Performance	ISO 14021:1999 Environmental labels and declarations-Self (Type II Envl. labelling)
ISO 14004:2004 EMS - General – Genl guidelines on principles, systems & support techniques	ISO/TR 14047:2003 EM Life cycle impact Assessment- Examples	ISO 19011:2002 Guidelines for quality and/or EMS auditing Examples of application of ISO 14042	ISO 14024:1999 Envl labels & declarations – Type I Envl labelling – Principles & Procedures
ISO/DIS 14005 Guidelines for phased implementation of EMS, including the use of envl performance evaluation	ISO/TS 14048:2002 EM .- LCA Data Documentation format	—	ISO 14025:2006 Environmental labels and declarations – Type III Envl declarations - Principles & Procedures
—	—	—	ISO/AWI 14033 EM - Quantitative envl information – Guidelines
Address environmental aspects in products and product standards	—	Evaluate greenhouse gas performance	—
ISO Guide 64:2008 Guide for addressing EM environmental issues in product standards and scope definition and inventory analysis	ISO/TR 14049:2000 LCA - Examples of application of ISO 14041 to goal	ISO 14064-3:2006 Greenhouse gases - Part 3 Specification with guidance for validation and verification of GHG assertions	ISO 14063:2006 EM Environmental. Communication - Guidelines and examples

ISO/CD 14006	ISO/CD 14051	ISO 14065:2007
EMS – Guidelines on Eco-design General principles and framework for accreditation	E M. – Material flow cost accounting & verification bodies	GHG- Requirements for GHG validation —
ISO/WD 14045		
—	Eco-efficiency Assmt – Principles & requirements	—

5.16 REQUIREMENTS OF ISO 14001:2004

5.16.1 Concept of ISO 14001

The EMS model is shown in Fig. 5.5. This can be integrated with other management systems to achieve environmental and economic goals.

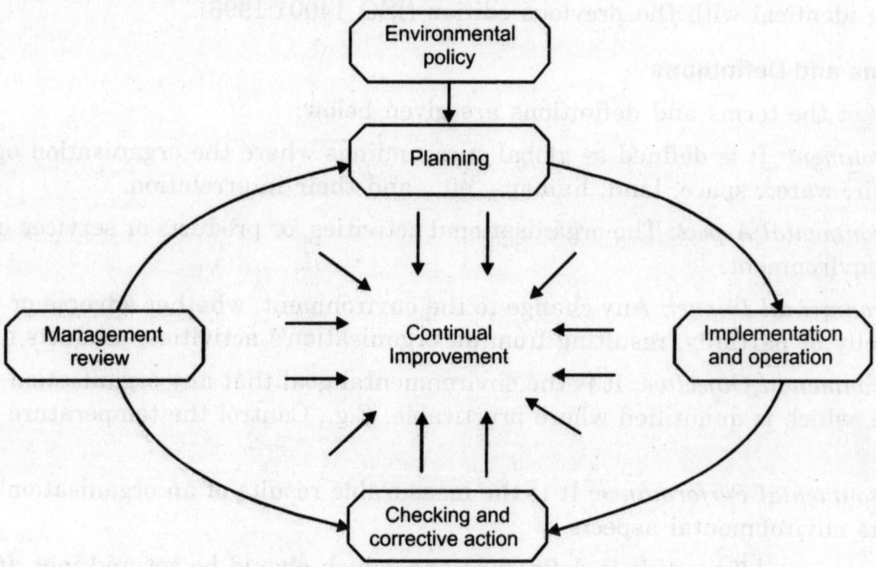

Fig. 5.5

This International Standard contains only those requirements that can be objectively audited. Those organisations requiring more general guidance on a broad range of EMS issues are referred to ISO 14004.

CL 1 SCOPE

This Standard specifies requirements for an EMS to enable an organisation to develop and implement a policy and objectives which take into account legal and other requirements to which the organisation subscribes, and information about significant environmental aspects. It applies to those environmental aspects that the organisation identifies as those which it can control and can influence. It does not itself state specific environmental performance criteria.

This Standard is applicable to organisations that wish to (*a*) establish, implement, maintain and improve an EMS, (*b*) assure itself of conformity with its stated environmental policy, (*c*) demonstrate conformity with this International Standard by (1) making a self-determination and self-declaration, or (2) seeking confirmation of its conformance by parties having an interest in the organisation, such as customers, or (3) seeking confirmation of its self-declaration by a party external to the organisation, or (4) seeking certification / registration of its EMS by an external organisation.

All the requirements are intended to be incorporated into any EMS. The extent of the application depends on factors such as the environmental policy of the organisation, the nature of its activities, products and services and the location where and the conditions in which it functions.

CL 2. Normative References

No normative references are cited. This clause is included in order to retain clause numbering identical with the previous edition (ISO 14001:1996).

CL 3. Terms and Definitions

A few of the terms and definitions are given below:

Environment: It is defined as global surroundings where the organisation operates. It includes air, water, space, land, humans, etc., and their interrelation.

Environmental Aspect: The organisational activities, or products or services interacting with the environment.

Environmental Impact: Any change to the environment, whether adverse or beneficial, either wholly or partially, resulting from an organisation's activities, products or services.

Environmental Objective: It is the environmental goal that any organisation sets itself, to achieve, which is quantified where practicable. E.g., Control the temperature of the air, 26 ± 1°C.

Environmental Performance: It is the measurable results of an organisation's management of its environmental aspects.

Environmental Target: It is defined as one, which should be set and met. It gives the detailed performance requirement applicable to the organisation or parts thereof. It is to be quantified where practicable.

CL 4. Requirements for ISO 14001:2004

CL 4.1 General requirements

An organisation must establish, document, implement, and continually improve its EMS and show how they meet all the requirements of this standard. The organisation defines the scope of the EMS, i.e., the boundaries of the organisation to which the EMS applies.

4.2 Environmental Policy

The organisation must have a policy, or commitment statement, developed by top management. This short statement drives the remainder of the EMS. Specific items that must be committed are: compliance with legal and other requirements, prevention of pollution, and the continual improvement. Further, the policy must be communicated to all employees, and others working on behalf of the organisation, and be also available to the public. The policy provides a framework for reviewing objectives and targets and be appropriate to the nature and scale of the entity included in the scope. This policy must be documented, implemented, and maintained. It means that it is kept current through the EMS review and continual improvement process, and is implemented through the remainder of the EMS elements.

4.3 Planning

4.3.1 Environmental aspects

This element requires a procedure to identify environmental aspects and related impacts that the organisation can control or has influence, and determine those which are significant to the organisation. ISO 14001 does not prescribe what aspects should be significant, or how to determine significance. However, a consistent and verifiable process is used to determine significance.

Aspects are defined as how an organisation's activities products and/or services interact with the environment. An impact is how an aspect changes the environment. The intent of this element is to help the organisation identify how it affects the environment, prioritize aspects, and use the EMS to manage, control, and improve upon the aspects. The organisation must make sure that the significant aspects are taken into account in the EMS. In order to ensure that the system is continually improving and current, this information must be kept up to date.

4.3.2 Legal and other requirements

This requires a procedure to explain how the organisation obtains information regarding its legal and other requirements, and makes that information known to key functions within the organisation. The intention is to identify the environmental, legal and other requirements pertaining to its operations and activities so that the organisation can ensure that they are taken into account in the EMS. This includes legislation by the government and regulatory bodies, industrial codes of practice, contracts, agreements with public authorities and non-regulatory guidelines.

4.3.3 Objectives, targets and programs

Although there is no specific requirement for a procedure, there must be some process to ensure that the objectives and targets are consistent with the policy. This includes the commitments to compliance with legal and other requirements, continual improvement, and prevention of pollution. Further, the organisation must take into consideration significant aspects, legal and other requirements, views of interested parties, and technological, financial, and business issues when deciding what it wishes to accomplish as objectives. The objectives and targets need to exist at different functions and levels of the organisation, and be measurable, where practicable. The objectives include:

(*a*) Reduction of waste and depletion of resources

(*b*) Reduction or elimination of the release of pollutants

(*c*) Design products so as to minimise the environmental impact in production, use, and disposal.

(*d*) Promotion of environmental awareness among employees and the community. A typical target can be: By using recycled water for gardening, reduce the water consumption by 15% every year.

Management programs (MPs) are the detailed plans and programs explaining how the objectives and targets will be accomplished. Such programs shall note persons responsible, dates and milestones, and measurement of success. Such monitoring and measurement parameters facilitates conformance to 4.5.1 on Monitoring and Measurement.

4.4 Implementation and operation

4.4.1 Structure and responsibility

14001 requires that appropriate management and accountability structure be defined herein. Top management is expected to make sure that the human resource, organisational structure, financial and technological resources are available so that the EMS can be implemented, maintained, and improved. Roles, responsibilities, and authorities must be defined, documented and communicated. The MR is responsible to oversee the EMS and report to management on its operation. MR must ensure that the EMS is established, implemented and maintained consistent with 14001. MR reports on the performance of the system including recommendations for improvement, to the top management.

4.4.2 Competence, training and awareness

This element is to ensure that persons performing tasks that have significant impact on the environment and/or relate to the legal and other requirements are competent to do those tasks. Competence is ensured through appropriate education, training, and/or experience. The organisation has to identify EMS training needs, the significant aspects, and the legal and other requirements and ensure that this training is provided and recorded. A procedure is needed to make sure that such persons are aware of the need to conform to EMS procedures and requirements and what they need to do, the legal and other requirements associated with their respective responsibilities, why improved performance is beneficial and the consequences of not following these procedures. In addition to job-specific knowledge, it is expected that all personnel within the EMS (including contractors) have general awareness on the policy and emergency response.

4.4.3 Communications

Procedures are required for both internal and external communications. 14001 only requires procedures, and allows the organisation to decide for itself the degree of openness and disclosure of information. But the decision process must be recorded. There is a specific requirement that the organisation considers external communications, about its significant environmental aspects and records its decision. It has to specify how the external communications are received, documented, and a response provided. For internal communications, the procedure has to explain how it is done among the levels of the organisation.

4.4.4 EMS documentation

The organisation has to document the system in either electronic or paper form such that it addresses all the elements, describes how the organisation conforms to each element, and provides direction to related documentation. All the required procedures need not be documented, so long as the system requirements can be verified. But, documentation must be provided to ensure the effective planning, operation, and control of processes related to the significant aspects, and to demonstrate conformance to 14001. Such documentation at a minimum includes policy, objectives and targets, the scope of the EMS and other main elements.

4.4.5 Control of documents

The organisation is required to control documents, such as system procedures and work instructions, to ensure that current versions are distributed and obsolete versions are removed. The document control procedure makes sure that documents are approved prior to use, reviewed and updated, changes to versions are identified, that the current versions are available at points of use, that they are legible, identifiable, and that obsolete ones are so noted to avoid unintended use. It is acceptable to use documents of internal origin, but those must be identified as being essential to the EMS and their distribution controlled.

4.4.6 Operational control

The critical functions related to the policy, significant aspects, the legal and other requirements, and objectives and targets are identified and procedures and work instructions are required to make sure proper execution of activities. The required procedures need to provide instructions such that the organisation conforms to the policy, objectives and targets, the legal and other requirements, and addresses any impacts from significant aspects. The needed procedures can be determined by review of the significant aspects, objects and targets, the legal and other requirements, and policy and then deciding what must be described as procedure and documented to make sure that deviations from planned arrangements do not occur. Regarding the contractors, the organisation will need to establish procedures related to the significant aspects the legal and other requirements, of the goods and services it uses, and communicating the relevant elements of those procedures to the suppliers and contractors.

4.4.7 Emergency preparedness and response

The conventional emergency response plans typically address this situation. This element requires that a process must exist for identifying the potential emergencies, in addition to planning and mitigating them. Emergency incidents include those that may not be regulated, but may still cause significant impact. As part of continual improvement, the organisation is required, besides responding to emergency situations, to review the emergency procedures and make improvements as necessary. This may involve periodic testing of emergency procedures, if practicable.

4.5 Monitoring and measurement

4.5.1 Monitoring and measurement

In order to properly manage the system, measurements must be taken of its performance to provide data for action. Procedures are required describing how the organisation will monitor and measure key parameters of operations. These parameters relate to the operations that can have significant impacts, to monitor performance towards the objectives and targets, and to monitor conformance to the legal and other requirements and other EMS requirements.

Equipment related to environmental measurements, such as thermometers, pH meters and pressure gauges, must be calibrated according to procedures, and records maintained.

4.5.2 Evaluation of compliance

The organisation is to have a procedure to periodically evaluate its compliance with applicable legal requirements as defined in 4.3.2. It will need to keep records of these periodic evaluations. It also requires a similar evaluation for compliance with other requirements that are defined in 4.3.2 and the procedure can be the same as, and even part of 4.5.2.

4.5.3 Non-conformances, corrective and preventive action

This element requires procedures for acting on non-conformances identified in the system, including corrective and preventive action. A non-conformance is a situation where the actual condition is not in accordance with planned conditions. Someone not following a procedure, a regulatory non-compliance and an incident, are the examples of possible systemic non-conformances.

Non-conformances may be identified through audits, monitoring and measurement, and communications. The intent is to correct the system flaws by addressing root causes, rather than just fixing the immediate incident only. This element also requires that trends in corrective actions be evaluated to see if deeper-rooted preventive actions can also be implemented.

The procedure is to make ensure that non-conformances are not only initially addressed to mitigate environmental impact, but also the further investigation done to determine their cause, and action taken to avoid recurrence. Preventive actions are those actions resulting from an evaluation as to why nonconformities are occurring and taking action to prevent their recurrence. The corrective action is to be appropriate to the magnitude of the problem and the impacts encountered and to avoid either over-compensating or under-compensating for a problem. The organisation must record the results of corrective actions taken, and must also review the effectiveness of actions taken.

4.5.4 Control of records

Records are expected to serve as verification of the system operating and the organisation's conformance to the EMS requirements. Procedures are required for the maintenance of records, and specifically require that records are identifiable, retrievable, safely stored, and legible, retained as appropriate, and traceable.

4.5.5 Internal audit

The internal audit procedure could include methodologies, schedules, checklists and forms, and processes used to conduct the audits. The purpose of this audit is to determine whether the system conforms to ISO 14001 requirements and the organisation's own EMS requirements, and if the EMS has been properly implemented and maintained. The procedure for internal audits has to address responsibilities and requirements for planning and executing the audits, reporting results, and what records will be generated and maintained as per

4.5.4. The procedures also address determination of audit scope, how often they will be conducted, and specifically how they will be done. Auditors are to be selected such that objectivity and impartiality of audit process is ensured.

4.6 Management review

Periodically, the top management will review the EMS to ensure it is operating as planned, and is suitable, adequate, effective and continually improved. The organisation make sure that they review and discuss the following:

(*a*) Results of internal audits (EMS and compliance)

(*b*) External communications

(*c*) environmental performance

(*d*) Status on objectives and targets

(*e*) Status of corrective and preventive actions

(*f*) Follow up on actions from prior management reviews

(*g*) Changing conditions or situations and

(*h*) Recommendations for improvement.

Results and records of management review include: agendas, attendance records, minutes, and documented items of agreed upon actions.

❑ ❑ ❑

CHAPTER 6

Additional Topics

6.1 POKA YOKE

6.1.1 What is Poka Yoke?

There are many ways of doing an act wrongly; but only a fewer ways of doing it correctly. In the manufacturing situations, this is very true. A hole may be missing or wrongly drilled on the left or wrong side and this may lead to rejection or rework or even recall of the assembled product. To avoid such wastage of product, money, and time, fool-proofing or Error-proofing is adopted in the industries. In Japanese, this principle is called poka-yoke, which means avoiding (yokeru) inadvertent errors (poka). This system was first introduced in Japan by Shingeo Shingo.

For example, consider the product, shoes. We know for sure, that a shoe is for the right or left foot. We can not use, if both are right shoes or left shoes. In case of D.C power connection, we can not change the terminals. On the other hand, the hand gloves are not easily distinguished as left or right. However, it may not matter very much in this case, as we can use the gloves for the left or right hand interchangeably, without problem.

A two-pin A.C. electric plug can be connected in any way, and it will not matter at all. But a three-pin plug has to be connected in a unique way, since the earth line should be separate from the other two terminals. For computer terminals, connectors are provided with lugs or projections or recess, to get the parts connected in unique and correct way. Even in X-ray photographs of teeth or ears or lungs, the right or left side is marked on them for the easy and correct identification and interpretation and subsequent operation. In spite of such practices, it was reported in the press a few years back, that a person was operated upon the left side of the brain instead of on the temporally right side!

Thus it can be seen that errors are harmful and can not be tolerated in many situations. In those cases, it is necessary to design or redesign the shape (form) and size (dimensions) or mark to indicate the unique and correct interpretation, assembly, and even usage.

6.1.2 Different Types of Human Errors

Various types of causes attributed to the occurrence of human errors are listed as follows:

1. *Forgetfulness:* We forget activities, when we do not concentrate on safeguards. e.g., Alerting the operator in advance, by checking at regular intervals or alerting him whenever he releases the grip of the steering wheel.

2. *Errors due to misunderstanding:* Either by not understanding or understanding incompletely or by wrong understanding, we jump to wrong conclusions. E.g., Switching-off instead of switching-on, and opening the valve instead of closing. Safeguards: Training and vigilance.
3. *Errors in identification:* We misjudge a situation, because we view it with pre-conceived notions or too quickly, or use wrong tools. Parallax error is an example of this type.
4. *Errors made by amateurs:* Mistakes through lack of experience. Safeguards: Skill building and training.
5. *Deliberate or Wilful or Intentional errors:* Errors occur when one decides to harm or damage the equipments or instruments. This may harm one's colleagues, environment, and one's own self. Safeguards: Education, counselling, and experience.
6. *Inadvertent errors:* Absent minded actions, mistakes committed unaware of how they happened, and wrongly used tools and instruments. Safeguards: Attentiveness, Work standardization.
7. *Errors due to slowness:* Actions are slowed down by delays in understanding and judgment. Safeguards: Skill building.
8. *Errors due to lack of standards:* Absence of appropriate instructions or work standards, use of non-calibrated measuring instruments. Safeguards: Work standardization and periodical calibration of instruments.
9. *Surprise errors:* When an equipment or machine runs differently than expected. Safeguards: Total Productive Maintenance.
10. *No supervision.* Safeguards: Necessary and sufficient supervision.
11. *Confusion upon sudden and unexpected events around Safeguards:* Sufficient attention but not remaining 'at tension'.

6.1.3 Different Types of Chance Errors

Other types of random or chance errors are identified as:

1. Ignoring certain activities, e.g., this occurs in repair of alarm time-piece.
2. Errors in activities, e.g., Driving the screw in wrong position, or with wrongly matched thread.
3. Set-up errors: Set up without checking for accuracy or alignment or dirt particles.
4. Missing components, e.g., Repair or assembly of wrist watch.
5. Wrong connections, e.g., Electric circuits, and hydraulic circuits.
6. Errors during repair or correction: e.g., Putting a wrong replacement or causing damage due excessive force or torque.
7. Wrong tools or instruments, e.g., wrong size or type of screw driver.

6.1.4 Countermeasures Towards Poka-Yoke

1. Appropriate fool-proof designs.
2. Do activities right first time, every time.

3. Continuous education and training.
4. Coordinated efforts.
5. Free and frank discussions in meetings such as quality circle and grapevine communication.

6.1.5 Eight Principles of Poka-Yoke to Achieve Zero Defect

1. Build quality into processes.
2. Eliminate all inadvertent errors and defects.
3. Stop doing it wrong and start doing it right-from now on!
4. Don't think of excuses, think of how to do it right.
5. A 60% chance of success is good enough.
6. Defects can be reduced to zero, when every one works together!
7. Two heads are better than one, provided they think and act in one direction.
8. Seek out the true causes (Truth), using five Ws and two Hs. i.e., What? Why? Where? When? Who? How? and How much?

6.1.6 Detection Devices used for Poka-Yoke

One of the common methodologies for elimination of source or cause of errors is the design and use of automatic sensors of one of the following types:

Based on the principle of operation, the sensors used are classified as:

(*a*) Optical sensor
(*b*) Thermal
(*c*) Resistive (potentiometer type)
(*d*) Inductive and
(*e*) Capacitive sensors.

Based on the parameters measured, they are classified as:

(*a*) Force or torque (strain gauge)
(*b*) Displacement
(*c*) Velocity
(*d*) Acceleration
(*e*) Pressure
(*f*) Vibration (amplitude or frequency) and
(*g*) Temperature (Thermocouples, thermiators)

Another type of classification is:

(*a*) Contact devices and
(*b*) Non-contact or proximity devices.

6.1.7 Case Study

Case—6.1

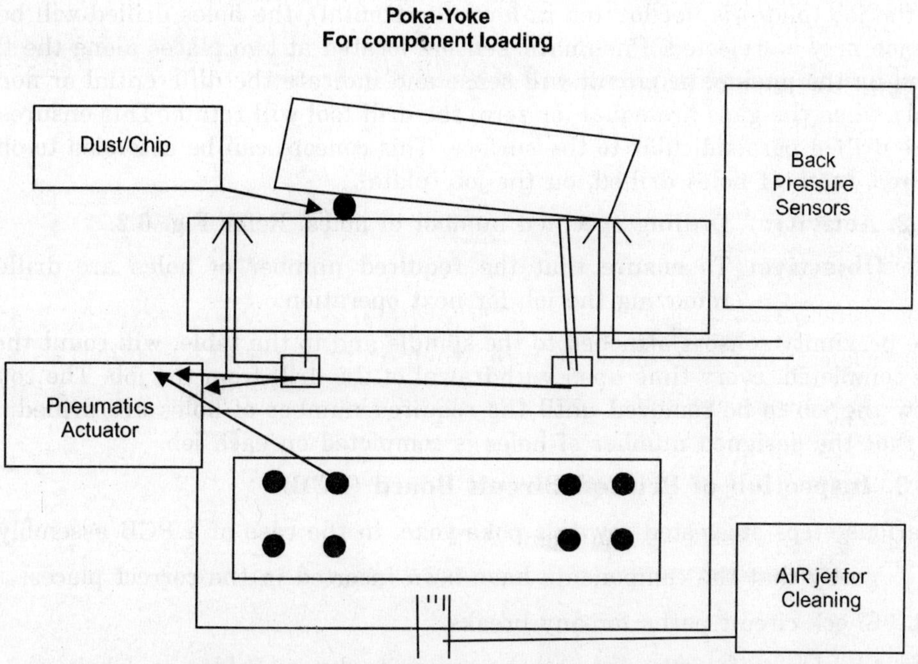

Fig. 6.1 Poka yoke for component loading

Case–6.2

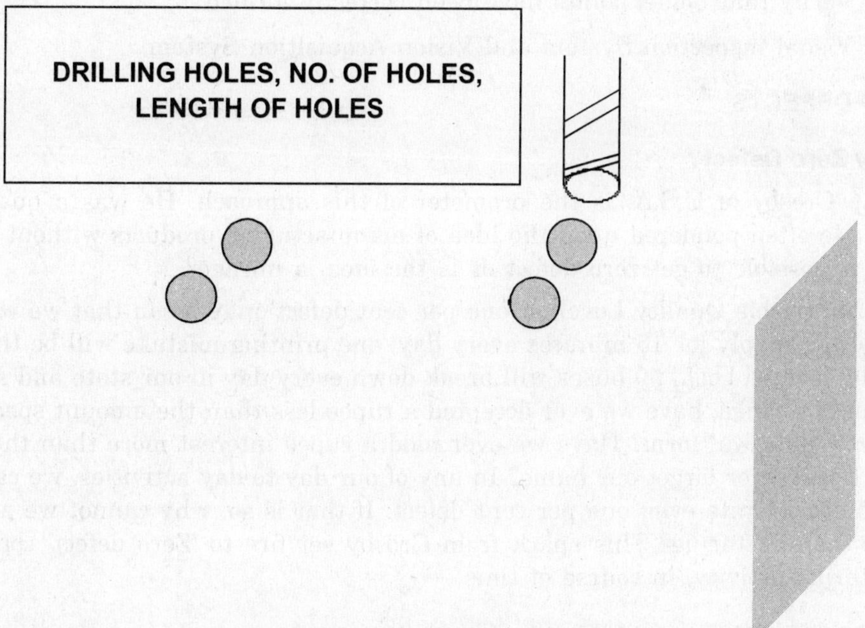

Fig. 6.2 Poka yoke for drilling holes

Case 6.1. Activity: Loading the work piece correctly on the table. Refer Fig. 6.1.

Objective: To ensure that the job (plate) is placed in level on the work table and get the holes drilled perpendicular to the surface.

If the job (plate) is not located in level (horizontal), the holes drilled will be inclined and the job may be rejected. Pneumatic sensors located at two places along the table, and energized by the pneumatic circuit will sense and indicate the differential or non-uniform gap. Only when the gaps are equal (or zero) the drill tool will rotate. This ensures that the holes are drilled perpendicular to the surface. This concept can be extended to obtain also the desired depth of holes drilled, on the job (plate).

Case 6.2. Activity: Drilling specified number of holes. Refer Fig. 6.2.

Objective: To ensure that the required number of holes are drilled before removing the job for next operation.

The proximity sensors attached to the spindle and to the table, will count the number of holes completed, every time upon withdrawal of the drill from the job. The counter will not allow the job to be removed until the required number of holes are drilled. This will ensure that the designed number of holes is completed on each job.

Case 6.3. Inspection of Printed Circuit Board (PCB)

Various steps suggested towards poka-yoke, in the case of a PCB assembly are:

1. Verify that the components have been inserted in the correct places.
2. Check circuit paths for any breaks.
3. Check circuit paths for any short circuits due to bolder or debris.
4. Check for any defect in the leads of attached components to the board.
5. Verify that bolder joints have been correctly formed.
6. Visual inspection System and Vision Acquisition System.

6.2 ZERO DEFECTS

6.2.1 Why Zero Defect?

Philip Crosby of U.S.A. is the promoter of this approach. He was a quality control engineer. He often pondered upon the idea of manufacturing products without any defects at all. Is it possible to get zero defect or is the idea, a mirage?

The Acceptable Quality Level or 'one per cent defect' may mean that we will not have electric power supply for 15 minutes every day; one printing mistake will be there in each page of the printed book, 50 buses will break down every day in our state and so on! When we transact in banks, have we ever accepted a rupee less than the amount specified in the cheque or withdrawal form? Have we ever paid a rupee interest more than the stipulated amount? Do we ever forget our name? In any of our day-to-day activities, we cannot afford to and do not tolerate even one per cent defect. If that is so, why cannot we achieve 'zero defect' in manufacturing? This spark from Crosby set fire to 'Zero defect' concept in the manufacturing activity, in course of time.

Some of the *guidelines* for zero defects would be relevant in this context:

1. Procrastination is the thief of time and honor. What can be done now, should be done immediately.
2. Have the courage to admit your mistakes. Do not throw the blame on others. Own your mistake and it will give you a chance to rectify errors, progress, succeed, and ultimately excel. All great people have committed errors in the early part of their life.
3. Be honest. Do not compromise on quality. Do not pass on the defective component to the customer. You will be considered incompetent and demotivated.
4. No compromise on quality. Do not accept sub-standard product or supplies. Exhibit moral autonomy, based on facts, without fear or favour.
5. A change in the mind set or cultural change is required to achieve zero defects.
6. Training and sustained efforts are needed. Rome was not built in a day! The Independence Day flag was raised in one minute. But the freedom fight went on for over one hundred years! Many a human lives were sacrificed.
7. Never-ending Faith and Enthusiasm are needed not only to reach but also continue to stay at Zero defects.
8. On the top of all these, the Management commitment in providing the means and directions are the most important to realise the Zero defects.

6.2.2 Definition

Zero defect is defined as a management concept, aimed at the reduction of defects while manufacturing, through 'prevention'. It is achieved by motivating people to prevent mistakes, by developing a constant and conscious desire to do their job right the first time and every time. It is achieved by aligning their desire, knowledge, and actions, i.e., aligning Ichcha sakthi, Gnana sakthi, and Kriya sakthi or in other words, *the heart, the head, and the hands!*

In the order of importance, the sources of defects have been identified as:

1. Omitted process
2. Errors in the process
3. Errors in setting the work piece
4. Missing parts
5. Wrong parts
6. Processing wrong work piece
7. Disoperation
8. Adjustment errors
9. Equipment not set up properly
10. Improperly prepared tools and jigs
11. Improperly stored tools and jigs

6.2.3 How Achieved?

The steps to achieve Zero Defect are:

1. Setting objectives for improvement
2. Adopt the identified procedures

3. Compare the achievements and objectives, and continue the corrective actions towards the objectives
4. Understanding, acceptance of concepts and participation in action by all employees
5. Motivation to change from 'tolerate a few defects' (AQL) to 'no defects at all'
6. Standardise the systems for the removal of the cause, as a way of life and
7. Continue to improve and stay at Zero defect.

6.2.4 Award for Zero Defect

It is worth mentioning that, Sarva shri Raghunath Medge and Talekar, the two Mumbai dabba-wallahs were honoured with the 'Lucas-NIQR' award on behalf of their organisation for making only one mistake in six million tiffin box deliveries across Mumbai. Their organisation, which is 115 years old, has been serving lunch to two lakhs office-goers every afternoon. Their success is attributed to the preference of the people for home-cooked meal, and the super-efficient suburban rail system which effects delivery of lunch 'on time, every time'. It is reported that these people are able to compete with General Electric and Motorola with near zero-error and that too with 'no investment, no working capital and no modern technology'.[14]

6.3 JIT–PHILOSOPHY OF ELIMINATING WASTE

6.3.1 The Concept

The Just-in-time concept can be explained as follows: Production is viewed as a system of stream. The water level in the stream is analogous to inventory. At the bottom of the stream are rocks, that is the problems relating to quality, vendor, delivery, and machines. The traditional approach is to hold inventory high enough to cover up the rocks and thereby keep the stream flowing. The JIT approach is just the opposite; the water level is lowered to expose the top of the rocks. And the rocks are pulverized, i.e., the problems solved, the water is lowered again and more rocks are exposed. This process is repeated until all rocks are turned into pebbles and the stream flows smoothly at a low level. This analogy appropriately highlights the problem-solving approach of JIT. The JIT philosophy involves continuing improvement, simplification and elimination through problem solving.

When JIT is applied to manufacturing, the products are manufactured to order, in right quantity and in time for the immediate delivery to customers. The raw materials also arrive just-in-time, before the manufacturing activity begins.

Product cost = Material cost + Overhead costs + Direct Labour.

To keep the product cost low, it is essential to reduce the material cost and overhead costs. The carrying costs (rentals and maintenance of stores or go-down and salary for the stores staff, and transportation costs) increase with quantity of inventory and time, since the materials deteriorate over storage, or the demand for the end products may fall. According to this concept, keep the inventory to bare minimum or even zero.

The Just-in-time philosophy aims at focusing the efforts towards elimination of wastage of resources, by procuring the right materials as well as manufacturing the right quantity of products in right time. It means zero inventories and no surplus of materials or products. It is said in the lighter vein, that while the Japanese philosophy insists on Just-In-Time, we people follow *Just-In-Case* philosophy!

This concept can be applied even in our households. Weekly purchase of vegetables and fruits, storing in the refrigerator and spending for electric energy can be avoided or minimized, by purchasing them in smaller quantity or daily. Gone are the days when people in the villages were used to buy paddy and grocery items such as *toor dhall*, chilli, oils, and jaggery and store them in earthen vessels or pots, for a long time before use.

6.3.2 Reduce Waste

JIT attacks waste. A waste is defined as, 'any thing other than, minimum amount of equipment, materials, parts, and working time that is absolutely necessary for manufacture'. The Japanese principles list three Ms to be avoided, namely:

1. MUDA or Muddling, i.e., waste, cut or minimize the waste
2. MURI or Muscling, i.e., fatigue, over-burden or strain
3. MURA or Murkiness, i.e., Instability or discrepancy

The Seven Deadly Wastes

The automobile industry in Japan has classified the wastes into the following seven types:

1. *Overproduction:* Because of poor production planning and over estimation of sales, more than what is required is produced and kept idle.
2. *Waiting time:* This exists for the work in progress in the shops or finished products in trnsit.
3. *Unnecessary transportation:* Proper layout planning will reduce this.
4. *Processing waste:* Total productive maintenance will eliminate this waste.
5. *Inventory waste:* J.I.T., and Good house keeping will reduce this waste.
6. *Wasted motion:* Proper training on the job and availability of appropriate tools will eliminate this.
7. *Waste from defective products:* Zero defect program, proper planning of the production, up-keep of the tools and measuring devices, are definite to eliminate this type of waste.

Absolute Minimum Resource is achieved by the following ways:

1. Having one or more, but reliable suppliers
2. No safety stock of raw materials or equipment or instruments
3. Minimise the time for product planning and process planning
4. No excess lead time
5. No testing or inspection beyond the optimum level
6. People not executing the jobs that do not 'add value'. Eliminate the following:
   (*a*) Persons waiting for work or the machine or getting tools
   (*b*) Machines waiting for workers
   (*c*) Unnecessary transportation, handling, and storing of raw materials or work in-process or finished products
   (*d*) Setting up of the jobs as well as the tools, and rework and
   (*e*) Cleaning up the oils or chemicals for subsequent operation.

7. Increasing the operator utilisation: An operator can attend upon more than one automatic machine. While the first machine continues its operation (in automatic mode), the operator fixes the job in the second machine and so on. After fixing the job in the fourth machine, the person goes to the first machine, which by then has completed the operation, and removes the job and so on. Neither the machine nor the operator is kept waiting. Both are fully utilized.
8. Prevention of the causes of errors at their sources. Prevention is better than cure, from the point of view of time and money. The cost of rejection is more than the cost of rework. The cost of rework is more than the prevention cost. This is the basic approach towards anticipatory management.

6.3.3 Components of JIT

1. *Planning:* Establish balance between capacity (requirements) and Flow. A well documented system is to be laid.
2. *People:* Employee involvement. The mental make-up of people from top to bottom, appropriate education and training, motivation, and recognition and reward system are the essential ingredients of employee involvement. Quality circles play important role in this direction.
3. *Philosophy:* Doing it right first time, and every time.
4. *Technology:* Good Information Technology infrastructure is vital. Enterprise Resource Planning, Continuous monitoring of the inventory, automatic reordering at specified inventory levels, automated delivery process and productive maintenance of machinery are some of the essential features to be incorporated to achieve success.

6.3.4 Essential Requirements of JIT

1. Flow manufacturing: that is, manufacturing without any in-process inventory
2. Simplified production process:
   (*a*) More general purpose machines and simplified set-up are recommended
   (*b*) Lesser movement of materials
   (*c*) Use of jigs and fixtures
   (*d*) Simplified purchase activity
3. Uncovering problems buried by inventory
4. Emphasis on Total quality management, including documentation
5. Good productive maintenance
6. Good house keeping (5S) and
7. Continual improvement

In some of the automobile tyre manufacturing industries, the long wait for the realization of money after the delivery, no longer exists. There is no need of sending the bills every day. From the sales department, the number of cars rolled out of the factory at the end of the day, and the tyres (four plus one spare) fitted are known, and hence the bills are prepared automatically and the payments are made daily, accordingly.

6.3.5 Aims and Techniques for JIT

AIMS	TECHNIQUES ADOPTED
Zero inventory	(*a*) JIT purchasing
	(*b*) Kanban pull system
Zero Lead time	(*a*) Reduction of queuing time by automatic production level controls
	(*b*) Standard operations
	(*c*) Line balancing
	(*d*) Manual relief
	(*e*) Small lots for production and transport
	(*f*) Reduction of processing time by production layout
	(*g*) Reduced set up time
	(*h*) Reduction of transport time by production layout
	(*i*) Quick means of transport
Zero set up Time	(*a*) By converting internal set up, as far as possible, to external set up
	(*b*) Abolish the setup wherever possible
Zero defects	(*a*) TQM (Do not use AQL)
	(*b*) Poka-Yoke
	(*c*) Preventive maintenance
	(*d*) House keeping
Zero material handling	(*a*) U shaped layout
	(*b*) Group technology

6.3.6 Limitations of JIT

However JIT is not without any limitations. Some of the specific problems (limitations) listed by JIT users include:

1. Initial investment and cost of implementation is high.
2. Time needed to get improvements.
3. Reliance on perfect quality of materials needed from vendors.
4. Inability of vendors to adapt to JIT methods.
5. Variable demand from customers.
6. Difficulty of reducing setup times.
7. Lack of commitment with the organisation.
8. Need to change layout of facilities.
9. Increased stress on workforce.
10. Vulnerable to plant shutdowns.
11. It cannot accommodate frequent new product introductions because of the need to introduce 'Kanban' cards for all components and parts.

12. Frequent delivery of small lots can generate highway congestion, a phenomenon that has been observed in crowded cities.

6.4 KANBAN SYSTEM

The KANBAN system was introduced in 1950 at Toyota by Taiichi Ohno, with the following objectives:

1. Eliminate waste or scrap and reduce costs
2. Design work stations to create mutual trust and support among human beings
3. Design work stations to adapt and respond to changes quickly and
4. Promote achieving and assuring quality improvement

'Kan' means card and 'ban' means signal. Originally Kanban referred to the cards along with boxes or craters used to transport materials or semi-finished components from one work station to another, in the production line. The components are moved only when needed (on demand) by the next station, such that there is no waiting of parts for operation or further movement. A set of cards, one for each component being produced, move from one station to its subsequent station.

Two types of Kanban commonly used are 1. Withdrawal Kanban and 2. Production Kanban. In the withdrawal system, the authorisation is passed for the movement of components from one station to another. The card remains with the components until the last piece is consumed by the following station. The card is sent back to the preceding station to get another batch of components. These cards contain the details of the component number, name, batch size, route, name and location of the next work station, name and location of the preceding work station and the details of the boxes/craters.

In the production Kanban system, the order is released to the preceding work station for the required batch size. This card contains details of the materials or components required in the previous station and details mentioned in the previous paragraph. In actual practice, the withdrawal Kanban is issued first to allow the component to enter the production stage. Upon entry, a production Kanban is issued and retained with the components until all work steps listed in the Kanban are completed.

Thus it can be seen that in the Kanban system, the components are pulled to the production line, as against the conventional forecast oriented method, wherein the components are *pushed to* the line and *through* the line. As the components are supplied to the work stations only when needed for manufacture, work in process as well as idle inventories are reduced to a large extent.

Other advantages of the Kanban system are:

(*a*) It responds quickly to the increase or decrease in demands.

(*b*) Defective parts are isolated and moved out of line.

(*c*) Precise information on movements and delays are quickly monitored and so controlled.

(*d*) Over production is avoided.

(*e*) Facilitates cellular manufacturing system.

(*f*) promotes kaizen by the team members involved.

6.5 QUALITY CIRCLE

6.5.1 Introduction

Japan was defeated in the World War II, in 1945. All the industries were destroyed and there was no food, clothing, and housing. Most of the people were starving. Around 1946, the U.S. Forces instructed Japanese industries to use statistical quality control and the JIS marking. It was at this juncture, that The Japan Union of Scientists and Engineers (JUSE) was established.

In 1949, the quality control research was promoted to rationalize the Japanese industries to export quality goods, and to raise the living standards of the people. The first basic course on quality was conducted in Japan in that year.

When Dr Edward Deming visited Japan in 1950, he organized seminars on SQC for managers and engineers on: How to use P-D-C-A in Design, Production, Sales, Service, and Redesign to enhance quality. He trained them for process control, through control charts. He stressed the importance of statistics. But SQC created problems. No standards were available. Workers could not use SQC. The data were not available. Data were not collected properly. The workers suspected the motives, because SQC was over-emphasized. Top managers did not show any interest.

In 1954, Dr. J.M. Duran was invited to help the Japanese industries. He conducted seminars for top and middle level managers. He emphasized that QC is a management tool. This created an opening for the establishment of Total Quality Control. SQC emphasized sample inspection, correction and control. TQC stressed on production of defect-free components through control of manufacturing process, design, planning, and service.

In 1958, Dr. Ishikawa modified the QC. He involved workers and called it 'Company-Wide Quality Control'. JUSE started publishing QC Journals for the foremen and workers. He requested them to form groups to read and understand the articles. Upon this, the foremen and workers tried to use QC techniques in their work area.

It was in 1962, the quality circles were initially launched. The tools such as brain-storming, flow diagrams, data collection through check sheets, stratification of data, pareto charts, cause and effect diagram, histogram, control charts, and scatter diagram were developed and applied to identify and solve the problems.

Quality was never an accident; it is always the result of high intention followed by actions. Then to succeed, people should develop confidence and faith, work as team, involving everybody. Taiwan is a good example in this respect. The per capita income of Taiwan was \$ 48 in 1952, \$ 500 in 1972, which rose to \$ 6000 in 1992! The secret of success was that they gave priority for solving internal constraints. They understood and accepted the reality and the need for changes. The inflation was reduced to 0 %. The unemployment rate was reduced 2 %. That is the success story of Taiwan.

The rapid industrial developments in Japan were attributed to the successful functioning of the quality circles. It was in 1982, the quality circles were introduced for the first time in our country, at the Bharath Heavy Electricals Ltd., Hyderabad. The quality circle Forum of India, with its headquarters at Hyderabad, and branches all over the country, has been offering guidance, training, and motivation through awards for best performance.

6.5.2 Objectives of Quality Circle

The Quality circle is a voluntary activity and its function and success depends upon:

(*a*) Commitment of the top management,

(*b*) Involvement of all the members, and

(*c*) the recognition and reward system existing in the organisation.

The commitment of the management should be available always for the success of this circle. This success stories in the Indian scene show ample evidence of the top management visiting the shop floors, mixing with the workers, encouraging their actions and recognizing their achievements and appropriately rewarding them.

PEOPLE BUILDING is a basic principle of quality circle. Japan has risen from the ashes of Nagasaki and Hiroshima, through the sustained hard work of the people. The patriotic fervour, sufferings, discipline, sacrifice and tolerance have united the people in their journey towards prosperity. The people grew with the organisations. The heads of the commercial organisations are more familiar to the Japanese (and to the world outside also!) than their religious or political heads.

The SYNERGY in team work is another philosophy of the quality circle. Two people put together, can perform better than the sum of two individuals. 'Union is strength' is the proven proverb.

'NO BLAME' is a fundamental concept of quality circle. Instead of investigating 'who was wrong?', the objectives will be realised soon, if 'what went wrong?' was analysed. Ego problems, mental tension, enmity, and arguments will only drive the solutions farther away. It has been proved in the long run that, *what* is right is more important than *who* is right! This is said to be the typical Japanese way of living. It is said that they always view the life as with '*no problem*'. They believe that, if one ponders upon problems always, the person himself *becomes* a problem to the Society! They attempt to innovate and solve the problems.

It is of relevance to narrate what happened twenty five years back in our country. There was power cut every where, many times undeclared. It existed even during the winter months. But then, we were blaming each other. We blamed the governments, the Electricity Board staff and so on. A Japanese trade team visited then, many parts of India for about two months. They took note of the situation. A few months after their return home, the Indian market was flooded with portable diesel and petrol generators of capacities of 1.5, 2.5 and 4 kVA. Even small vegetable vendors, betel-nut shop owners, and hut dwellers owned the portable generators and all the people were happy. It must be pointed out that at that time our country had capability of manufacturing 1000, 1500 and 2500 kVA diesel generators for the services. Nobody ever thought of making small capacity generators, but we spent our energy only in blaming each other. Everybody was thinking and talking about, what the other person should do. Nobody gave thought to "what I can do to solve the problem?" The *threat* that existed in India was converted into *a gift or an opportunity*, by the Japanese minds.

Yet another basis for success of quality circle is its *Voluntary nature*. People come forward without anticipating any personal gain or results, but with faith, willingness to experiment and hope to succeed. Quality circle members exhibit also a 'Sense of owning', that is, selflessness and willingness to work for the development of the organisation and so for themselves. Another characteristic feature of the quality circle is its 'bottom-up' approach. Normally in the 'top-down' approach, the top management plan and issue orders to the lower cadre. Whereas, in quality circles, the employees discuss on the problems, study, solve, implement solutions, and report to the top management.

The objectives of Quality circle are illustrated in Fig. 6.3.

Fig. 6.3 Objectives of quality circle

6.5.3 Structure of Quality Circle

A typical structure of the quality circle is shown in Fig. 6.4.

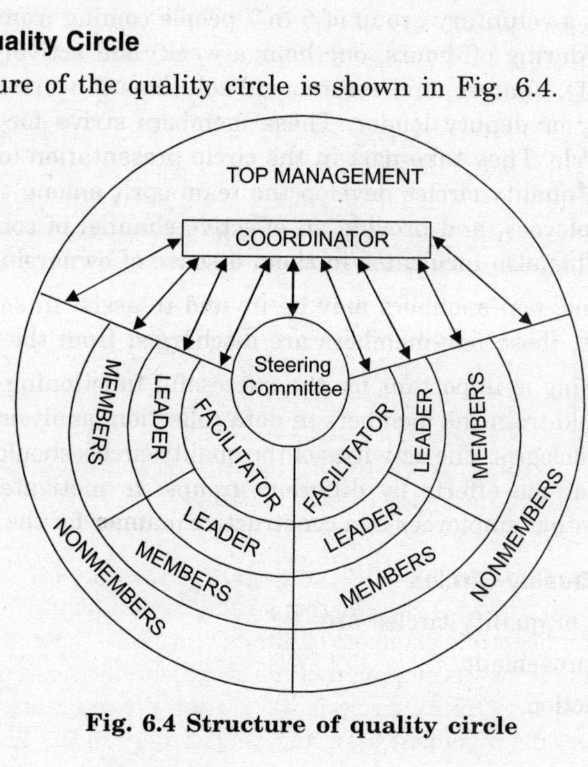

Fig. 6.4 Structure of quality circle

1. Top Management—The Chairperson, Managing Director, Directors, General Managers and other top Executives should lend support to the philosophy and activities of QC. They motivate the people by meeting circle leaders and members periodically. They should incorporate QC promotion as one of the company's objectives.

2. Steering Committee—The steering committee comprises of representatives of all major functions. It is responsible for establishing objectives and resources. They meet regularly once in two or three months with facilitators as invitees. This committee provides guidance and direction. It gives the thrust by promoting QC as a way of life. This committee attends top management's presentation and annual social get together. These activities demonstrate visibly the management's commitment, support and faith.

3. Facilitator—A senior officer heading an area or department is chosen as the facilitator. This person is responsible for the successful function of the circles in one's area. The facilitator trains members by assisting leaders, and solves interface problems between circles. He/she demonstrates support of the management, and works closely with the steering committee. The facilitator maintains the activity level records of circles, reports to the steering committee, and takes timely and corrective actions to revitalize the inactive circles.

4. Leader/Deputy Leader—The Leader is chosen by the members. The leader guides, trains the members, involves every member in circle activities. He/she prepares the agenda and conducts the meetings regularly and effectively and ensures discipline and decorum. The leader chalks out action plan. He/she maintains records and interacts with other agencies for solving problems. The leader organizes management presentation. In essence, the leader catalyses the attitudinal changes in the people.

5. Members—It is a voluntary group of 5 to 7 people coming from the same work area. They meet regularly (during off-hours, one hour a week) and actively participate in circle meetings. They identify, analyse, and recommend solutions to work-related problems, and thus assist the leader or deputy leader. These members strive for highest standards of performance of the circle. They take part in the circle presentation (on problem solving) to the management. The quality circles develop the team sprit among the members, improve the morale of the employees, and provide an effective channel of communication upwards in the organisation. This also inculcates in them a sense of ownership of the organisation.

On a few occasions, non-members may be invited to assist in solving problems. Upon reaching the solutions, these non-members are discharged from the quality circle.

Appropriate training is important for the successful functioning of the quality circles. The management should train the members in data collection, analysis, decision making and problem solving methodologies. The activities of the quality circles should be made transparent, to avoid duplication of the efforts by different groups, to motivate the members of the circles, and to involve other employees in a constructive manner for the process improvements

6.5.4 Advantages of Quality Circles

The advantages of quality circles are:

1. Quality improvement.
2. Waste reduction.

3. Attitudinal change.
4. Cost reduction.
5. Safety improvement.
6. Improved communication.
7. Higher productivity.
8. Increased job satisfaction.
9. Team building.
10. Improvement in skills.
11. Self esteem.

6.5.5 Quality Circles in Educational Institutions

Although the quality circles were adopted in manufacturing industries, they have spread into service industries such as hospitals, banks, transportation, and educational institutions, in the present. As per the University regulations, the class committee consisting of the concerned teacher, student representatives, and a chairperson who is not teaching the class is to be formed for each class. Three or four meetings per semester are prescribed. The class committee functions towards solving problems experienced by the students, communicating the schemes of assigning weightage for various modules of evaluation, identifying the weak students and recommending necessary corrective actions and preventive actions by the teachers. Thus the class committee serves as a 'quality circle'.

CASE STUDIES

Case 6.4 The absenteeism in the industry as well as in the educational institutions is the most common problem existing in the country, for a long time. By discussion in the quality circle, and class room, using brainstorming and other techniques, various causes and the recommended remedies are listed in Table 6.1

Table 6.1 Absenteeism in class/factory

Causes/symptoms	Remedies
A. PHYSIOLOGICAL:	
1. Laziness	1. Physical exercises
2. Health problems or illness of the self or a member in the family	2. Camps for health check up by college/factory
3. Liquor habits, and drug addiction	3. Meditation and introspection
4. Physically challenged persons (Deaf, or blind or lame)	4. Counselling the students on habits, health and hygiene
5. Early marriage (during education)	5. Counselling the parents, in some cases, against liquor habits, consanguineous marriages and on parenting
	6. Provision of food with nutrients
	7. Schemes sponsored by the Govt. or charitable organisations for physically challenged persons

	8. Open occupational health centers for periodical check up, preventive services, biological monitoring/tests, health risk assessment study and audits on exposure to materials/and chemicals 9. Health awareness programs by medical teams to address life-style diseases (hyper tension, diabetes, heart diseases) (e.g., RIL)
B. MENTAL HEALTH: 1. Habits 2. Illness of the self or a member in the family 3. Mentally retarded	1. Counselling 2. Exercises for mental health 3. Counselling students against drug addiction, and to prevent consanguineous marriages
C. COMMUTING PATTERN: 1. Tiresome travel by long distance by bus or train 2 No bus transport available 3. Changing of bus due to breakdown or remoteness	1. Locate a room or house nearby 2. Join a college nearby 3. Provision of bus facility by the organisations, from specific vantage terminals
D. POOR INFRASTRUCTURE: 1. Crowded canteen and crowded mess 2. Unhygienic canteen or mess	1. Stagger the timings of mess 2. Provide students co-operative stores to issue stationery 3. Integrated management system encompassing the requirements of ISO 9000 (Quality), ISO 14001 (Envt.) and OHSAS 18001 (Occupational health and safety assmt) (e.g. RIL.)
E. FAMILY ENVIRONMENT: 1. Parents' disinterest 2. Separated family, divorced parents, men marrying second time and deserting the first wife and children 3. Children living with grand parents since either of parents is in jail or employed elsewhere away 4. Loss of either of or both the parents	1. Family counselling of the parents 2. Programs for drop-outs 3. Social service schemes effected by non-profit organisations such as Rotary club or Lions club 4. Public-private partnerships to contain spread of diseases such as TB and HIV/AIDS though counselling, education, training, social and nutritional support (e.g., RIL)

5. Physical or mental damage to the parents 6. Parents sending their wards on errands or for work to earn livelihood 7. Drop-out from educational institutions due to poverty or bonded labour 8. Sickly wife/ husband/ parents/ child or other elders	
F. PHYSICAL ENVIRONMENT (HOUSE):	
1. Mosquito problem leading to sleepless nights	1. Supply mosquito nets
2. Gambling and boot-legging activities in or near their house	2. Train the parents with rural sanitation
3. Contagious diseases prevailing during seasons (cholera, dysentery, typhoid, chickenpox, etc.)	3. Counselling parents against liquor habits and drug addiction
4. Parents' personal or political enmity, caste enmity in the village, preventing the free movement of students	4. Conduct awareness camps in villages against boot-legging, child marriage, infant mortality, and on sanitation 5. Conduct family welfare health camp and administer inoculation/vaccination against communicable diseases 6. Promote sports and recreational activities in the residential area

Case 6.5. LATE-COMING

Late coming is often the problem in industries and educational institutions existing in the rural area as well as in the outskirts of the cities. Hence an attempt was made to study the causes and the remedies. Table 6.2 illustrates this example.

Table 6.2 Late coming or late reporting

Causes/Symptoms	Remedies
A. LACK OF DISCIPLINE:	
1. No attendance register	1. Awareness of duties and responsibilities, besides rights 2. Teachers/officers to be punctual 3. Automated (using proximity card) entry registration 4 Counseling the students/workers
B. POOR PHYSICAL HEALTH:	
1. Falling sick frequently	1. Appoint Medical Officers 2. Appoint Physical Education Director

	3. Start daily activities after a brief physical exercise (drill), as practised in Japanese industries 4. Ensure hygienic and subsidised food in the mess/canteen 5. Conduct awareness program on environmental management.
C. POOR MENTAL HEALTH: 1. Not punctual 2. Liquor habits	1. additional counselling 2. Promotion of recreational activities 3. Course in personality development, and team work
D. POOR INFRASTRUCTURE: 1. Over crowding of the hostel mess during lunch 2. Insufficient lunch interval 3. No vehicles of transport for students. Hence they travel even in trucks and tractors, which are unscheduled and unsafe	1. Make lunch interval longer, by 10 minutes (50-60 min) 2. Stagger the timings for the lunch interval 3. Employ the full time Physical Education Director 4. Stagger the postal delivery timings 5. Provide vehicles for transport to and fro, especially after sports and long library assignments 6. Promote hostel (social) life culture and allow better utilisation of the infrastructure (gymkhana, library, and internet) facilities.

Case 6.6 PRODUCT DEFECTS

A problem prevailing in the manufacturing industries, especially the small scale industries, is the occurrence of product defects. Accordingly, the reasons and remedies are observed and presented in Table 6.3.

Table 6.3 Product defects

Causes/Symptoms	Remedies
A. EQUIPMENTS: 1. Worn-out parts of machines 2. Use of equipments beyond the stipulated (useful) life 3. Overloaded equipments 4. Frequent break down of equipments	1. Total productive maintenance 2. Promote autonomous maintenance groups 3. Regular calibration of equipments and tools 4. Regular calibration of measuring instruments

5. Use of erroneous instruments	5. Operation manual must be made available, updated, and operators communicated
6. Use of non-calibrated instruments	6. Ensure availability of spare parts adequately.
7. Design specifications too tight for adjustments during manufacture	
8. Installation subcontracted and inadequately supervised	
9. No operation manual ready	
10. Inadequate supply of spare parts	
B. OPERATORS:	
1. Lack of training in setting-up	1. Appropriate training in setting up of machines, and tools
2. Wrong use of tools and fixtures	2. Training in handling and using the measuring instruments
3. Wrong measurements	3. Updating the 'know how' and 'do how' through periodical training
4. Poor or rough handling of materials before and after machining	4. Knowledge and training of test standards
5. Unsafe workplace conditions	
6. Disregard for stress due to repetitive motion, in workers	
C. MANAGEMENT:	
1. No clear replacement policy prescribed or enforced	1. Specify investment and replacement policies
2. No quality mgt. system in effect	2. Implement total productive Maintenance system
3. No OHAS system in effect	3. Promote autonomous maintenance group and activities
4. No TPM system in operation	4. Obtain ISO certification
5. Training subcontracted or inadequate	5. Implement OHAS system
6. No formal procedure for following life cycle of product, its effects on society and environment	6. Promote quality circles
	7. Install recognition and reward system
	8. Conduct family welfare and health camps for employees
D. MATERIALS:	
1. Faulty materials	1. Education and training in handling materials and products

2. Poor inspection	2. Training in quality control methods and principles
3. Poor handling including stacking	3. Supplier rating and partnering and development
4. Inadequate testing of purchased materials or parts	
E. METHODS:	
1. Lack of training and instructions	1. Training the workers
2. Not updating the drawings	2. Continuous education and training on practices of standard tests
3. Faulty material handling	3. Use of computers to learn drawing including specifications
4. Faulty or incomplete processing	4. Promotion of quality circles
5. Wrong measurements	5. Provision of browsing facility to familiarise with standard testing and updating on developments
6. Non-standard or faulty testing	
7. Tests rushed or results falsified	

6.6 SIX SIGMA

6.6.1 Introduction

Six Sigma is defined as a statistical measure of the performance of a process or a product. It establishes a measurable status on yield as defects per million opportunities, a goal that reaches near perfection for performance improvement. It reduces variation to achieve very small standard deviations, so that almost all products and services meet or exceed customer expectations. It is a system of management to achieve lasting business leadership and World Class performance. It is a management philosophy focused on eliminating mistakes, eliminating rework, waste and scrap.

Six Sigma efforts target three main areas, namely,

1. Reducing defects to Retain the customer, get new markets.
2. Reducing cycle time for Cost savings.
3. Improving Customer satisfaction.

The objectives of this approach are: (1) Decrease manufacturing and design cycle time, (2) Enhance customer satisfaction and market position, (3) Decrease costs due to inventory, scrap and rework, (4) Cultivate new business and hold on to old business and (5) Increase profitability and shareholder value.

The Six Sigma is implemented in the following steps:

1. Emphasizing 'dpmo' as a standard metric that can be applied to all parts of an organisation – manufacturing, engineering, administrative, software and so on.

2. Providing extensive training followed by project team deployment to improve profitability, reduce non-value added activities and achieves cycle time reduction.

3. Focusing on corporate sponsor responsible for supporting team activities, helping to overcome resistance to change, obtain resources, and focus the teams on overall strategic objectives.

4. Creating highly qualified process improvement experts who can apply improvement tools and lead teams.

5. Ensuring that appropriate metrics are identified early in the process and that they focus on business results.

6. Setting objectives for improvement.

6.6.2 Approach for Six Sigma problem by General Electric

The steps recommended by the General Electric Co. in solving Six Sigma problems, called DMAIC are detailed below:

1. Define (D) (1) Identify customers and their priorities, (2) Identify a project suitable for six sigma efforts based on business objectives as well as customer needs and feedback and (3) Identify critical-to-quality characteristics that the customer considers to have the most impact on quality.

2. Measure (M) (1) Determine how to measure the process and how is it performing and (2) Identify the key internal processes that influence CTQs and measure the defects currently generated relative to those processes.

3. Analyse (A) (1) Determine the most likely causes of defects and (2) Understand why defects are garneted by identifying the key variable that are most likely to create process variation.

4. Improve (I) (1) Identify means to remove the causes of the defects, (2) Confirm the key variable and quantify their effects on the CTQs, (3) Identity the maximum acceptable range of the key variable and a system for measuring deviations of the variables and (4) Modify the process to stay within the acceptable range.

5. Control (C) (1) Determine how to maintain the improvements and (2) Put tools in place to ensure that the key variables remain within the maximum acceptable ranges under the modified process.

Example 6.1 If there are 9 defects among 150 invoices, and there are 8 opportunities for errors for every invoice, what is the dpmo?

dpu = no. of defects / total no. of product units = 9/150 = 0.06 dpu

dpo = no. of defects / (no. of units × no. of defect opportunities per unit)

= 9/ (150 × 8) = 0.0075 dpo

dpmo = dpo × 1,000,000 = 0.0075 × 1,000,000 = 7,500 dpmo

Example 6.2 **What are the equivalent sigma and C_p values, given a proportion defective of 1%?**

Yield $= 1 - p = 1 - 0.01 = 0.990$ Z table value for $0.990 = 2.32\ \sigma$

Estimate the process capability by adding $1.5\ \sigma$ to reflect the 'real world' shift in the process mean, $2.32\ \sigma + 1.5\ \sigma = 3.82\ \sigma$

This σ value can be converted to an equivalent C_p, by dividing it by $3\ \sigma$:

$C_p = 3.82\ \sigma / 3\ \sigma = 1.27$

Figure 6.5 and Table 6.4 illustrate clear pictures of six sigma approach, compared to the conventional approach.

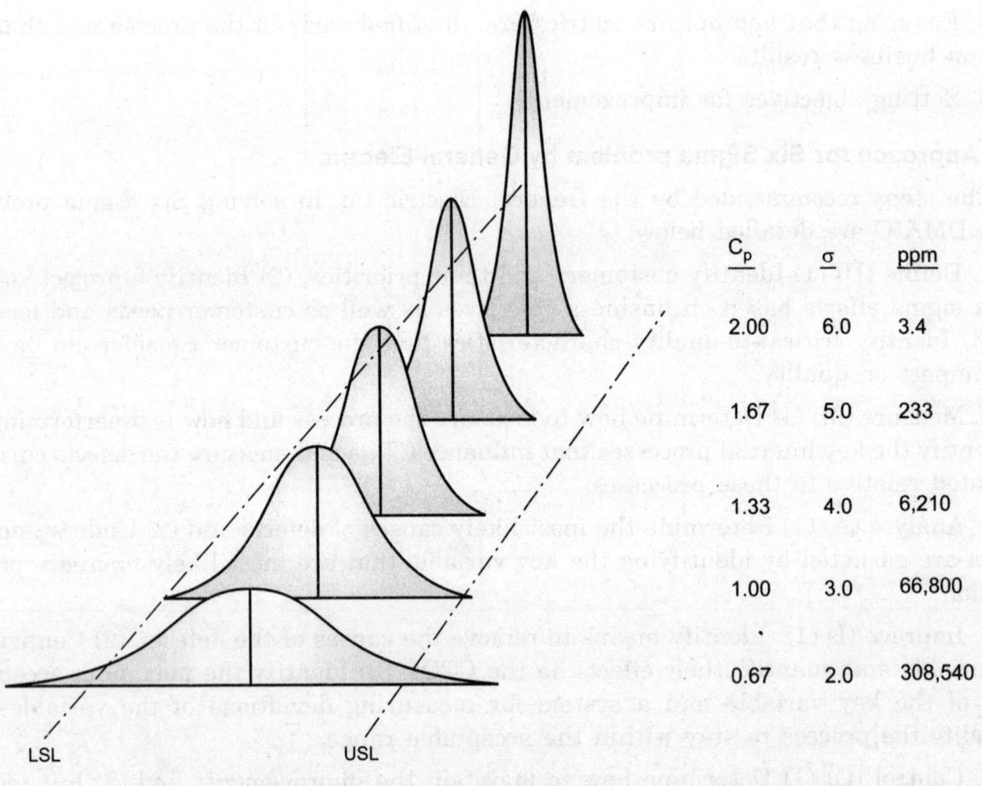

Fig. 6.5 A comparison between 2σ and 6σ approaches

Table 6.4 Sigma Table

Yield	dpmo	Sigma (ó)	C_p Equiv.	COPQ (Cost of Poor Quality)
0.840	160,000	2.50	0.83	40%
0.870	130,000	2.63	0.88	
0.900	100,000	2.78	0.93	
0.930	70,000	2.97	0.99	
0.935	65,000	3.01	1.00	
0.940	60,000	3.05	1.02	
0.945	55,000	3.10	1.03	30%
0.950	50,000	3.14	1.05	
0.960	40,000	3.25	1.08	
0.970	30,000	3.38	1.13	
0.980	20,000	3.55	1.18	20%
0.985	15,000	3.67	1.22	
0.990	10,000	3.82	1.27	
0.995	5,000	4.07	1.36	
0.998	2,000	4.37	1.46	
0.999	1,000	4.60	1.53	10%
0.9995	500	4.79	1.60	
0.99975	250	4.98	1.66	5%
0.99998	20	5.61	1.87	
0.9999966	3.4	6.00	2.00	

❑ ❑ ❑

CHAPTER 7

Additional Case Studies

Many of the case studies that are presented herein were poked, provoked, and developed with our students and colleagues. They have been further modified and presented in the following pages, with the objective of inducing the minds of the teaching fraternity and student community, towards identifying and focussing on the solutions. These case studies serve as examples and are neither unique nor exhaustive, in solving the problems. Certainly they will guide and ignite the imagination of the creative minds of the individuals. The knowledge gained by these case studies, the authors trust fully, will create concrete and feasible ideas and solutions to the problems of the present as well as train us to meet the problems of the future.

CASE 7.1 BRAINSTORMING (REFER # 3.9.5)

Problem: Poor Academic Performance of Students

This is a common and perennial problem. This has been presented in many elite forums, challenged, discussed and had generated heat and fire, but the problem persists. Especially in the technical education scenario in our country, the institutions have been continuously exerting their energy towards raising the human excellence in education, training, innovative thinking, and promoting problem solving abilities. Institutions as well as the teachers have definite roles in developing the skills, experience, and confidence of students, in surviving of the changes and challenges of the future. Towards that objective, this exercise has become quite relevant.

Table 7.1 is the summary of the results of the 'poking and provoking' all the stakeholders namely, the students, teachers, administrators, experts, and the parents

Table 7.1 Poor academic performance of students[15,19].

Causes/Symptoms	Solutions
A. Students:	
1. Lack of preparation	1. 100 % attendance in the class
2. Lack of good and current (updated) text books	2. Buying necessary text books
3. Poor physical health	3. Inculcate library study habits
4. Poor mental health	4. Regular physical exercises

5. Difficulty with the medium of instruction, when different from that at the higher secondary level (e.g., Tamil/Telugu to English)	5. Practice of relaxation and meditation
6. Poor communication ability assessment, by attending C.I.A tests	6. Counselling by teachers or by professionals
7. Poor presentation because of lack of grammar, vocabulary, modulation, and errors in pronunciation	7. Participation in continuous internal and model examination and by submitting assignments in time
8. Uncertainty of employment upon activities. E.g. students' quiz Graduation, leading to disinterest	8. Participation in co-curricular seminar, sports, cultural activities and contribution in the form of creative works, news-letters, magazines and journals
9. Distraction due to T.V. Cinema, and cricket matches held for days/weeks	9. Participation in extra-curricular activities such as N.C.C., N.S.S., and Social service clubs
10. Involvement in crime/sex scandal due to association with gangs	10. Enrolment in Professional Societies e.g., I.E.E.E., I.E.I., C.S.I, and I.S.T.E.
11. Frequent power cuts in the nights especially during the examinations	11. Training on time management
12. Brainwash by political and religious forces, luring the youth	12. Training in personality development towards nurturing confidence, courage, involvement, and commitment, leading not only to success but also to *excellence*
13. Home-sick students extend their leave from home to be with parents	13. With the guidance of teachers, perform SWOT analysis and identify and develop their *core competencies*
14. Students with many arrears prefer to go for project work (on package deal) in centers outside the college, cutting classes in their final semester	14. Students should not speculate questions or skip some chapters
15. Students tamper mark lists in the university records, in collusion with some employees	
16. Students speculate questions and skip some chapters/units	
B. Teachers:	
1. Poor preparation	1. Teachers should report to the class on time (nay, a few minutes earlier)
2. No updating of knowledge	2. Teachers should keep the course-file including lesson plans, notes, and teaching aids, updated

3. No research activity	3. Encouraged to enrol as members in professional societies
4. Models or visual aids are not used	4. Promote research activity (MODROB, TAPTEC, R & D, and DST projects)
5. Reading or dictating from the text books	5. Subscribe for national and international journals and trans. of profnl. societies.
6. Teachers skip some chapters either for want of time or on speculation	6. Teachers motivated to write text books, and e-books on subjects of their specialisation
7. Teachers go late to the class	7. Encouraged to attend winter/summer schools conducted by ISTE, AICTE, university on thrust areas/themes 8. Teachers should work a few numerical/ tough problems in the class 9. Conduct special/coaching classes for poor performers and report to parents 10. Giving handouts/brief notes and definitions, and miss-spelt words wherever needed 11. Use of teaching aids (e.g., 2 D colour charts, 3 D models, and colour video shows) 12. Plan and conduct students' seminar at state level and motivate their participation 13. Encourage students to participate in group discussion/mini-projects (e.g. yoU EXCEL) 14. Teachers should train students on SWOT analysis and help them to identify and develop their *core competencies* 15. Teachers have to train the students on *conformity,* and yet through unlimited *creativity*
C. College:	
1. Low teacher-students ratio	1. Appointment of teachers in terms of quantity and quality (qualification and experience)
2. Poor infrastructure facilities such as transport, communication including internet access	2. ISO 9001:2008 Certification (periodic audit inclusive)
3. Absence of or weak recruitment policy	3. Establish and follow transparent and uniform recruitment policies
4. Absence of or weak promotion policy	4. Establish and follow transparent and uniform promotion policies

5. Poor pay scales	5. Implement appropriate pay scales
6. Poorly designed and unhygienic mess/canteen/room facilities	6. Obtain accreditation by NBA, AICTE
7. Insufficient number of books	7. Encouragement of teachers to write textbooks and data books
8. Inconvenient library timings	8. Library with adequate textbooks, reference books and journals
9. Courses not oriented to jobs	9. Library with reprographic facility and with adequate and convenient timings
10. No grievance-redressal mechanism	10. Implement career development schemes for teachers and non-teaching staff
	11. Provision of comfortable seating/rooms for teachers, with ventilation, illumination, and privacy (especially for women)
	12. Orientation program for newly inducted teachers by senior faculty/experts
	13. The essence of the feed back from the students and Professors, given to teachers
	14. Feedback from alumni to the teachers as well students, on current requirements of skills from employers/industries
	15. Counselling by professionals for the teachers and students
	16. Provision of well ventilated and illuminated lecture and drawing halls
	17. Laboratory commissioned with necessary equipments and with all of them in working condition
	18. Promotion of sports activities, provision of gymkhana, track, stadium and auditorium for students
	19. Placement cell to liaise with prospective employers, and for career guidance and counselling
	20. Entrepreneurial development cell
	21. Establish science and technology park and innovation centers as incubators, to nurture young entrepreneurs
	22. MOU with industries and higher institutes of learning such as I.I.T, and I.I.Sc., for short term programs or lectures on thrust areas/topics

	23. MOU with foreign universities for exchange of teachers and students in specific fields, and for twinning programs for students
	24. Open Higher education bureau and conduct coaching for GATE, TOEFL, GRE, etc.
	25. Establish the students' cooperative stores, telecommunication facilities, and common room
	26. Establish hobby center and recreational facility
	27. Establish music club and film club and conduct functions periodically
	28. College administration should start allied industries and run sandwich courses
	29. Initiate steps for autonomous status or deemed university
	30. Schedule lectures from industrial experts and consultants including environmental management.
	31. Arrange industrial visits and short tours
	32. Arrange students' seminar at the national and international levels each year, on current topics of importance and relevance
	33. Conduct language courses in English, Japanese, German and French
	34. Conduct courses even in Indian languages such as Hindi or Bengali
	35. Conduct 'open house' meet and serious follow-up of grievances/complaints.
D. University:	
1. Frequent revisions in syllabus	1. Revise the syllabus once in 2 or 3 years
2. Prescribing textbooks which are either obsolete or not available in the country	2. Schemes to promote teachers to write textbooks or learning materials in selected subjects/topics
3. Setting of question papers by teachers who have not taught the subjects in the immediate past	3. Educational broadcasts (T.V with interactive participation)
4. Passing examination question papers that are wrongly worded or out of syllabus or with insufficient or wrong data	4. Permit, with broad mind but planned controls (act as facilitator as well as controller), the autonomy or deemed

	University status to colleges, and they are encouraged to experiment with novel and job-oriented courses
5. 'Drill and kill' approach to curriculum, robbing the *joy* of learning.	5. Setting the syllabus by the experts from industries and senior teachers, who are currently teaching or doing research in that specialisation
6. Canvassing and enrolment by foreign universities or even Indian deemed universities through distance education mode.	6. Benchmarking of syllabus with that of leading national and international institutions, finding gaps, and taking corrective actions
	7. Select responsible examiners as question paper setters and valuers and making them accountable
	8. Provision for revaluation/re-totalling on demand, at reasonable fees
	9. Examinations reform: Examinations to test the creativity, thinking capability, understanding, and applications in changed situations, but not merely the memory; CIA to carry 50% marks
	10. Valuation system: Transparent (mistakes or wrong answers to be highlighted), proportionate marks for steps also
	11. Grading rather than marks system
	12. Choice-based credit system, to provide flexibility and yet promote healthy competition among students
	13. Promoting and financing the centers of excellence for training and updating the teachers' knowledge (e.g., COE in TQM and nano-technology at SRMIST DU, with Japanese collaboration)
	14. Promote technology parks/innovation centers/high tech. Clusters of small firms and promote them as incubation centers, where research theses are realised as products (e.g., WEDGE flat L.C.T.V. screen

	by Adrian Travis, a Cambridge University group, U.K) 15. Frame codes of ethics for regulating the behaviour/activities of students including day scholars, off the campus 16. Initiate steps to teach 'value based' education
E. Parents: 1. Not following reports of their wards 2. Separation of wards due to litigation, divorce proceedings between parents, or death of parents 3. Parent trap or Parents push: thrusting the study options/branches of specialisations on their wards 4. Grand parents/parents allowing their wards to enjoy care-free holidays and extend their stay at home 5. Parents retaining their wards for some personal errands	1. Guide and facilitate their wards to decide upon the courses of choice, and pursue 2. Follow-up on the progress reports of their wards 3. Visit their students in the college as well as their place of stay (hostel/lodge/room) once a semester 4. Frequently remind and convince their wards, not to extend their stay at home and/or miss the class, even for a single working day
F. Industries: 1. Lack of interaction with educational institutions 2. Lack of funding for research either in the industry or sponsored at the educational institutions	1. Promote industry-institution interaction (e.g., Bannari Amman Sugars with BIT) 2. MOU with educational institutions, not only to sell products and training package, but also for collaborative or sponsored research (e.g., Adastral Park, in U.K. housing the R&D center in photonics and nano-technology) 3. Corporate trust should offer scholarships /research grant/sponsor research and promote innovation at institutes of higher learning 4. Corporate industries are to run higher institutes of learning (e.g., IRTT, Erode, PSG. Institutes, Coimbatore, Nirma Institute of Mgt., Ahmedabad) 5. Promotion of off-line multimedia activities (e.g., TryScience and EXITE through IBM kiosks)

G. Government:	
1. No effective legislative controls on admission, starting of colleges and courses	1. Enact laws to supervise and for effective and timely control. The Govt. should act as a *facilitator* for growth and a *controller* to sustain the development of institutions
2. Education being in the concurrent lists of the State and the Center, views and measures have become divergent, time variant, and politically oriented	2. Allow the deemed universities to establish and experiment, but not to proliferate on commercial lines
	3. Motivate corporate industries to start colleges, deemed universities, and centers of excellence of education and training. (E.g., D.A.Instt. of I.C. Techy., G Nagar, Gujarath, by RIL)
	4. Tax industry to establish research, development, and innovation centers/ laboratories
	5. Govt. should watch on enrolment by foreign universities, especially upon globalisation.
	6. Laws regulating the behaviour/activities of students, off the campus
	7. Bringing 'education' to the state list.

CASE 7.2 SIX SIGMA

Case Study: A specialty hospital in a city uses diagnostic imaging of the body to identify the area of abnormality or disease in any of the human organ. Stress tests are conducted to study the damage or disease of heart and the images are taken before and after the stress tests.

The complaints from the patients were that excessive turn around time for tests was consumed. The TAT is the time interval between the time of order for nuclear test and when the radiologist signs off on the test report. This led to inordinate waiting time for the patients with negative results. A project to improve TAT with six sigma was planned. A preliminary study for 4 months provided the base line data.

Four primary drivers were identified as:

1. Order to stress test
2. Procedure time
3. Study dictation and
4. Procedure sign off.

Target was established for each driver with upper specification limit as per customer requirements.

(a) Define

The team began 'define stage' by identifying five goals, namely:

1. Create a team charter critical to quality (CTQ)
2. Identify issues that are critical
3. Create a process map of the project
4. Address organisational resistance to process change and
5. Decrease overall TAT for stress tests.

Voice of customer-critical to quality-process mapping-surveys with people to set USL for TAT as 36 hours.

Six major requirements are listed in Table 7.2.

Table 7.2 Major requirements

1. Test scheduled quickly	Schedule time	Patients will undergo procedure in < 18 hrs upon order received
2. Patient transported to test area with minimum waiting time	Transport time	Patient received in < 30 min. of transport requirement
3. Test performed quickly	Procedure time Room turn around time	Procedure time < 2 hrs Room is available for next patient in < 15 min.
4. Test read quickly	Examine read process	< 8 hrs of procedure time
5. Test transacted quickly	Transcription procedure	Test report transcribed and signed by Radiologist in < 8 hrs of reading
6. Test report signed quickly	Report process	

Table 7.3 Critical to quality tree

PROCESS MAP	Supplier	Input	Process	Output	Customer
	Physician	Patient	Test ordered	Images	Patient
	Nurse	Isotope	Patient transport	Verbal report	Family
	Isotope vendor	Procedure order	Resting scan	Transcription	Physician
	Transporter	Examination schedule	Stress test Stress scan Results read Results transcribed	Read, and write report	Isotope vendor

In the change acceleration process, the support of the stakeholders of the organisation to the project was studied. The team has to plan, change efforts through communication, mobilizing political and moral support, and creation of measures and rewards.

Table 7.4 Stakeholders analysis

Customer	Strongly against	Moderately Against	Neutral	Moderately supportive	Strongly Supportive
Cardiologist					X
Technician			X		
Administration				X	
Patients/ Family			X		
Radiologist			X		

(b) Measure

Actual TAT was 68 hrs with a variation of 30 hrs. The target was fixed, from the voice of customer at USL 36 hrs. and from the physicians at a mean 24 hrs.

The analysis of the four key variables was made, as shown in Table 7.5. The drivers (1) and (4) are found to be vital, causing most difficulty.

Table 7.5 Process map

Components	Goal	Actual	Opportunity
1. Order to test begins	18 hrs	28	10 hrs
2. Test time	2	2	Zero
3. End of test to read file	8	11	3
4. Film read to sign-off	8	27	19
	36	68	32

(c) Analyse

The team used the following tools for analysis:

1. Fishbone diagram
2. Control/Impact matrix
3. Test for equal value and
4. Regression analysis

1. Cause and Effect Diagram or Fish Bone Diagram

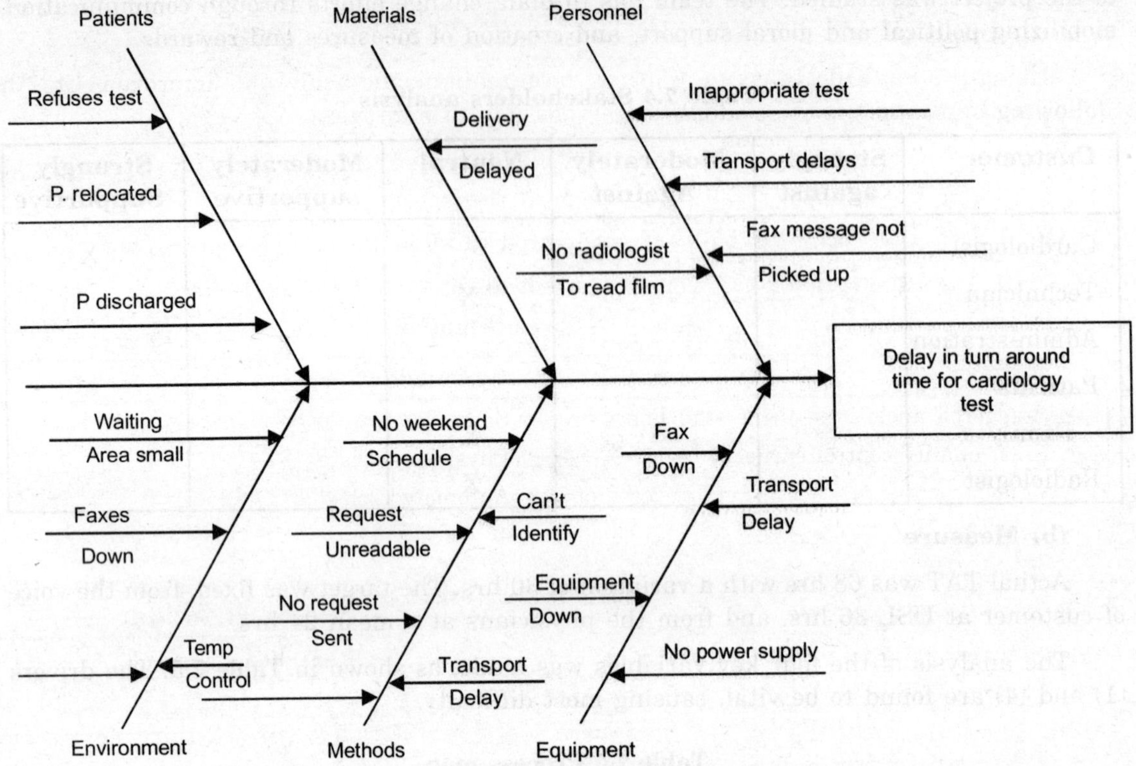

Fig. 7.1 Cause and effect diagram

2. Control/Impact Matrix

Table 7.6 Control impact matrix

	High	**Medium**	**Low**
In our control	• Transcriptionist delay • No voice recognition	• Dictaphone/medical system not interfaced • File clerk delays tracking • Clerk delays in bringing to transcription area	• Technician did not track to end of procedure • Old equipment
Out of our control	• Radiologist schedules	• Outside service delays transcribing	• Outside transcriber can't trace due to voice cut off or is misunderstood • Bar coding done incorrectly; system does not indicate error • Radiologist wants report redone

Using regression model, (1) the patient arriving in the department and (4) the time it took from transcription to results sign off by radiologist were both found to be statistically significant.

(d) Improve

Using the Pay Off Matrix to prioritise both realistic and achievable improvements, the following opportunities were identified as possible to improve:

(*a*) Prescheduled times for stress test did not exist

(*b*) Patient transport was part of overall transport

(*c*) Technologist hours were not staggered to allow for quality control work and

(*d*) Nuclear medicine radiologist was not always available each day.

Table 7.7 Pay off matrix

Pursue	**Rescope/Reconsider**
• Staggered nuclear medicine staff hours • Start quality control earlier • Change phone message to include prompt • Dedicated transporter ELIMINATE • Patient education video	• Same day scheduling policy • Physician assistance • Automated scheduled protocols ELIMINATE • Education of specific cardiologists

(e) Control

Results were achievable and sustainable. Using check lists, SPC charts, and periodical status reports to ensure process inputs were sustained, it was confirmed that the process inputs were sustained. Further, the pilot tests were conducted for one week every month, for six weeks.

The results were:

(*a*) The turn around time was reduced to 32 hrs with a variation of 8 hrs. and

(*b*) The department was able to increase the capacity *without* increasing the costs.

Case 7.3 DECISION MATRIX

In the maintenance shop of a steel rolling mill, a study team investigated and identified many problems causing frequent break down and large down time existed. Further study short listed three problems and the team wanted to establish the priority. The following is the resulting summary, presented as a matrix.

Table 7.8 Matrix for problem selection

		Themes				Nature of work			
S. No.	**PROBLEMS**	**QUALITY**	**COST**	**DELIVERY**	**SERVICE**	**DESIRABLE**	**ESSENTIAL**	**VITAL**	**PRIORITY**
1.	ROLL BENDING FACILITY DOES NOT EXIST		√				√		SECOND

2.	DIFFICULTIES DURING IN-HOUSE RECONDI-TIONING OF FAN IMPELLER	√			√		√	FIRST
3.	NO MACHINING FACILITY FOR RUBBER ROLL		√	√		√		THIRD

Case 7.4 AFFINITY DIAGRAM

In continuation of the Case 7.3, the problem of 'reconditioning of the fan impeller' was considered as top priority. Various constraints were listed and classified as shown in Fig. 7.2, as the affinity diagram. Three distinct groups have been marked for further investigation and remedial measures.[11,14]

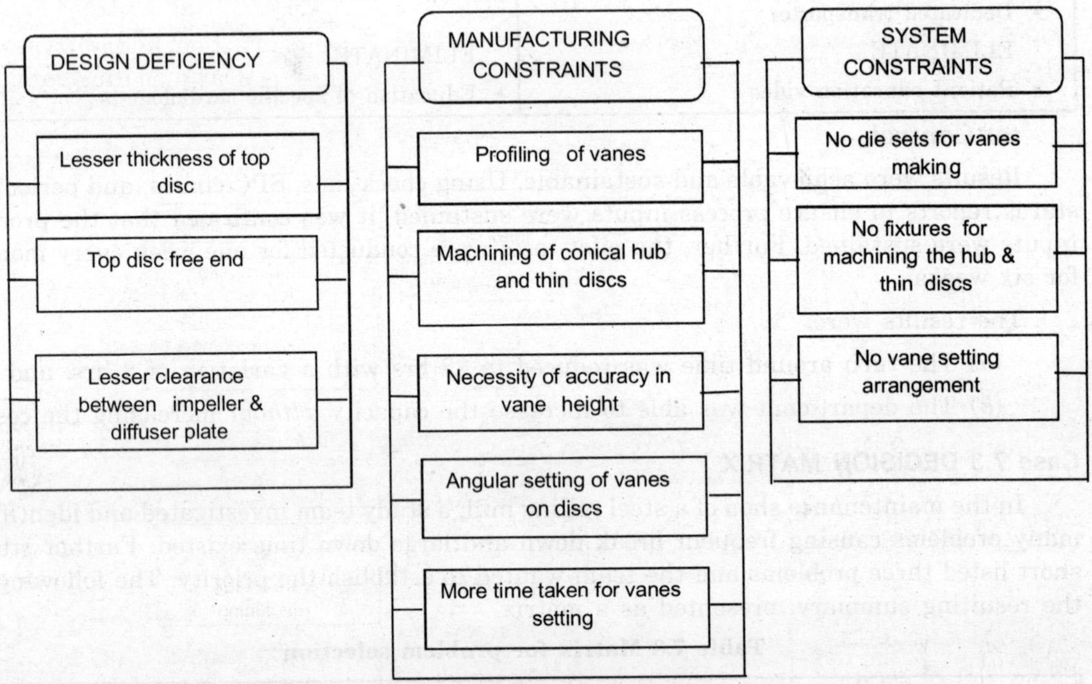

Fig. 7.2 Affinity diagram

Case 7.5 P D P CHART

The case presented is on providing a financially secured future for most of the employed people. As an illustrative example, the common activities, What to do if they are wrong? and the possible counter measures are shown in Fig. 7.3.

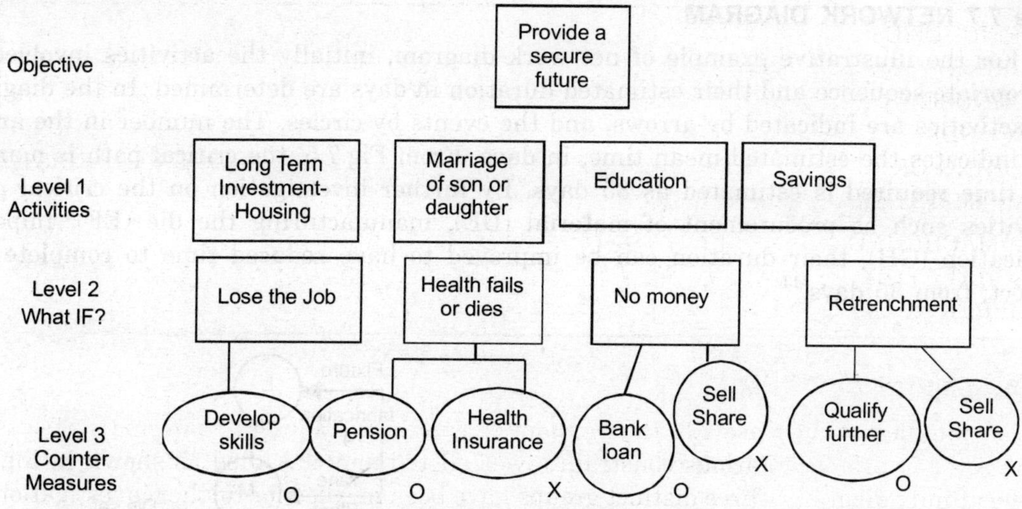

Fig. 7.3 Example of PDP chart

Case 7.6 TREE DIAGRAM

For further identifying the (*a*) approaches, (*b*) areas/components of action, and (*c*) types of action for Cases 7.3 and 7.4, the development of the tree diagram is drawn as illustrated in Fig 7.4.[11,14]

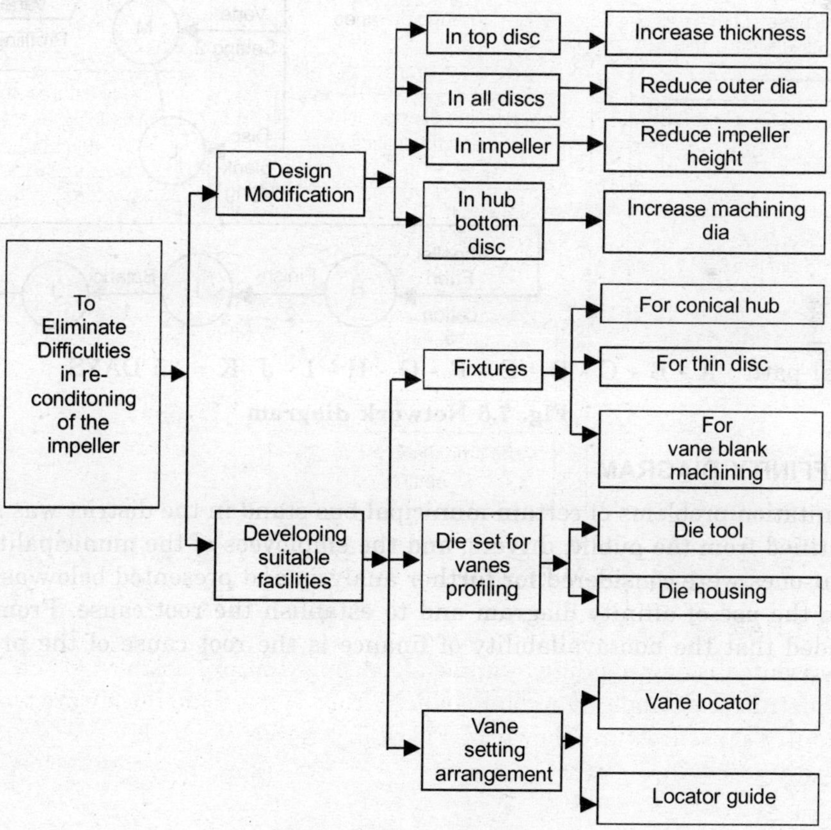

Fig. 7.4 Tree diagram

Case 7.7 NETWORK DIAGRAM

For the illustrative example of net work diagram, initially the activities involved in appropriate sequence and their estimated duration in days are determined. In the diagram the activities are indicated by arrows, and the events by circles. The number in the arrow line indicates the estimated mean time, in days. From Fig.7.5, the critical path is marked and time required is estimated as 35 days. By further investigation on the critical path activities such as procurement of material (DE), manufacturing the die (EF). Impeller fabrication (GH), their duration can be improved to have reduced time to complete the project, from 35 days.[11]

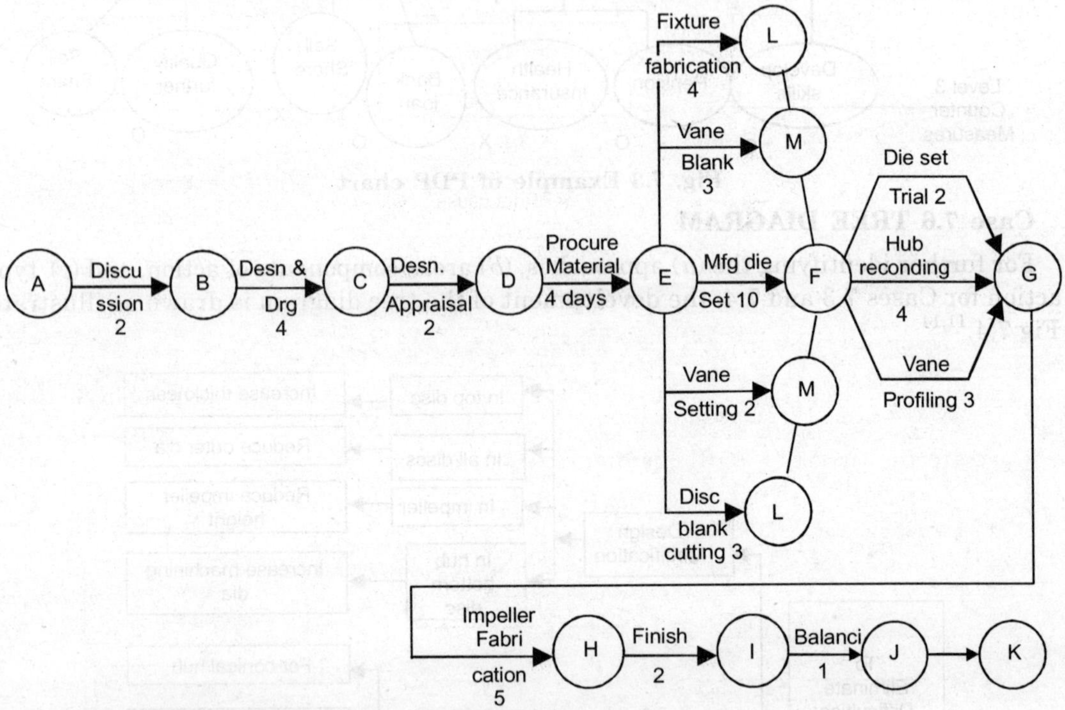

Critical path : A - B - C - D - E - F - G - H - I - J -K = 35 DAYS

Fig. 7.5 Network diagram

Case 7.8 AFFINITY DIAGRAM

The sanitation problems of certain municipal bus stand in the district was studied. The causes identified from the public, drivers, and the employees of the municipality are listed. The relevant ones were considered for further analysis and presented below as an example to illustrate the use of affinity diagram and to establish the root cause. From Fig. 7.6, it may concluded that the non-availability of finance is the root cause of the problem.

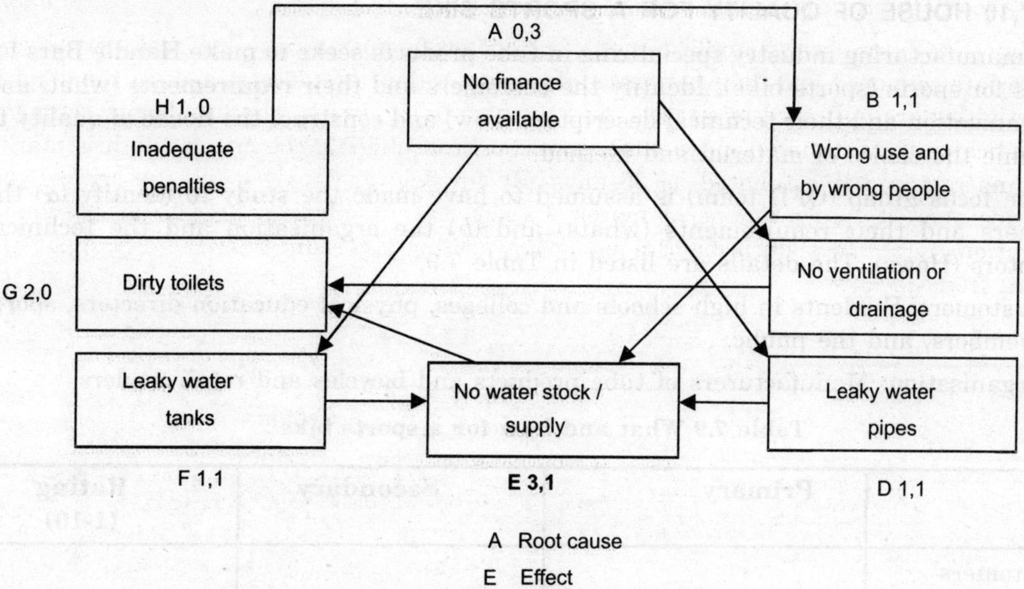

Fig. 7.6 Affinity diagram

Case 7.9 AFFINITY DIAGRAM

Another case study was done to identify the causes of the problem of high mobility (turn over) in rural educational institutions. A sample tree diagram is presented in Fig. 7.7, to illustrate the use of the affinity diagram.

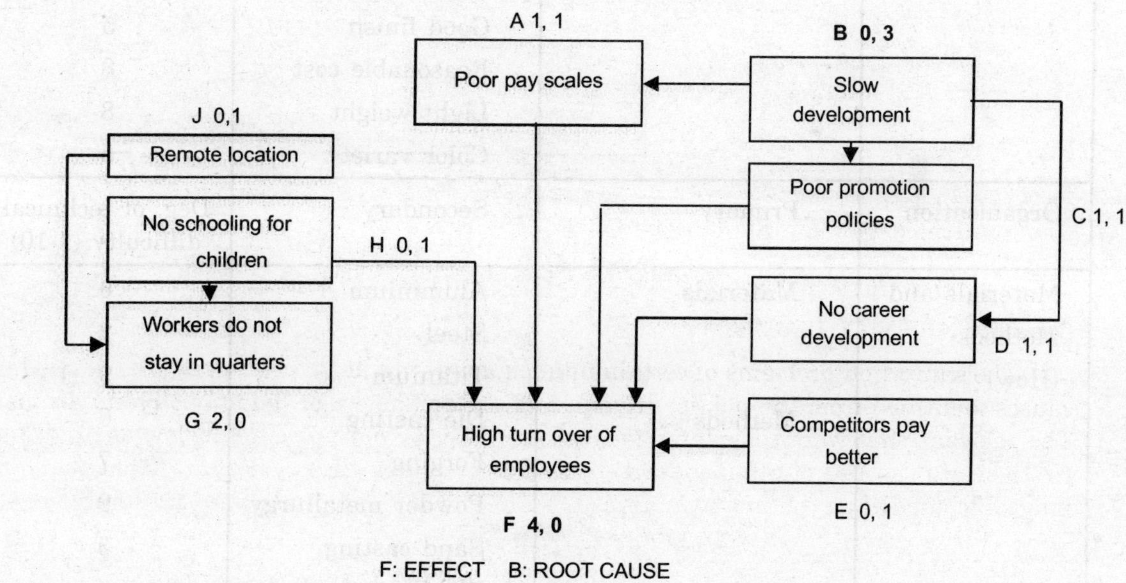

Fig. 7.7 Affinity diagram (High turn over of employees)

Case 7.10 HOUSE OF QUALITY FOR A SPORTS BIKE

A manufacturing industry specializing in tube products seeks to make Handle Bars for bicycles for sports (sports bike). Identify the customers and their requirements (what) and the organisation and their technical descriptors (how) and construct the house of quality to determine the choice of material and method.

The focus group (QFD team) is assumed to have made the study to identify (*a*) the customers and their requirements (whats) and (*b*) the organisation and the technical descriptors (Hows). The details are listed in Table 7.9.

Customers: Students in high schools and colleges, physical education directors, sports club members, and the public.

Organisation: Manufacturers of tube products and bicycles and retail traders.

Table 7.9 What and how for a sports bike

	Primary	**Secondary**	**Rating (1-10)**
Customers' requirements (What)	Performance	High Strength	6
		Durability	4
		Corrosion resistance	3
	Aesthetics	Aerodynamic design	5
		Good finish	5
		Reasonable cost	8
		Light weight	8
		Color variety	5
Organisation	Primary	Secondary	Deg. of technical difficulty (1-10)
Materials and Methods (How)	Materials	Aluminium	6
		Steel	2
		Titanium	9
	Methods	Die casting	6
		Forging	7
		Powder metallurgy	9
		Sand casting	3
		Welding	4

Further calculations by the design team are presented in the next page.

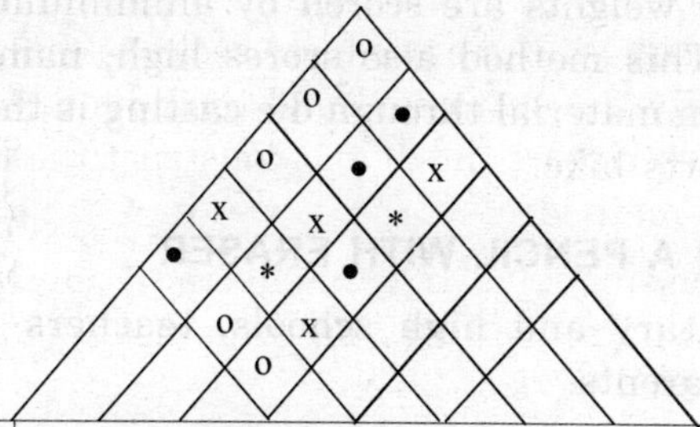

● strong +ve
o positive
X negative
* strong-ve

WHAT ?		HOW ? MATERIALS: Aluminium	Steel	Titanium	MANUFRG. PROCESS: Die casting	Forging	Powder metalgy	Sand casting	Welding	Our product	Y's product	Z's product	Imp to customers	Target value 1-5	Scale up factor	Seales point 1-2	Absolute wt., d_i
PERFCE	Strength	o	●	●	o	●	o	o	Δ	3	4	3	6	4	1.3	1	7.8
	Durability	o	●	o	●	●	o	o	Δ	3	3	4	4	4	1.3	1	5.2
	Corrosion resistance	o	Δ	●	o	o	o	o	Δ	4	4	2	3	4	1.3	1	3
AESTHETICS	Aero dyn design	o	o	Δ	●	o	●	o	Δ	4	5	3	5	5	1.25	1.5	9.4
	Good finish	●	o	●	●	o	●	Δ	Δ	4	3	5	5	5	1.25	1	6.3
	Reasonable cost	●	●	Δ	o	o	Δ	●	●	3	4	2	8	4	1.3	1.5	15.6
	Light weight	●	Δ	o	o	Δ	Δ	Δ	Δ	3	4	2	8	3	1	2	16
	Color variety	o	o	Δ	o	o	Δ	o	o	4	3	3	5	4	1	1	5
	Our prodt.	5	0	0	5	0	0	0	0								
	Y's prodt.	0	5	0	0	0	0	0	4								
	Z's prodt.	0	0	5	0	0	4	0	0								
	Deg of tech. dify.	6	2	9	6	7	9	3	4								
	Target value	5	5	5	5	0	0	0	4								

9 ● Strong
3 o medium
1 Δ weak

Absolute	25	21	18	21	17	15	15	108
weight, aj	8	8	0	6	6	0	4	
Relative	43	33	24	33	25	22	25	193
weight, rj	2	8	9	1	1	7	3	

Example: $a_2 = 9 \times 6 + 9 \times 4 + 1 \times 3 + 3 \times 5 + 3 \times 5 + 9 \times 8 + 1 \times 8 + 3 \times 5 = 218$

$r_2 = 9 \times 7.8 + 9 \times 5.2 + 1 \times 3 + 3 \times 9.4 + 3 \times 6.3 + 9 \times 15.6 + 1 \times 16 + 3 \times 5 = 338$

Maximum absolute and relative weights are scored by aluminium namely 258 and 432. This material can be die cast. This method also scores high, namely 216 and 331. Hence we can conclude that aluminium material through die casting is the most favourable choice, for the handle bar for the sports bike.

Case 7.11 HOUSE OF QUALITY FOR A PENCIL WITH ERASER

Customers: Students of elementary and high schools, teachers (of kindergarten, elementary, and high schools), and parents.

Organisation: Pencil manufacturers and retail traders.

Table 7.10 What and how for a PENCIL

Parts	Customers' requirements	Importance to customer (1-10)
Body	1. Light weight	7
	2. Non-toxic	8
	3. Easy to hold	5
	4. Does not roll	2
	5. Less costly	9
	6. Easy to sharpen	7
	7. Durable body	8
	8. Glue strength	1
	9. Colour	1
	10. Smells good	1
Lead	1. Hardness	2
	2. Non-smearing	2
	3. Thickness/diameter	1
	4. Strong	8
	5. Legible marking	2
	6. Erasable	2
Eraser	1. Non-smearing	2
	2. Not brittle	2
	3. Colour	1
	4. Perfumed	1

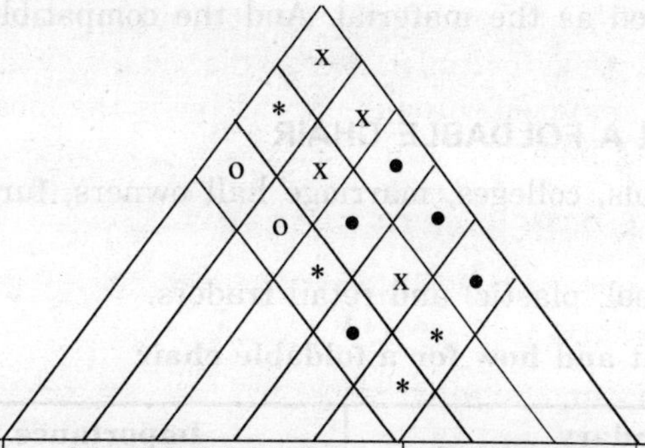

9 ● Strong

3 o medium

1 Δ weak

		MATERIALS					MFG PROCS										
		Ceramics	Glass	Plastic	Steel	Wood	Casting	Injctn. Moulding	Turning, drilling	Our product	Y's product	Z's product	Imp to customers	Target value 1–5	Scale up factor	Sales point 1-2	Absolute wt. d_j
PERFORMCE & APPEARANCE	Light weight	●	o	●	Δ	●	Δ	Δ	Δ	4	5	3	7	4	1	1.5	10.5
	Non-toxic	Δ	Δ	Δ	Δ	●	Δ	Δ	Δ	4	4	2	8	5	1.25	1.5	15
	Held easily	●	●	●	Δ	o	●	●	Δ	3	5	3	5	4	1.33	1	7
	Strong lead	Δ	Δ	o	●	Δ	Δ	Δ	Δ	3	4	2	8	3	1	1	8
	Easy 2 sharpn	Δ	Δ	●	Δ	●	Δ	Δ	Δ	3	4	2	7	4	1.3	1	9
COST	Less costly	Δ	Δ	o	Δ	●	o	Δ	●	3	3	4	9	3	1	1.5	13.5
	Durable body	o	Δ	●	o	●	Δ	Δ	o	3	3	4	8	4	1.3	1	10.4
	Our prodt.	3	3	4	2	5	2	4	5								
	X's prodt.	3	4	5	2	0	3	4	1								
	Y's prodt.	5	2	3	3	4	4	1	2								
	Deg of Techl. difclty	3	3	6	2	6	3	4	4								
	value Target	3	3	4	2	5	2	4	5								
	Abs. wt. a_j	164	106	302	132	**374**	110	92	140								
	Rel. wt r_j	234	150	412	158	**555**	156	129	202								

Highest score is obtained by wood as the material. And the compatible methods as turning and drilling are favoured.

Case 7.12 HOUSE OF QUALITY FOR A FOLDABLE CHAIR

Customers: House holders, schools, colleges, marriage hall owners, furniture hirers, and public.

Organisation: Manufacturers (steel, plastic) and retail traders.

Table 7.11 What and how for a foldable chair

Primary Requirements	Secondary requirmnts	Importance to Customer (1-10)
Performance	Load bearing capacity	4
	Durability	8
	Unbreakable	5
Cost	Less costly	9
Aesthetics	Light weight	7
	Safety	5
	Minimum space	6
	Color variety	6
	Cushioned	2

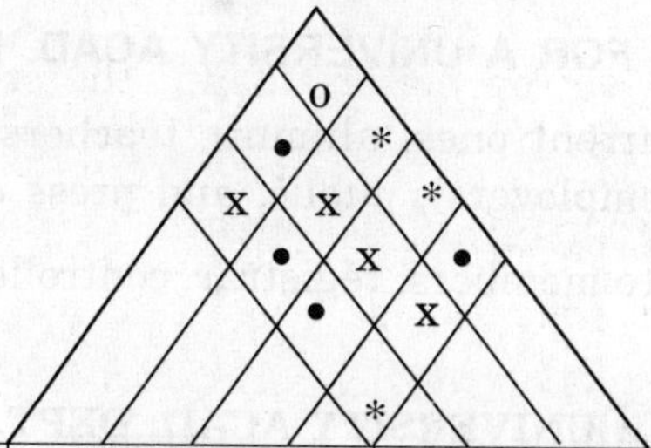

		MATERIALS				PROCESS			9 —Strong; 3 o medium; 1 Δ weak; 0 b							
		Plastic	Timber	Teak wood	Steel	Carpentry	Moulding	Welding	Our product	Y's product	Z's product	Imp. to customers	Target value	Scale up factor	Sales point	Absolute weight
PERFMCE	Load bg capacty	o	o	•	•	o	Δ	•	2	4	3	4	3	1.5	1	6
	Durable	o	Δ	•	o	Δ	Δ	•	3	4	3	8	4	1.3	1.2	12
	Unbreakable	Δ	o	•	•	Δ	Δ	o	3	5	3	5	3	1	1	5
COST	Less costly	•	o	Δ	o	•	o	o	4	2	3	9	4	1	2	18
AESTHETICS	Light wt.	•	o	Δ	o	Δ	Δ	o	5	1	3	7	5	1	1.5	10.5
	Safety	•	Δ	o	o				4	3	4	5	4	1	1	5
	Minm space	•	o	Δ	o				4	2	3	6	4	1	1	6
	Color varty	•	Δ	Δ	o		•		4	2	3	6	4	1	1.3	7.8
	Our prodt.	5	0	0	1	0	5	1								
	X's prodt.	0	2	4	0	5	0	0								
	Y's prodt.	1	0	0	5	0	1	4								
	Deg of Tech difclty	5	6	9	7	8	4	6								
	Target Value	5	2	5	0	5	5	0								
	Abs. wt. a_j	338	112	196	204	113	105	171								
	Rela. wt. r_j	485	161	224	277	208	152	263								

Plastic as material and its compatible method of manufacture as moulding are preferred.

Case 7.13 INTER-RELATIONSHIP MATRIX FOR A UNIVERSITY ACAD. DEPT.

Customers: Students (from schools, current ones, alumni), teachers, parents, clerical staff, local administrators, industrialists (employers), public, and press correspondents.

Organisation: Vice Chancellor, syndicate members, registrar, controller of examinations and PRO.

Table 7.12 IR matrix for a UNIVERSITY ACAD. DEPT.

		H O W ?										
What	**Imp to cust**	**Teachr Qlty**	**Teachr Qnty**	**MOU (projt, &trng)**	**Indstry sponsd courses**	**Res pub licn**	**Place ment**	**Coun sellg**	**GRE, GATE trng**	**Profl socy mem**	**Centl valua tion**	**Com ptrsd recrd**
Hi pass % & hi Marks	10	•	o	o	o			o				
Guidance to higher Studies	7	•		o	o	o		o	•	•		
Job Opportuaity	9			o	•	o	•	o		o		
Reasonble Cost	6	Δ	Δ							Δ		
Quick valn, issue certificate	8	o	o								•	•
Accrdtn & ISO certification	5	•	o	o	o	o	o	o		o		o
Soft Skills	4	o	o					o	o	o		
Deg of tech. difficulty	(1-10)	2	4	6	8	3	8	8	7	9	10	10

Case 7.14 INTER-RELATIONSHIP MATRIX FOR A CALL CENTRE

Customers: Employees, investors, press correspondents, public, local administrators, and government.

Organisation: Banks, insurance companies, and travel agents.

Table 7.13 IR Matrix for A CALL CENTER • 9 o 3 < 1

What?	Imp to Custr	H O W ?				
		Computerised records	Branching enquiry	Multi-Lingual response	24 hours service	Good Training
Quick service	8	•	•	o	o	o
Reliability	9	•				o
Updated informn.	7	•			o	
Variety of service	5	•	•	•		o
Friendly response	6			•		
Deg of techl. difficulty	(1–10)	9	8	6	7	8

Case 7.15 INTER-RELATIONSHIP MATRIX for a RESTAURANT

Customers: Customers [public, students, house holders, children, 5/7 bachelors (5 out of 7 days!), tourists], employees (servers, kitchen workers).

Organisation: Restaurateurs, Banks.

Table 7.14 IR matrix for a restaurant

What	Imp to cust	H O W ?					
		Membership	Improve quality	Prime Area	Good Training	Classify items	Environment
Reasonable Cost	8	•		o			Δ
Qlty., taste & hygiene	9		•		•		o
Home delivery	7	o					
Variety	6		o			o	
Gd locn & car parkg.	5	o		•			o
Friendly service	8		o		•		
Pleasant rooms	5		o				•
Deg. of techl. difficulty	(1-10)	6	8	9	7	5	6

Case 7.16 INTER-RELATIONSHIP MATRIX FOR A DEPARTMENT STORE

Customers: House wives, bachelors, sales persons, delivery persons, and suppliers.

Organisation: Traders.

Table 7.15 IR matrix for a dept. store

What?	Imp to cust	H	O	W ?			
		Comput-erised	Member -ship	Door delivery	Credit cards	Improve quality	Packed, stacked
Quick service	9	•	o	o	•	•	
Variety	7	o		o			o
Frozen / readymade	6			o		o	o
Reasonable cost	8		•	o			
Quick reach	5		o			o	o
Deg of Techl. difficulty	(1-10)	5	7	7	6	9	6

Case 7.17 INTER-RELATIONSHIP MATRIX for a HEALTH CARE CENTER

Customers: Patients, physicians, health assistants, lab. technicians, medical equipment suppliers, pharmaceutical manufacturers, medical representatives, customer Service personnel, press correspondents and the public.

Organisation: Senior physicians, corporate hospitals.

Table 7.16 'What and how' for a health care center

What ?	Customer Reqirements	Importance to Customers (1–10)
	1. Quick service	7
	2. Reasonable cost	6
	3. Accurate reports	8
	4. Friendly response	3
	5. Prompt response	4
	6. ISO certification	3
	7. EMS certification	3

How	Methods & Facilities	Deg of teach difficulty (1-10)
	1. Good training	8
	2. Good equipment maintenance	8
	3. Adequate resources	9
	4. Environment (Temp, Aesthetics, Hygiene, Play room for children etc)	6
	5. Reduce wastes	7
	6. Improve quality	8
	7. Diagnostics/test labs.	7
	8. Pharmacy shop	5

Table 7.17 IR Matrix for a health care centre

What?	Imp to cust	HOW?							
		Good train-ing	Good Equpt mtce	Adeq resou rce	Envi ronm ent	Reduce wastes	Impr-ove quality	Diag/ test labs	Phar macy shop
Quick service	7	•	•	o		Δ		o	
Reason -able cost	6		Δ		Δ	•	o		o
Accur -ate report	8	o	•				•	o	
Prompt response	4	•	o	Δ				o	o
Friendly response	3	•		Δ	o				
ISO and EMS Certi-fication	3	o	o					•	o
Deg of Technical difficulty	(1-10)	8	8	9	6	7	8	7	5

❑ ❑ ❑

CHAPTER 8

Bibliography

1. Besterfield D.H., et al., *Total Quality Management*, Pearson Educn., III edn. 2004.
2. Bounds et al., *Beyond Total Quality Management*, Mc Graw Hill, Interntl. Edn. 1994.
3. Arora K.C., *Total Quality Management*, and ISO 14000, Kataria Publication, New Delhi, 1998.
4. Subir Chowdhary, *The Power of Six Sigma*, Pearson Educn., Asia, India, Reprint, 2001.
5. William J.Kolarik, *Creating Quality*, Mc Graw Hill, Interntl edn., 1995.
6. John Bichengo, and M.R.Gopalan, *A Management Guide to Quality and Productivity, Wheeler*, New Delhi, 2000.
7. Amitava Mitra, *Fundamentals of Quality Control and Improvement*, II edn. Pearson Educn., Asia, Addison Wesley-Longman, Delhi, 2001.
8. ISO 9000:2005 *QMS (Fundamentals and vocabulary)*

   ISO 9001:2008 *QMS (Requirements)*

   ISO 9004:2009 *QMS (Guidelines for performance improvement).*
9. BIS: 397-1975 (Parts 1, 2, 3), *Control Charts for Variables.*
10. Naagarajan R.S., and Muralidharan C., *Statistical Data Book*, New Age International, New Delhi, II edition, Nov. 2005.
11. *How to Implement 5 S Practice*, ABK-AOTS DOSOKAI, T. N. Center, Chennai, 2004.
12. Lecture notes, *Faculty Development Training Program on TQM*, C.F.D., Anna University, Chennai, Nov. 16-21, 2004.
13. Nakkeeran P.R., Muzhuthara Melaanmai, *TQM in Thamizh*, Pavai Pub, Chennai, 2002.
14. *'Mumbai Dabbawalahs Get a Standing Ovation'*, The Hindu, April 25, 2005.
15. *Proceedings of the National Symposium on TQM*, Arunai Engineering College, Tiruvannamalai, Feb. 12, 2005.
16. Godin et al., *6s Faster Test Results, A Case Study, Quality Progress*, Vol. 37, no. 1, 2004, pp. 33-9.
17. Jack Welch, Winning, Harper Collins., N.Y., 2005.

18. Annual Report 2004-05, *Growth is Life*, Reliance Industries Ltd., June 2005.

19. *Innovative Practices in Technical Educational Institutions*, AICTE, New Delhi, 2004

Recommended Websites

1. www.iso.org <http://www.iso.org>
2. www.asq.org <http://www.asq.org>
3. www.theacsi.org <http://www.theacsi.org>
4. www.bis.org <http://www.bis.org>
5. www.qcin.org <http://www.qcin.org>
6. www.tqmi.com <http://www.tqmi.com>
7. www.abk-aots-alumni.org <http://www.abk-aots-alumni.org>
8. www.qfdi.org <http://www.qfdi.org>
9. www.6sigma.com <http://www.6sigma.com>
10. www.isixsigma.com <http://www.isixsigma.com>
11. www.treqna.com <http://www.treqna.com>
12. www.aicte.ernet.in <http://www.aicte.ernet.in>
13. www.ficci.com/qualityforum <http://www.ficci.com/qualityforum>
14. www.adviceonqualitymanagement.com <http://www.adviceonqualitymanagement.com>

❑ ❑ ❑

CHAPTER 9

Appendix I-SQC Table and Worked Out Examples

Table 9.1 Factors for quality control charts[9,10]

Sample size	A_2	A_1	D_4	D_3	B_4	B_3
4	0.729	1.888	2.282	0.0	2.266	0.00
5	0.577	1.596	2.114	0.0	2.089	0.00
6	0.483	1.410	2.004	0.0	1.970	0.03
10	0.308	1.028	1.777	0.223	1.716	0.284

Ex. 9.1 $\overline{X}$ and R chart

Draw the $\overline{X}$ and R charts, for the following observations and determine the trial and revised control limits. Sample size is 4. Total number of sub groups is 25.

Table 9.2 Data for $\overline{X}$ and R charts

$\overline{X}$	476	466	484	470	466	494	487	496	488	482	463	498	484
R	32	24	32	26	24	24	28	23	24	26	24	25	24
$\overline{X}$	482	506	496	478	484	506	476	485	490	463	469	474	
R	22	23	23	25	24	23	25	29	25	22	27	22	

Answer:

$$UCL_x = 482.52 + 0.729 \times 25.04 = 500.8$$

$$LCL_x = 482.52 - 0.729 \times 25.04 = 464.2$$

$$UCL_R = 2.266 \times 25.04 = 57$$

By scanning, we find the readings 11, 15 and 19 are to be removed, and the limits to be revised.

Ex. 9.2 $\overline{X}$ and s chart

The following are data on the results of life testing on 10 samples carried out on PC monitor picture tubes manufactured by a company. The values are in thousands of hours.

Construct mean and standard deviation charts for the process. Check whether the process is in control. Revise the control limits, if necessary.

Table 9.3 Data for $\overline{X}$ and s charts

$\overline{X}$	1850	1725	1910	2425	2000	2050	1770	1820	1780	1805
s	48	42	24	31	55	35	40	40	42	35

$\overline{X}$ = 1913 s = 39.2 UCL_s = 1913 + 1.028 × 39.2 = 1958.3

It is found that the observations 4, 5, and 6 are showing out of control points.

Ex. 9.3 p chart, with sample size constant

The following are the data on number of non conforming units, collected for 25 days on a process manufacturing safety helmets. The number of helmets each day is constant and equals 1750. Construct suitable chart with control limits. If necessary, revise the control limits.

Table 9.4 Data for p chart

Day	1	2	3	4	5	6	7	8	9	10	11	12	13	14	15	16	17
No.of non conforming	47	42	48	58	32	38	53	68	45	37	57	38	53	37	39	51	44
Day	18	19	20	21	22	23	24	25									
No. of non-Conforming	61	48	56	48	40	47	25	35									

Answer: $\overline{p}$ = 1147 / (25 × 1750) = 0.0262 and σ = 0.0038

Control limits for *p* are = 0.0379, and 0.0147

By scanning the record, it is found that the day readings 8 and 24 are outside the control limits. Hence they are removed. The revised control limits are then, 0.037 and 0.015.

Ex. 9.4 p chart, with varying sample size

The following are the data on number of samples, and number of non- conforming units every day, upon sampled inspection for statistical control. Compute the control limits and check if the process is in statistical control.

Table 9.5 Data for p chart, with varying sample size

Day	n_i	n_{nc}	p	UCLp	Day	n_i	n_{nc}	p	UCLp
1	145	8	0.055	0.119	14	158	11	0.070	0.117
2	160	6	0.038	0.116	15	140	11	0.079	0.120
3	165	15	0.091	0.115	16	140	8	0.057	0.120
4	136	18	0.132	0.121	17	155	6	0.039	0.117
5	153	10	0.065	0.118	18	..	.	..	...
6	150	9	0.060	0.118	19	..	..	..	...
7	148	5	0.034	0.119	20	139	10	0.072	0.120

8	135	0	0.0	0.121	21	151	11	0.073	0.118
9	165	12	0.072	0.115	22	..	..	...	...
10	143	10	0.069	0.120	23.	..	..	...	...
11	138	8	0.057	0.121	24	149	7	0.046	0.118
12	144	14	0.097	0.119	25	158	7	0.044	0.118
13	161	20	0.124	0.116					
					Total	3893	233		

$\overline{p}$ = 233/ 3893 = 0.060

$$\text{UCLp} = 0.060 + 3 \text{ SQRT} \left\{ \frac{0.060 \times 0.940}{n_i} \right\}$$

The data 4 and 20 are out of control situations, hence removed. After homogenisation, the process average is:

$$\overline{p} = \frac{233-(18+20)}{3893-(136+161)} = 0.054$$

By checking again, it is found that, all other data are within the control limits.

Ex. 9.5 np chart

A factory that produces video cassettes inspects a random sample of 40 units each day, after the assembly, at a final inspection station. The following are the data of the results for fourteen days. Determine the type of chart to be used to study the process. Compute the necessary statistical limits for a control chart, and interpret the results.

Table 9.6 Data for np chart

Day	1	2	3	4	5	6	7	8	9	10	11	12	13	14
No. of non-conformities	28	21	23	32	29	33	19	30	21	19	34	37	24	18

Answer: $\overline{np}$ = 368/14 = 26.8 $\overline{p}$ = 368/(14 × 40) = 0.657

Control limits are obtained as, 35.3 and 17.3

Hence remove the 12th day reading. The revised control limits for np are then calculated as 34 and 16.35. Now the chart may be used as reference for further inspection.

Ex. 9.6 c chart

The number of nonconformities on 10-gear-boxes inspected daily, from the manufacturing line, is obtained as shown in Table 9.7. Construct the c chart and comment.

Table 9.7 Data for the c chart

Lot number	1	2	3	4	5	6	7	8	9	10
No. of non-conformities	15	12	10	14	8	12	7	9	7	22

Lot number	11	12	13	14	15	16	17	18	19	20
No. of non-conformities	8	14	7	9	15	8	7	8	7	11

Answer: $\bar{c} = 210 / 20 = 10.5$ $\sigma = \sqrt{(c)} = \sqrt{(10.5)} = 3.24$

UCLc = $\bar{c}$ + 3 SQRT $\bar{c}$ = 10.5 + 3 × 3.24 = 20.22

LCLc = $\bar{c}$ – 3 SQRT $\bar{c}$ = 10.5 – 3 × 3.24 = 0.78

The point 10 is the outlier, hence removed.

Now the revised process average is 10.0 and σ = 3.16 and the control limits are then, 19.48 and 0.52, i.e., is zero.

Ex. 9.7 u chart

The number of non-conformities and the varying sample size of the certain electronic components, when inspected yielded the results, as shown in Table 9.8. Compute the control limits and comment.

$$\text{Let } k = \frac{\text{Actual sample size}}{\text{Size of the basic sample}}$$

$$\text{and } u = \frac{\text{Number of non conformities}}{k}$$

Table 9.8 Data for the u chart

Sub group number	n	number of non-conformities	k	u = c/k	$3\sigma = 3\sqrt{\frac{9.48}{k}}$	UCLu
1	100	5	1.00	5.00	3 × 3.078 = 9.24	18.72
2	90	4	0.90	4.44	3 × 3.24 = 9.72	19.20
3	110	6	1.10	5.45	3 × 2.23 = 6.69	16.17
4	80	12	0.80	15.00	3 × 4.33 =12.99	21.47
5	120	21	1.20	17.50	3 × 3.82 =11.46	20.94
				$\bar{u} = \frac{47.39}{5} = 9.48$		

Answer: Assuming the basic sample size as 100, the values in the fourth and fifth columns are calculated, as shown the table. σ varies with each sample size and k value. Hence 3σ values are calculated accordingly and shown in the sixth column. The upper control limits are then estimated as shown in the last column. These values are compared with the actual results obtained (column 5). All the values of u are found to within the limits.

Ex. 9.8 MX and MR chart

Estimate the Average of the moving averages and the moving ranges, for the data shown in Table 9.9.

Table 9.9 Data for the moving average and the moving range method

Sub group number	X	MX	MR
1	8	—	—
2	7	—	—
3	8	40/5 = 8.0	2
4	9	37/5 = 7.4	4
5	8	36/5 = 7.2	4
6	5	35/5 = 7.0	4
7	6	31/5 = 6.2	3
8	7	31/5 = 6.2	3
9	5	...	..
10	8	...	..
		$\overline{MX} = \frac{42.0}{6} = 7.0$	$\overline{MR} = \frac{20}{6} = 3.3$

The control limits for MX are, 7.0 + 0.577 × 3.3 = 8.90 and

7.0 – 0.577 × 3.3 = 5.10

The control limits for MR are, 1.114 × 3.3 = 3.67 and 0.0

BASIC STATISTICS

Ex. 9.9 A machine produces alloy steel pins. The length of the pins was measured after machining and the data obtained were recorded as shown in Table 9.10. Find (*i*) mean, standard deviation and variance, and (*ii*) What percentage of pins manufactured has length between 95.2 and 95.6 mm?

Table 9.10 (a) Test results

Length in mm	Frequency
95.05–95.15	5
95.15–95.25	4
95.25–95.35	20
95.35–95.45	30
95.45–95.55	22
95.55–95.65	10
95.65–95.75	6
95.75–95.85	3

Assuming the trial mean value as 95.4 mm, the deviation (d), square of deviation (d^2), the terms such as fd and fd^2 were calculated and shown in Table 9.10 (b).

Here, interval i = 0.1; deviation d = $(\overline{X}_n - \overline{X})/i$; $\overline{X}$ assumed is 95.4 mm. The total number of observations, N = 100 (= Σf).

Table 9.10 (b) Calculations

$\overline{X}$	f	d	d^2	fd	fd^2
95.1	5	– 3	9	–15	45
95.2	4	–2	4	–8	16
95.3	20	–1	1	–20	20
95.4	30	0	0	0	0
95.5	22	1	1	22	22
95.6	10	2	4	20	40
95.7	6	3	9	18	54
95.8	3	4	16	12	48
	Σ = 100			Σ = 29	Σ = 245

(*a*) The mean, $\overline{X} = \overline{X}$ assumed + i (Σfd) / N

= 95.4 + 0.1 (29) / 100 = 95.43 mm

(*b*) Standard deviation, σ = i SQRT { (Σf d^2/N) – $(\Sigma fd/N)^2$}

= SQRT {(245/100) – $(29/100)^2$}

= SQRT (2.450 – 0.084) = 0.1538 mm

(*c*) Variance $\sigma^2 = 0.0237$

(*d*) Percentage of pins between 95.2 and 95.6 is found as follows:

$$Z_L = \frac{95.20 - 95.43}{0.1538} = -1.495$$ Area in Table 9.11 pL at –1.495 σ = 0.0675

$$Z_H = \frac{95.60 - 95.43}{0.1538} = 1.105$$ Area in Table 9.11 pH at + 1.105 σ = 0.8654

The area between –1.495 σ and + 1.105 σ is 0.8654 –0.0675 = 0.7979

Hence the answer: 79.7953 % of pins manufactured will lie between 95.2 and 95.6 mm.

For the quick reference to the normal probability distribution values by the students and teachers, brief data are reproduced in Table 9.11.

Table 9.11 Normal probability distribution[9]

$$\text{Area from } -\infty \text{ to } Z = \int_{-\infty}^{Z} \frac{1}{\sigma\sqrt{(2\pi)}} \text{ EXP } \{-(X-\mu)^2/2\sigma^2\}$$

Z	Area / Probability
– 4.0	0.000 03
– 3.5	0.000 23
– 3.0	0.001 35
– 2.5	0.006 21
– 2.0	0.022 75
– 1.5	0.066 81
– 1.0	0.158 66
– 0.5	0.308 54
0	0.500 00
0.5	0.691 46
1.0	0.841 34
1.5	0.933 19
2.0	0.977 25
2.5	0.993 79
3.0	0.998 65
3.5	0.999 77
4.0	0.999 97

Ex. 9.10 The life of an electronic amplifier is a random variable following normal distribution with a mean of 2000 hours and standard deviation of 400 hours.

Find the expected number of amplifiers from a sample taken at random of 2000 amplifiers having life

(*a*) more than 3000 hours

(*b*) between 2600 and 2800 hours.

Given, $\overline{X}$ = 2000 hours, and σ = 400 hours

(*a*) Amplifiers having life more than 3000 hours,

$$Z = \frac{3000 - 2000}{400} = 2.5\ \sigma$$

From Table 9.11, area up to + 2.5 σ is 0.99379

Hence, P (L > 3000 hrs) is 1 – 0.99379 = 0.00621

N (L > 3000 hours) = 0.00621 × 2000 = 18.42 amplifiers

(*b*) $Z_1 = \dfrac{2600-2000}{400} = 1.5\ \sigma \qquad Z_2 = \dfrac{2800-2000}{400} = 2.0\ \sigma$

$a_1 = 0.93319 \qquad a_2 = 0.97725$

Prob $(2600 < L < 2880) = a_2 - a_1 = 0.04406$

N $(2600 < L < 2800) = 0.04406 \times 2000 = 88.1$ amplifiers

Ex. 9.11 A process average of 36.0 gm and a standard deviation of 1.00 gm were obtained for an electronic component which is under statistical quality control. This product is presently sold to two consumers who have prescribed two different specification limits. Consumer 1 has prescribed a specification limit of 38.0 ± 4.0 gm for the component, and the consumer 2 the specification limit of 36.0 ± 4.0 gm.

(*a*) What percentage of the component will not meet the specifications set up by consumer 1 with the current process set up?

(*b*) What percentage of the component will not meet the specifications set up by consumer 2 with the current set up?

(*c*) Assuming that the needs of these consumers are equal, a process average target was suggested at 37 gm. At this value, what percentage of the component will not meet the specifications of consumer 1?

(*d*) At this suggested target, what percentage of the component will not meet the specifications of consumer 2?

(*e*) Would this shift of target to 37.0 is desirable? Why?

Given, $\overline{X} = 36.0$ gm and $\sigma = 1.00$ gm

Specification limits of consumer 1: CL 38.0 ± 4.00 gm

consumer 2: CL 36.0 ± 4.00 gm

(*a*) For consumer 1 specification limits are 34 and 42 gm i.e., $-2\ \sigma$ and $+6\ \sigma$

the corresponding probabilities are 0.02275 and 1.00000

Prob. of not meeting the specification limits 0.02275 i.e., 2.275 %

(*b*) For Consumer 2 Specification limits are 32 and 40 gm i.e., $-4\ \sigma$ and $+4\ \sigma$

the corresponding probabilities are 0.00003 and 0.99997

Prob.. of not meeting the specification limits 0.00006 % , i.e., 0 %

At $\overline{X} = 36.0$ gm, total rejection for consumers 1 and 2, is 2.275 %

(*c*) Suggested process average $\overline{X} = 37.0$ gm and $\sigma = 1.0$ gm

For Consumer 1, SL are 34 and 42 gm (remains same) i.e., $-3\ \sigma$ and $+5\ \sigma$

Corresponding probabilities are 0.00135 and 1.00000

Probability of not meeting the specifications is 0.00135 i.e., 0.135 %

(*d*) For Consumer 2, SL are 32 and 40 gm, i.e., $-5\ \sigma$ and $+\ 3\ \sigma$

Corresponding probabilities are 0.00000 and 0.99865

Probability of not meeting the specifications ia 0.00135, i.e., 0.135 %

(*e*) At $\overline{X} = 37$ gm, the total rejection for consumers 1 and 2, is 0.27 %. This is less as compared to, when $\overline{X} = 36$ gm, which was 2.275%. Hence the shift of process average to 37 gm is preferred.

Ex. 9.12 Six Sigma

(*a*) If there are 10 defects among 200 castings and there are 10 opportunities for error for each casting, find the 'dpmo'.

Defect per unit, dpu $= 10 / 200 = 0.05$

Defect per opportunity, dpo $= 10 / (200 \times 10) = 0.005$

Defect per million opportunities

$$\text{dpmo} = \text{dpo} \times 1\ 000\ 000 = 5\ 000 \text{ dpmo (or) ppm}$$

(*b*) Given a nonconforming proportion, p of 2 % find the C_p ?

$$\text{Yield} = 1 - p = 1 - 0.02 = 0.98 \text{ and dpmo} = 20\ 000$$

From the normal distribution table, Z for 0.980 = 2.054

Process capability is estimated by adding 1.5 σ to reflect the 'real world' shift in the process mean. Accordingly, the shift in the process mean is $2.054\ \sigma + 1.5\ \sigma = 3.554\ \sigma$

Equivalent $C_p = 3.554\ \sigma / 3\ \sigma = 1.185$ (Note: C_{pk} can not be estimated in this way)

❑ ❑ ❑

CHAPTER 10

Appendix II TQM Question Bank

PART A (2 MARKS QUESTIONS)

Chapter–1

1. Define at least two forms of definitions of 'quality'.
2. What does the word 'total', in TQM signify?
3. List at least four dimensions of quality.
4. Name two basic concepts of TQM.
5. Name two quality gurus and indicate their major contributions.
6. Distinguish between reliability and durability.
7. Name two organisations (Society) in India, dedicated to the promotion of quality.
8. List the people under internal customers.
9. List the persons, classified as external customers.
10. List the characteristics of quality leaders.
11. Name four behaviours of employees.
12. Give two examples to illustrate the reactive and proactive behaviours.

    Ans. I can not———I choose; I must———I prefer

    Things are going from bad course———What can I do?
13. What is the primary step, in win-win situation?

    (View the problems, from the other side, yield but get others involved)
14. Name the principle of synergy.

    (Synergy, means, the whole is more than the sum of the individuals)

Chapter–2

1. Define external customers?

   Ans. A person who uses a product/service, purchases the product/service or who influences the sale of product/service.

2. Define reputation.

   Ans. Qualitative judgment of an organisation and understanding of the mind set and principles of an organisation.

3. What is the merit of 'visit to customers', in customer service?
4. What is the merit of employee feed back, in customer service?

   Ans. 1. What to solve, is known from the customer. How to solve, is known from the employee. 2. The employee's understanding and cooperation are ensured.

5. List the developments that make mass customisation, beneficial?

   Ans. FM technology, JIT and cycle time reduction.

6. Name the characteristics of front-line people, towards customer care.
7. What does the customer expect in (*a*) Field repair and (*b*) Warranty?
8. What are the factors explained in Herzberg theory?
9. Name the personality characteristics of employees, related to customer service.
10. Name the job attitudes of employees, with reference to customer service.
11. Differentiate between empowerment and delegation.
12. List basic features that lead to success in team work.
13. What are the roles of a team facilitator?
14. How is facilitator, different from the leader of a team?
15. List two barriers to the progress of team work.
16. Name two forms of intrinsic rewards.
17. List two forms of extrinsic rewards.
18. List the factors considered in performance appraisal system.
19. Name the three stages in Juran's trilogy.
20. List the four steps in Deming cycle.
21. List the five activities under Kaizen.
22. What is the non conformance rate as per (*a*) 3σ and (*b*) 6σ concepts?
23. List the key elements of supplier partnering.
24. List different types of sourcing.
25. What are the advantages of rating the suppliers?
26. List some performance measures, in manufacturing.
27. List some performance measures, in marketing.
28. List some performance measures on customer satisfaction.
29. List some elements, in determining supplier performance.
30. List some elements, in determining performance in innovation.
31. List some cost elements in purchasing, under preventive costs.
32. List some cost elements in quality administration under prevention costs.

33. List some cost elements of external appraisal costs under appraisal costs.
34. List some product/service design failure cost elements, under internal failure costs.
35. List some elements on warranty claims, under external failure costs.
36. List some penalty claims, under external failure costs.
37. List some elements on lost sales claims, under external failure costs.
38. Name the ways of reducing the appraisal costs.
39. List the factors considered in Malcom Baldridge International Quality Award.

Chapter–3

1. State the principle of Pareto analysis. (Vital few and trivial many).
2. List the merits of the cause and effect diagram.
3. Define 'standard deviation' of the (*a*) sample and (*b*) population.
4. Differentiate between a run chart and a control chart.
5. Why do we need 25 trials to construct a control chart?
6. What is meant by homogenisation?
7. List some unnatural patterns that may occur in the control charts.
8. Define 'process capability'.
9. What is the significance of process capacity?
10. Define C_{pk}.
11. What is the significance of C_{pk}?
12. When do we use attribute chart in QC?
13. What is meant by tree diagram, as a management tool?
14. What is the merit of matrix diagram, as a management tool?
15. What is the advantage of PDP Chart?
16. Highlight the features of activity network diagram.

Chapter–4

1. What are the advantages of bench marking?
2. What are the limitations of bench marking?
3. Define, 'break through' performance.
4. Write briefly on the house of quality.
5. What is meant by technical competitive assessment?
6. What is meant by customer competitive assessment?
7. Define 'loss function'.
8. Define 'signal'.
9. Define 'noise' and its types.
10. Define robust design.
11. Define TPM.

12. Define productive maintenance.
13. Define preventive maintenance.
14. Define breakdown maintenance.
15. Define periodic maintenance.
16. Define maintenance prevention.
17. Define 'availability' in maintenance.
18. Define performance efficiency.
19. Define equipment effectiveness.
20. Define 'rate of quality'.
21. List different types of FMEA?
22. Define the 'voice of customer'.
23. What is meant by 'design FMEA'?
24. What is meant by 'process FMEA'?
25. Define RPN.
26. Define occurrence.
27. What is meant by potential failure work?
28. Define detection.
29. What is meant by potential effects of failure?

Chapter–5

1. List the documents, used in QMS?
2. Write briefly on two parts of audit system.
3. Write briefly on three parts of audit system.
4. What are the benefits of QMS?
5. Name the elements in ISO 9001 that are similar to ISO 14001.
6. List the basic principles of quality management and explain briefly each of these.
7. Define 'environment'.
8. Define environmental impact.
9. Define environmental aspect.
10. Define environmental objective.
11. Define 'process'.
12. Define 'process approach'.
13. Define 'a product'.
14. Define customer satisfaction.
15. Define 'management'.
16. Define 'quality management system'.
17. Define 'quality policy'.

18. Define 'quality objectives'.
19. Define 'quality planning'.
20. Define 'continual improvement'.
21. Define 'an organization'.
22. What is the purpose of an organisation?
23. Define 'customer'.
24. Define 'supplier'.
25. Define 'characteristic'.
26. Define 'rework'.
27. Distinguish between 'effectiveness' and 'efficiency'.
28. Distinguish between a non-conformity and a defect.
29. Distinguish between 'corrective action' and 'correction'.
30. Distinguish between 'corrective action' and 'preventive action'.
31. What are the contents of a 'quality manual'?
32. Name a few needs and expectations of
    (*a*) Customer and end user, related to organisations' product / service
    (*b*) Employees
    (*c*) Owners / Investors.

Chapter–6

1. What is meant by poka yoke?
2. Give two common examples to stress the need for poka yoke.
3. What are the problems anticipated while implementing the JIT practice?
4. What are the four components of JIT?
5. List the merits of zero inventory practice.
6. What are the duties of leader, in a quality circle?
7. What are the duties of non-members, in a quality circle?
8. What is the purpose of inducting non-members, in quality circle?

PART B (16 MARKS QUESTIONS)

CHAPTER–1

1. Explain the basic concepts of TQM? (Or) Explain the TQM framework and awareness.
2. What are the obstacles in implementing the TQM?
3. Explain on various dimensions of quality.
4. What are the benefits of TQM?
5. Explain on the concept of leadership and list out the characteristics of a successful leader.

6. Explain the characteristics and features of deming philosophy.
7. Classify quality costs. Explain how cost of quality can be reduced.
8. Explain the process of TQM implementation.
9. Explain the phases of evolution of TQM.
10. What are the duties of quality council?
11. Write short notes on the following:
    (*a*) Vision statement
    (*b*) Mission statement
    (*c*) Goals
    (*d*) Objectives
    (*e*) Strategic planning
    (*f*) Quality policy
12. Discuss on steps to implement the TQM in
    (*a*) An International Public School or
    (*b*) A Deemed University

CHAPTER–2

1. Comment on the following statements:
    (*a*) "Employee satisfaction must be the top priority which leads to customer satisfaction".
    (*b*) "Price alone is not the only aim of a product. Product and service count for its success".
    (*c*) Recognition and award systems lead to motivation.
2. Explain the Maslow's needs Hierarchy theory.
3. What are the merits of empowerment?
4. Explain the types of team and elements of team's success.
5. List out the general guidelines for handling customer complaints.
6. Explain the steps involved in PDCA cycle.
7. What is performance appraisal? Explain the various methods of performance appraisal.
8. Write short notes on the following:
    (*a*) Customer retention
    (*b*) Partnering
    (*c*) Supplier rating
    (*d*) Juran trilogy
    (*e*) Team recognition and reward
9. Discuss on the steps involved in designing customer satisfaction surveys.
10. Explain the concept of 5S and kaizen briefly.

CHAPTER–3

1. List the new seven management tools for TQM. Explain any two of them.
2. Explain the conventional 7 QC tools.
3. Explain the various charts involved in QC tools.
4. Explain the steps to construct control charts for variables and attributes.
5. Explain the significance of control charts to ensure quality of the products.
6. Explain in detail how process capability values C_p and C_{pk} help to improve the process.
7. Explain the six sigma concept.

CHAPTER–4

1. Explain the concept of benchmarking.
2. Discuss on various types of benchmarking.
3. Discuss on the reasons for benchmarking including the merits and demerits.
4. Explain the basic principles of QFD? What are the principal benefits of QFD?
5. Draw the basic structure of house of quality by listing customer requirements and corresponding technical descriptors for the following. List at least three WHATs and four HOWs for

   (*a*) Pencil and

   (*b*) Computer
6. Outline the process of building the house of quality.
7. Explain Taguchi's 'quality loss function'.
8. What are the goals of TPM? And explain the six losses of TPM.
9. What are all the overall effects of TPM implementation? Discuss.
10. Briefly explain the various types of FMEA.
11. Explain different stages involved in FMEA.

CHAPTER–5

1. List five benefits that could be realized by implementing an ISO 9000 quality management system.
2. Describe the four phases of quality documentation.
3. What is quality auditing? Explain various types of quality audits.
4. Write short notes on QS 9000, ISO 14000.
5. What are the key requirements of a firm's quality program on which ISO 9000 standards focus? Explain briefly.
6. What are the benefits of environmental management systems?
7. Explain on various elements of quality system.

CHAPTER–6

1. Discuss on the need for poka yoke.
2. What are the roles of facilitator and leader in the quality circle?
3. Through 'brain storming session' in quality circles, determine the causes and the remedies for the following problems:
   (*a*) Poor research activities in engineering colleges.
   (*b*) Poor sanitary conditions in the municipality.
   (*c*) Poor performance by rural students in B.E./B.Tech. I Sem. examinations.
   (*d*) Violence in panchayath elections.

❑ ❑ ❑